REAL ESTATE INVESTING FROM A TO Z

The Most Comprehensive, Practical, and Readable Guide to Investing Profitably in Real Estate

William H. Pivar

McGraw-Hill

New York   Chicago   San Francisco   Lisbon   London
Madrid   Mexico City   Milan   New Delhi   San Juan   Seoul
Singapore   Sydney   Toronto

The *McGraw·Hill* Companies

Library of Congress Cataloging-in-Publication Data

Pivar, William H.
    Real estate investing from A to Z : the most comprehensive, practical,
and readable guide to investing profitably in real estate / by William
H. Pivar.—3rd ed.
        p. cm.
Includes index.
    ISBN 0-07-141624-2 (pbk. : alk. paper)
    1. Real estate investment—United States.   I. Title.
    HD255.P58 2003
    332.63'24—dc21   2003005762

    3 4 5 6 7 8 9 0 AGM/AGM 0 9 8 7 6 5 4

ISBN 0-07-141624-2

This publication is designed to provide accurate and authoritative information in regard to the subject
matter covered. It is sold with the understanding that neither the author or the publisher is engaged in
rendering legal, accounting, or other professional service. If legal advice or other expert assistance is
required, the services of a competent professional person should be sought.

> *—From a declaration of principles jointly adopted by a committee*
> *of the American Bar Association and a committee of publishers.*

 This book is printed on recycled, acid-free paper containing a minimum of 50% recycled
de-inked fiber.

McGraw-Hill books are available at special quantity discounts to use as premiums and sales promo-
tions, or for use in corporate training programs. For more information, please write to the Director of
Special Sales, Professional Publishing, McGraw-Hill, Two Penn Plaza, New York, NY 10121-2298.
Or contact your local bookstore.

CONTENTS

PREFACE

If you follow the advice of Ben Franklin, "Neither a borrower nor lender be," you will spend your life working for wages.

Bob Bruss

No one gets rich working for wages. You get rich using money—yours or someone else's. By using your money, you make your personal worth grow. By using other people's money, you will have the ability to magnify your effectiveness in your investments. This book will show you how to use not only your own savings but borrowed capital as well.

It is not enough that you learn how to purchase property with no or low down payments. Actually, it is easy to buy with little or nothing down. This by itself is not the key to riches. The key is being able to purchase property that makes economic sense.

One of the seminar gurus of high-leverage purchasing proved to the press that everything he said was true about nothing-down properties. While he purchased several properties in a short period of time without any down payments, he ended up defaulting on the loans. The purchases just didn't make any economic sense. If a property is priced above its re-sale value, the anticipated income stream does not justify the price, or there is a negative cash flow you cannot live with, then that property likely won't make economic sense for you. Your investments must be related to your own situation and needs. Someone else's dream investment could turn out to be your worst nightmare. I will help you analyze your needs and give you direction in locating property to fulfill those needs.

A great many gurus conduct seminars aimed at would-be real estate investors. Most of these seminars are really the first-stage promotion to sell something else, like a special course outlining "secrets" of investing. Unlike the gurus, I don't want to sell you anything else. I will not promise you that you can obtain riches without working for them. I will not tell you how to get away with legally questionable tactics nor will I tell you how to fleece unsuspecting owners. I will, however, show you what can be done and point you toward opportunities.

This book will show that you don't have to have a Mensa mentality, good looks, or sparkling personality to succeed in real estate investing. You will learn that debt and appreciation are the dual engines that can power your future financial well-being.

The one thing this book cannot do is to get you to act. It is not easy to pull yourself out of a set of ruts and forge a new course for your life. It is far easier to let the ruts lead you where they may. It isn't even a matter of work because working for wages isn't easy. In working for wages, harder work generally results in blisters. On the other hand, smart work can equal riches.

This book can be worth millions to you. The advice and techniques set forth have made me and many others millionaires. On the other hand, you may find this book to be worthless. Its value is in your ability to transfer ideas into practical application.

While care has been taken to provide accurate and current information, this publication should not be used as a substitute for competent legal advice. State and federal laws, regulations, as well as court decisions can affect the principles and conclusions presented in this book. The reader is urged to consult legal counsel regarding any point of law.

WILLIAM H. PIVAR

1

Why Real Estate?

> Property is desirable, is a positive good in the world. Let not him who is houseless pull down the house of another, but let him work diligently and build one for himself, thus by example assuring that his own shall be safe from violence when built.
>
> *Abraham Lincoln, 1864*

The easiest way to gain wealth is to be born to it. A second-best method is to marry it, although many who have done so will argue that it is anything but an easy route to riches. Assuming that these two paths are closed to you, real estate investment should be your third choice.

More millionaires have achieved their wealth through real estate than from all other endeavors combined. Our tax system, which takes more as we earn more, actually serves to punish success. With our current economy, even with both husband and wife working and earning good salaries, most families find it impossible to accumulate much wealth. To send children through college or look forward to a retirement where coupon clipping isn't a necessity, investments are necessary.

In their search for sure and certain wealth, many Americans listened to the financial television channels, read the financial papers, and invested in the stock market. In investing in stocks, they left their future to others rather than trying to control their own destiny. We have learned that what goes up can go down without necessarily going up again. We have also learned that many in corporate management have been more concerned with obtaining obscene personal wealth than in the welfare of their investors. We are even finding out that brokers have hyped stocks for their own benefit in disregard to the merits of the investments. "Investing" in the stock market now appears to be more of a gamble than an investment, with the odds tilted against small investors. On the other hand, relatively low interest rates have made for an increased real estate demand and a healthy real estate market.

Real estate investments are different than stock market investments because the control is in your hands. You make the decisions that affect your future. You can also structure purchases as well as sales to meet your particular needs.

Profits can be realized from real estate investments in a number of ways:

1. Positive cash flow (excess of cash received from rents over cash expenditures).
2. Taxation benefits. You will see in Chapter 3 that real estate can both avoid and shelter income from taxation.
3. Appreciation in value:
   a. Realized upon sale.
   b. Realized by borrowing on equity.
4. Benefits of use.

But, as with any investment, you can lose money. Loss in real estate investment is realized in two ways:

1. Negative cash flow, where cash income is insufficient to meet required cash outlay. You will see in Chapter 3 that tax benefits in many cases will effectively overcome or significantly reduce the effect of a negative cash flow.
2. Loss realized at sale or trade.

This book will show you how to maximize your chances for profits and minimize them for losses.

ADVANTAGES TO OWNING REAL PROPERTY

Taxes Encourage Real Estate Investment

Our state and federal tax laws, while harsh on earnings, actually encourage ownership of real estate. Interest and property tax payments are still deductible expenses (see Chapter 3). So, a person buying a home can afford to make a significantly higher payment for a home purchase than for a nondeductible rent payment.

Here's an example. Suppose you and your spouse could buy a property with $2000 per month payments (including taxes and insurance) or rent a similar property for $1500 per month. Of the $2000 payment probably $1900 will apply to interest and taxes. An adjusted gross income in excess of $43,850 for a couple filing a joint return would place any additional earnings in a 28 percent federal tax bracket. If you add the applicable state income taxes (assume a 10 percent rate), you will probably be in a 38 percent combined federal and state tax bracket. In this case you would save $722 per month through lower tax liability (38 percent of $1900)—a true out-of-pocket cost of ownership of $1278 per month. Hence home ownership with monthly payments of $2000 per month would actually result in a gross monthly payment that would be $222 less than the nontax-deductible rent. In this case, the savings would likely be more than sufficient to cover maintenance and repair, which would normally be a landlord's responsibility.

Many states have homeowner-type exemptions that reduce the property tax liability of owner occupants. One purpose of these exemptions is to encourage home ownership. Homeowner tax exemptions are generally limited to the principal residence of the taxpayer.

Inflation

Right now, inflation is not a major concern for most Americans. Except for oil prices and medical expenses, most of our prices have not shown significant increases in recent years. However, we have had periods of great inflation in the past, and we will likely have inflationary periods within the lifetime of our investments. As prices for consumer goods rise, the net effect is that the value of each dollar decreases as it takes more dollars to buy the same goods.

Inflation is categorized as either cost-push inflation or demand-pull inflation. If the cost of wages and material increase, we can expect cost-push inflation to exert upward pressure on prices. Concern for our environment has led to greater development costs as well as time delays in development approvals, which have had a considerable effect on the cost of new construction. Price increases in new property will be reflected in increased prices on existing property as well.

Demand-pull inflation is the result of demand for a good or service exceeding the available supply. Because of the time it takes to build new units and the limitations on available land, an increase in the demand for housing in a particular area will result in price increases within the area. With a growing population caused by both natural increases and immigration, demand pressure on our housing stock has continued. Demand is really meaningless unless it is coupled with purchasing power. Our current low interest rates have made home ownership possible for millions of Americans. As long as the interest rates remain relatively low, there will be a strong demand exerting upward pressure on housing values. We are also seeing more singles uncoupling from their families, setting up their own households. Widows and widowers are more likely to live by themselves than to move in with their children. These factors have contributed to the fact that single person households are one of the fastest growing areas of our residential economy. It is the increase in the number of households, not raw population figures, that results in demand increases.

Remember: No one is making any more land. The supply and demand law of the marketplace dictates that even without cost-push inflation, increases in demand from qualified buyers must result in higher prices.

Investments that fail to keep pace with inflation actually result in an erosion of savings. To make matters even worse, investments generally produce taxable income so that with state and federal income tax, an investor might not only be losing purchasing power, but might have to pay up to 40 percent taxes on what is falsely labeled a gain.

To illustrate this point, suppose you earn 3.5 percent on a certificate of deposit while the Consumer Price Index rises 2.5 percent. The true value of your investment provides just a 1 percent return. You will nevertheless be taxed on the 3.5 percent you earned. A combined 40 percent tax (federal and state) means you will have lost 1.4 percent of your 3.5 percent earnings for taxes, leaving you with 2.1 percent earnings, which will in this case be less than the rate of inflation. You can readily see why such investments are really a formula for poverty and not for riches. Real estate is considered an inflationary hedge because values have increased at even a greater rate than inflation. Unlike gold or stocks and bonds, which fluctuate in value with every newspaper headline, real estate values have in most instances climbed upward since World War II.

Of course, there have been market corrections during recessionary periods following rapid construction or price increases. However, inflation runs in cycles. When the economy gets going, the demand for money and goods drives up interest rates and prices. While inflation is currently not of great concern, future inflationary periods can be expected. These can actually be periods of great opportunity.

While we cannot count on the annual double-digit appreciation in real estate values that we have been experiencing in some areas of the country, we can nevertheless expect real estate value increases to at least match the Consumer Price Index. If property is chosen carefully, you can expect long-term value to increase far in excess of the Consumer Price Index. More and more people who desire to protect their savings are turning to real estate.

An often-overlooked advantage of inflation—at least with respect to real estate—is that when you use borrowed funds you get to pay back loans using ever-cheaper dollars. By the use of borrowed funds, real estate investors are able to use inflation to their best interest. For example, a monthly house payment of $250 per month in 1970 would have been relatively high—beyond the means of a great many families. By the 1990s, such a payment would be easy to make by all but a few families. As the dollar becomes less valuable, payments become easier because you are using less valuable dollars to repay the expensive dollars you borrowed. Today's monthly $1600 house payment might be considered a bargain payment in just a few years.

The greater part of the net worth of average homeowners is the equity in their homes. This has been caused by the greater appreciation in value that homes have had over the past two decades. Housing for a homebuyer today is more than shelter. It is a long-term investment. Second homes are not looked at solely as luxuries anymore; they can be additional long-term investments. During protracted periods of real estate inflation, buyers should consider buying the finest home they can reasonably afford. As inflation continues, not only will the high payments become reasonable or low, but also the homeowner will benefit by greater value appreciation. Inflation does not have to rob you. You can harness it to help meet your financial goals.

If you want to be a millionaire, you can achieve your goal by going into debt and letting long-term inflation help you. If you can purchase real estate on which you owe $2 million and hold on to it for 15 years, you should be a millionaire. With only an average 3 percent inflation rate (and we can expect that real estate values will increase at least that much), within 15 years your equity for average purchases should give you your million-dollar equity. And that is without even compounding the inflation or considering debt reduction. In actual practice the inflation rate applies to the increased value, not the original cost. If you make careful selections of property, you should be able to obtain far better than average increases.

It may sound too simple to be true, but it is the formula that has turned thousands of people into millionaires. This book will show you many different ways to obtain real estate with relatively low down payments and even no down payments. You will find that it doesn't necessarily take money to make money in real estate.

Leverage (Other People's Money)

A major advantage of real estate is leverage, that is, financing. Financing real estate is the easiest way to find others to help you attain financial security.

As previously explained, your monthly payment will actually decrease each month for real estate investments. As inflation continues, you will be making payments with ever-cheaper dollars. The person who is most in debt therefore benefits the most in periods of great inflation. For example, if a person had $100,000 to invest and purchased a 6-unit building for $200,000, that person would get some benefit from inflation but nowhere near the benefit obtainable by buying a 24-unit apartment building for $700,000 and financing $600,000 of the purchase price (see Table 1–1).

TABLE 1–1

Percentage Return on Your Investment:
The Magic of Leverage

Percentage Increase in value	Down Payment and Return on Investment		
	Cash (%)	50% Down	10 % Down
10	10%	20%	100%
20	20%	40%	200%
30	30%	60%	300%
40	40%	80%	400%
50	50%	100%	500%
60	60%	120%	600%
70	70%	140%	700%
80	80%	160%	800%
90	90%	180%	900%
100	100%	200%	1000%

(When the value increases, the lower the down payments, the greater the return on the investment.)

REAL ESTATE INVESTMENTS CAN BUY THEMSELVES

If you can buy a property where the income is sufficient to make the payments, then the property buys itself. If you could buy a $250,000 building with $20,000 down with a 20-year loan and your income from the building makes the payments, in 20 years the building will be paid for. You will have turned $20,000 into $250,000, and there is nothing magical about it. This situation does not even consider the fact that income should rise with inflation, giving you an even stronger cash flow as the years progress. In addition, inflation should have increased the building's value at least several times, so that instead of a $250,000 building you very well might have one worth $1 million that is now free of debt. While spendable income is nice to have, income normally will not make you rich because spending tends to rise to meet income. Appreciation in value is what makes real estate investors wealthy.

The amount of your loan payment that applies to your loan principal may seem to be a cash expense, but it is really increasing your equity in the property by reducing the loan. This is phantom income because you don't actually see it in your pocketbook. Nevertheless, it is a positive element of ownership. This phantom income will be realized when the property is sold.

SAFETY IN REAL ESTATE

Real estate has proved to be one of the safest investments possible. While there is some element of risk to every investment, the safety of real estate investments, compared with business investments, is reflected in a foreclosure rate of less than 1 percent for residential property (see Figure 1–1).

The level of risk in real estate varies by area and type of real estate. For example, areas where the economy is based on a single industry or firm have a greater risk for investors than an area with a more diverse economic base. The type of property also affects risk. The lowest-risk real estate investments are rent-producing properties. Of rent-producing properties, residential properties present the lowest risk because of the sheer number of available renters. Office buildings, factory buildings, raw land, and commercial property have a far greater element of risk than residential property. Their demand is tuned more to the economics of the time. While people need housing, businesses can delay moving or expansion, and in a period of economic contraction, they generally do.

F I G U R E 1–1

Elements of Risk and Safety in Real Estate Investing

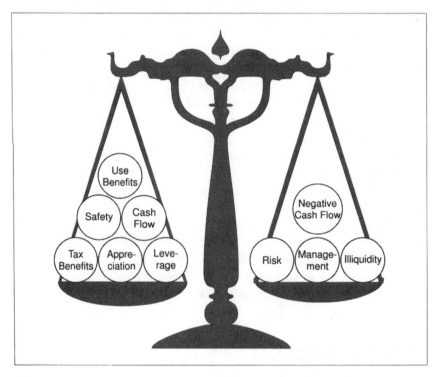

But you can hedge your "bets." By researching a property, an area, and the local economy you can gain the kind of knowledge that will allow you to evaluate the risk of an investment with a fair amount of accuracy. As an investor you must learn to evaluate risk and consider alternative courses of action. Never accept extraordinary risks unless you can also foresee extraordinary profits.

If absolute safety is your goal, you should stay away from real estate. Instead, consider government bonds or possibly GNMA securities (GNMA securities are government-backed mortgage interests). They offer absolute safety but a modest return. While you won't lose your investment, you also won't materially increase your net worth when inflation is considered. *Absolute* safety is incompatible with achieving financial independence. The person who offers you an investment without risk is either lying or offering you a minimum return on your investment.

PYRAMIDING

Pyramiding your investments can maximize your growth potential. Pyramiding is using your equity in property to acquire more or larger properties. This can be accomplished in a number of ways:

- Borrowing on your property (as equity increases due to inflation) to buy more property. This is known as *trading on your equity.* While real estate may be an illiquid investment (not readily convertible to cash), it is possible to pump money out of a real estate investment in a relatively short time. This can be accomplished by using the property as security for a loan or increasing an existing loan by refinancing. The beauty of borrowing on your equity is that you can take money out of your property, often more than you originally invested, without paying any taxes on the money, as this is not considered a taxable gain.

- Selling (or, better still, trading) property to obtain larger properties.

- Reinvesting the cash generated by real estate investments into further investments. This is like compounding interest. By reinvesting your equities, they continue to grow.

Some investors start out with plans to own many properties, but after obtaining a positive cash flow they begin using the cash flow for their living expenses. After a while there is no spendable cash and the "investment plan" becomes just a single property. By failing to reinvest in the early years, you will fail to maximize your investment potential.

A LOOK AT THE NEGATIVE SIDE

Negative Cash Flow

Many good investments have negative cash flows, which means that your monthly cash payments exceed monthly cash receipts. Unless you can correct this imbalance, it could be difficult to hold such property for a long period of time. When you find an investment with a negative cash flow, there are two ways to correct it:

1. Increase the income (raise rents, change use, reduce vacancies, etc.). Properties offered at what an investor considers a below-

market rent would be very attractive, as a negative cash flow might quickly become a very positive cash flow.

2. Reduce expenses (refinancing to cut expenses, more efficient spending, competitive bids, energy conservation, etc.). By performing work yourself that was formerly done by others, you might reduce or eliminate a negative cash flow until rents can be increased.

If there still is a negative cash flow, keep in mind that the government probably will be paying a good part of it for you. Because your cash loss and more (depreciation) will be fully deductible expenses for most investors (see Chapter 3), the net effect will be to significantly reduce the negative cash flow and in some cases eliminate it completely.

Keep in mind that inflation works on rents just as it works on value. Therefore, if rents increase 5 percent each year, it won't take long to turn a negative cash flow into a money machine throwing off significant positive cash amounts each month. As an example, if rents are $1000 per month and operating expenses are $200 per month, a 5 percent increase in both would mean $50 more in income but only $10 more in expenses.

Currently, residential rents have been stagnant, and in some areas they have actually declined. The reason for this is really low interest rates, which have made home purchases possible for many former renters; this has decreased rental demand in some middle-income apartments. The rents can be expected to increase as interest rates begin to rise, and they surely will.

Illiquidity

Another disadvantage of real estate is illiquidity. Depending upon the market and the type of property, it could require a significant time period to sell the property. Because price is related to the time available to sell, should a quick sale be required, the price would likely have to be discounted significantly. Single-family homes have greater liquidity than other real estate investments because greater numbers of potential buyers are available.

Safety

As previously stated, real estate investments do involve risk in that changes in the area, the local, or the national economy will affect income and value. Even political changes, such as rent control or zoning changes, can have a significant effect on value.

Keep in mind that increased risks are only acceptable if you can live with the risks and if the risks are offset by increased likelihood of profit on the investment. I will show you how to analyze risk so that investment decisions can be made with a realistic risk evaluation.

If we plotted a curve based on typical investments, we would discover that low-risk investments offer relatively low profit potential while high-risk investments offer relatively high profit potential. (Investors will not accept greater risk in the absence of the possibility of greater profit.) The curve in Figure 1–2 will help you understand this concept. An investment at point A would have a relatively low risk but would also offer a relatively modest profit potential. On the other hand, a relatively high-risk investment at point B offers significantly greater profit potential. An investment at point C (below the curve) would not appear economically sound, as the higher risk is not reflected in a profit commensurate with the risk. Investment D (above the curve) would offer an investor an interesting opportunity because the profit potential is greater than would be expected by the degree of risk. You will learn how you can reduce risk so that investments viewed by others to be undesirable can in fact be economically viable investments.

A young person with very few assets can often afford to be a high roller, risking all in a highly speculative investment. A person approaching retirement age who needs the capital for the coming retirement years is usually more interested in capital preservation coupled with a reasonable profit than in making a killing. Risk capital, capital that will not affect a person's lifestyle, can be invested in property offering a greater appreciation potential as well as greater degree of risk.

Personal Liability

While most people understand that if they cannot make payments, they will lose their property to foreclosure, many do not understand the implications of a deficiency judgment, which is a court judgment for the difference between what is owed against the property, and the amount that was realized at the foreclosure sale. This deficiency judgment could easily exceed the initial investment made.

While it is possible to avoid deficiency judgment by purchasing in a corporate name or as a limited liability company (LLC), these are unlikely solutions as lenders will be reluctant to lend to an entity set up for the purpose of being able to walk away if the investment sours.

A number of states will not allow deficiency judgments under any circumstances or restrict them to the point where they are the exception rather than the rule. If a deficiency judgment is not possible upon foreclosure, then the investor with the lowest down payment in some ways has the lowest risk. Should real estate values significantly decline, the big losers are those owners who made significant down payments to purchase properties. The smallest losers are those using the greatest leverage.

Knowing the law as to deficiency judgments in your state might affect the degree of risk you are willing to accept. Investors with few assets have the least to lose, so they frequently take risks that more affluent in-

F I G U R E 1–2

Risk–Profit Curve

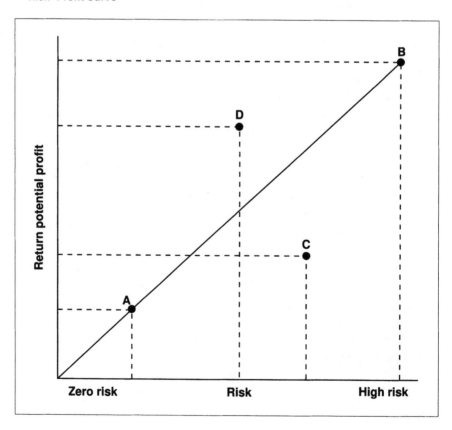

vestors avoid. However, other areas in this book will explain ways to reduce risks for almost any type of investment.

Management

Real estate investments require management. You must know what you want to do and have a plan to do it. This is true even if you hire professional management. To maximize yield you must know what is happening and be flexible to make changes as needed. Real estate is not like blue chip stocks that you buy, put in your portfolio, and forget. Real estate demands your attention. Chapter 15 will cover management of your real estate investments.

WHEN TO BUY AND SELL

The best time to buy real estate is when you don't have to buy the property. In such a situation you have the bargaining power to make an offer which is economically advantageous to you and which you are able to walk away from if negotiations become disadvantageous. When you don't have to buy, you are likely to have your emotions under control.

The worst time to buy is when you absolutely must buy, whatever the reason. The more stringent the time requirement, the less likely you will make the most advantageous purchase. Similarly, when you fall in love with a property, you are likely to make decisions based more on emotion than your economic benefits.

The best time to sell is when you don't have to sell. When you are not under any selling pressure, you are unlikely to make an agreement not in your best interests. Generally, you will not accept an offer to sell unless you have what you consider a better investment available for your money.

I have received unsolicited offers to sell properties that really were not on the market. In evaluating the decision to sell or to hold, I use a very simple technique. I ask myself, "If I didn't own this property and someone else offered it to me at the price and terms offered, would I buy it?" If I wouldn't, then I try to negotiate a sale. Otherwise, I would be bidding against myself. When you refuse a firm offer, you are saying, "No, I will pay more for it." If you wouldn't buy it at the price offered, you should sell it and buy something that you are willing to buy. Don't hold on to property without any economic basis for doing so. In making your decision, you must consider the tax implication of the sale. If you are going to have to pay taxes on your gain, you should consider the price after sales costs and taxes. If you wouldn't want to buy the property at that price, then you should sell it. In Chapter 12, I will show you how to defer any taxes with a tax-free exchange.

You are vulnerable when you must sell. You are the kind of person you would be seeking if you were in a buying mode. It is possible to protect yourself from becoming someone else's pigeon by a basic knowledge of negotiation techniques.

Real Estate Cycles

We have cycles of activities in real estate. When interest rates rise, real estate activities tend to slow down. Generally, a downturn in real estate activity precedes a general economic downturn. When interest rates fall real estate activity generally increases. A real estate recovery generally precedes a general business recovery. High sales activity is generally associated with what we call a seller's market. Great demand, often exceeding supply, forces prices up. In a buyer's market, sales activity is slow with few buyers and many sellers. Contrarians are the best investors. They like to buy when few other buyers are available. They are more likely to find highly motivated sellers whose expectations have been crushed by a lack of interested buyers. Must-sell sellers tend to get desperate in such a market. Similarly, contrarians like to sell when the market is rising and prices are going up. Actually, there are opportunities available in any market to buy or to sell.

When interest rates are high, one mistake many people make is waiting for interest rates to drop. While they wait, prices rise and interest rates still do not come down. In the last 40 years, there have only been a few years in which property values have failed to increase at a greater rate than the interest rates charged for real estate loans after tax benefits have been considered. Assume you are in the 40 percent tax bracket (total of federal and state income tax) for your top dollar of income. If you are paying 7 percent interest on a loan, it only costs you 4.2 percent. Since the interest is deductible, the government really pays the other 2.8 percent for you. With only moderate inflation, and an increasing population, an average real estate investment will likely increase in value over a 10-year period at a rate in excess of 4.2 percent each year.

Most people tend to look back as to where they have been rather than forward to where they are going. They tend to talk about deals available 2 years, 5 years, or 10 years ago that are now bargains rather than today's purchases that will become tomorrow's bargains. People who don't invest in real estate tend to say that others who did successfully invest were lucky. (They never say others were smart, as this would be saying they were dumb.) Well you can be lucky too if your definition of luck is preparation coming together with opportunity. I am going to show you how to prepare yourself, how to recognize opportunity, and how to then take advantage of the opportunity.

WHAT IT TAKES TO INVEST

You probably have heard and repeated the old maxims "It takes money to make money" or "Money goes to money." These slogans were probably written by real estate investors who wanted the game all to themselves. I am going to show you that having money is far from the most important attribute a real estate investor needs. There are many ways to make up for lack of cash. Personal qualities are far more important for success.

Personal qualities of successful real estate investors include:

- *Imagination:* The ability to visualize what will happen in the future and what can be done to increase desirability.
- *Resourcefulness:* The ability to solve problems. This includes the ability to structure purchases and sales in a variety of ways to meet both buyer and seller needs.
- *Persistence:* The plain gumption it takes to continue to work to find properties and to solve problems.
- *Self-Confidence:* The faith in oneself so that when an opportunity presents itself, the investor is mentally able to act.
- *Acceptance of Risk:* The ability to realistically analyze risk, work to reduce it, and to accept it in the light of the benefits.
- *Self-Organization:* A successful investor must be organized so that he or she continues to work toward his or her goals. It takes self-discipline to work when others are engaging in leisure activities. Work by itself is not enough; it must be directed. You need a financial plan to reach a financial goal. Planning is less difficult than

putting your plan into action. It is not that effective investing in real estate is difficult, it just takes courage.

- *Willingness to Sacrifice:* You can't have everything when you are just starting on your investment plan. Some part of your want list should be set aside so you can accumulate a cash reserve. While you will find opportunities to buy with little or no cash, having a cash reserve is an ace in the hole against unplanned expenses. Besides financial sacrifice, you must also be willing to sacrifice time. The hours in front of the television set or on the golf course might have to be reduced. You must determine where your priorities lie.

- *Support:* If you are married, it is going to take a supportive spouse to invest in real estate. Unless you have your spouse as an enthusiastic partner, the sacrifice in time and money can place an unbearable strain on a relationship.

- *Motivation:* You must have strong motivation to succeed in real estate investing for without strong motivation you will not expend the effort to learn the market and evaluate property properly. Without strong motivation, your success is unlikely.

- *Courage:* This is the most important trait for a real estate investor.

My father was successful in both business and real estate investments. He had a saying: "You lose your money and you have lost nothing, but you lose your courage and you have lost everything." While courage is required for every investment, the greater the downside risk, the more courage is required of the investor.

One of the smartest real estate investors I know of was wiped out financially in a building project. He had even borrowed on his cars, home, and furniture in an attempt to save his investment, but all was lost. He never recovered from the loss because he also lost his courage. He took a salaried job and was unwilling to take any risks. He has no faith in his own judgment anymore and asks friends their opinions on any important decision he must make. No one can give him back his courage; it must come from within. For many people an investment in other than a savings account causes great emotional stress that they are unable to overcome.

To the other extreme, a large Midwestern investor had been extremely successful. He owned over 800 fine residential units, lived on an estate with a household staff, and had all the trappings we associate with great wealth. His brother, a large developer, had a heart attack and he stepped in to handle his brother's projects. To keep the business going, he personally guaranteed large loans, but the business failed. When I first met this gentleman, he was $3 million in debt. Rather than go through bankruptcy, he went to his creditors and asked for their help. They agreed not to press him for the money, so he concentrated his efforts on recouping the losses. He moved to California, where he rented a two-bedroom apartment and started using many of the techniques covered in this book, especially options. Today, he has paid back the debt, lives in a beautiful home on a golf course, and drives a Mercedes. He never lost his courage and faith in his abilities.

Many people talk about investing in real estate but never do. Many of them even read books about it and attend seminars by know-everything gurus. Even these great motivators fail to persuade many of their disciples to actually make an investment commitment. There are a number of reasons for this. They include:

- *Inertia:* A body at rest tends to remain at rest. The easiest decision is no decision.
- *Fear.* Fear of the unknown, the paperwork or dealing with new situations often results in last-minute decisions not to commit.
- *Peer Influence:* Would-be investors who ask people who don't invest in real estate for advice will not be advised to invest. They will tell them to place their money in whatever venue they have placed their money. It will help validate the friend's decisions. They can't advise you to do what they fear to do themselves. In addition, many people feel that advice not to do something is the safest advice to give.

Preparing Yourself

While there are more real estate investors without real estate licenses than those having licenses, there are advantages to obtaining a license:

- The license training will provide familiarity with real estate contracts and language. Even if you do not take the license examination, this basic training can be valuable.
- Having a license will provide you with information about property being offered for sale.

A disadvantage of being licensed is that there can be a conflict of interest if you buy a property listed by your firm should you not fully disclose your intentions. If you buy a property listed by another firm and you share in the commission, then you will likely have the same disclosure requirements.

Even though you decide not to obtain a real estate license, you should still learn all you can about various aspects of real estate. Chances are your local community college offers evening courses in real estate principles, real estate finance, real estate law, and appraisal and property management. You can learn from these classes—knowledge is truly power when it comes to investing.

There are many books available about real estate investing. While some are primarily motivational and others propose courses of action that are unrealistic or unethical, many books will provide you with ideas to help you succeed. The comments of readers at *Amazon.com* will help you in selecting suitable books.

A great many seminar providers have focused on how you can get rich through real estate investing. Some of these providers are knowledgeable professionals and can help you succeed. However, there seem to be more charlatans than experts conducting seminars. They may be great speakers and get the audience excited, but if their ideas don't provide lasting benefits, the seminar is a waste of time and money.

Some presenters provide a "pie-in-the-sky" approach. You should avoid presenters who give you just a taste of what they are offering for your admission price and want you to spend hundreds of dollars for their secret detailed approach to wealth.

John Reed, a real estate author, provides a free review of what he thinks of the major real estate gurus at his Web site, *JohnTReed.com/rate-seminars.html*. While Mr. Reeds' evaluations are his own, he receives input from attendees of these seminars.

Every 50-year-old wishes he or she had invested in real estate 20 years earlier. In fact, many of us remember our fathers or grandfathers lamenting that the days of big profits in real estate were over. They, of course, were wrong, and you are also if you think as they did. The parade hasn't passed you by. Age is not a factor in real estate investment. Some investors who retired with modest incomes have become millionaires during their retirement years. At the other extreme I know of a college freshman that started out with $2000. He invested in a run-down rooming house and was a millionaire before he finished graduate school.

Your decision to invest in real estate should be your own, but it should be made only after careful consideration. You can't win in real estate until you get into the game, and you're not in the game until you commit yourself to buy. But a word of caution: Don't jump without looking, and that means a careful examination.

C H A P T E R

Investment Alternatives

> The first man to fence in a piece of land saying "This is mine . . . ," was the real founder of civil society.
>
> *Jean-Jacques Rousseau, 1754*

Real estate investments are divided into two categories: keepers and flippers. *Keepers* are property you buy for a long-term hold. You hold such property for income and/or appreciation in value and, in some cases, income tax benefits (see Chapter 3). *Flippers* are properties you intend to resell as soon as possible. These are properties where you feel you can make a profit either with or without renovation, repairs, or improvements. While the price paid is always important, the price being paid is not as critical for keepers as it is for flippers. As a general rule, I would not buy a property for resale unless I could anticipate a 30 percent markup in the selling price from my cost. I have learned that unexpected costs and extended holding time can quickly eat into this cushion. Types of property purchased depend on the individual investor's needs and the particular market. (In Chapter 18 I will discuss determining an investor's specific needs.)

You will quickly realize that there are a great many investment alternatives available for you. The amount of time you have to devote to real estate investing, as well as your individual talents and goals will help you to focus on the area or areas that will best meet your needs.

SINGLE-FAMILY HOMES

For many years the "experts" advised people not to invest in single-family homes, saying they provided a poor return on the investment. Those who failed to heed this advice prospered. When you measure income against price paid for a single-family home, it does appear to be a poor investment. However, income is not the sole criterion to use. The more important criterion is appreciation. Since World War II the appreciation of single-family homes has been phenomenal. Despite a business recession and a dismal stock market, single-family homes have continued to appreciate in value. The appreciation rate for single-family homes has been greater than all other real estate categories.

With construction costs continuing to escalate, with increasing demand, fueled by both population increase and low interest rates, and with a limited supply of land, we can expect significant increases in value for the future. Of course, there may be a temporary leveling off and even decline in value based on changes in local and national economies, but for the long haul we can expect further appreciation in value.

While real estate is generally considered an illiquid investment not readily converted to cash, single-family homes are the most liquid of real estate investments. Generally they can be sold in a far shorter time than other real estate, and home equity can be readily used as collateral for loans. A single-family home is also the most readily rentable of real estate investments, as everyone needs housing. The sheer abundance of homes is an advantage to an investor. There are new opportunities available every day.

A major advantage offered by single-family homes is financing. You can obtain both a lower interest rate and a higher loan-to-value ratio (LTV) for single-family homes than for any other investment. In many instances, such as Veterans Administration (VA) financing and some low-income Federal Housing Administration (FHA) loans, owner-occupied homes can be purchased without any cash down payment.

A disadvantage of single-family homes as investments is that rarely will the rent make the debt payments unless a very substantial down payment is made. When the dollars going out for payments and expenses exceed the income, an owner has a negative cash flow. This makes holding the property an economic burden for many would-be investors.

When a single-family house has a negative cash flow, this negative aspect is unlikely to continue for more than a few years because rents in most areas have been rising between 5 percent and 8 percent a year. The increase in gross income coupled with a fixed-debt service (mortgage payment) will mean that, in just a few years, what was a negative cash flow will likely turn into a significant positive cash flow.

Even if a single-family home has a negative cash flow, the negative cash flow might be effectively reduced or eliminated by the tax benefits. Depreciation (covered in Chapter 3) is a paper expense that can be used for income tax purposes. You will see that the effect of depreciation is to reduce your income tax liability.

If the buyer can live with the negative cash flow, and the appreciation and tax benefits are significant, then what would otherwise appear as a poor rental investment could make a great deal of sense.

Some buyers of single-family homes are able to avoid the negative cash flow aspect of their investments by offering them for sale on a lease option basis. On a lease option with a significant portion of the rent applying to purchase, a higher payment is possible. This technique will be covered in Chapter 13.

Keep in mind that no home purchased for resale is a bargain if you can't locate a buyer for it who will pay you more than your investment. Generally, be leery of:

- Floor plans unlikely to appeal to most buyers.
- Architectural styles likely to appeal to a very limited group of buyers unless modifications are economically feasible.
- Shoddy basic construction.
- Likely code violations.
- Work likely performed without building permits.
- Rapidly declining neighborhoods.

If you are going to invest in single-family homes, it is best to stick with one area you are familiar with. It also provides for more efficient use of your management time. Generally, it is not economical to use professional property management for single-family homes. While you can contract much of the maintenance and repair, the more work you can perform yourself, the greater your net return.

Your own home should be considered the start of your investment program. It is more than a shelter; it is an excellent investment. Today, buying the best home you can afford in the best area makes sense. This type of home will provide you with maximum appreciation and will improve your general quality of life.

Areas that have been hit by economic recession are especially attractive because homes can likely be purchased for less than reproduction costs and will likely realize a significant increase in value when the market recovers.

Many homes were built on double lots or large lots. If a lot can be split off from the home, it could be a good investment opportunity. A friend of mine recently purchased a home for $260,000, sold off a lot for $80,000, and then sold the home for $245,000.

Buying Prior to Subdivision Approval

In many states buyers can make reservations on homes but can't complete the purchase until a subdivision has received final local and state approvals. Until such time as a public report is issued by the state, the buyer can back out of the purchase and receive his or her deposit back in full.

If you live in such a state, it may be practical to consider speculating in condominium reservations when the market appears to be rising. Generally, units can be reserved with only a few thousand dollars down. If the demand increases and the units sell out, reservations can be sold at a profit. The downside risk for such an investment is only the interest lost on the deposit, which must be kept by the developer in a trust account. On the other hand, the upside profit could be many times the amount of the deposit.

Some developers have discouraged speculating by requiring larger deposits and by prohibiting purchasers from assigning their purchase contracts. In other words, the purchaser must buy before he or she can resell. Nevertheless, profits can still be made in this area.

> My name is Robert O. I sold my home in San Francisco in late 1977 to take a job in Southern California. I had almost $100,000 from the sale. After looking around, I put a $2000 deposit on a new home in an Orange County subdivision. Two weeks later, when I went to see the developer about upgrading the carpet, a salesperson for the developer told me that if I wanted to make a profit he could get me $10,000 for my reservation. It seems the phase I had purchased in had sold out. There were buyers willing to pay a premium to get a home.
>
> While I didn't sell my reservation, I discussed this with a neighbor where I was renting. My neighbor, who was an attorney, told me that investing in reservations was a no-lose situation. All I had to do was call developers to find out if final subdivision approval had been received for advertised openings (in most cases it hadn't), get there early, and put down a deposit that was really refundable at will.
>
> I may not be the brightest guy in the world, but I don't have to be hit over the head with a two-by-four when opportunity is knocking. After some convincing and her own checking, my wife agreed that we should start putting in reservations. We went to different subdivisions on weekends and my wife went alone during the week. We never paid more than $2500 for a deposit and often only

$1000. We placed 41 deposits in a month and a half. We wanted midmarket, three-bedroom, two-bath, two-car-garage homes in desirable areas.

When I exhausted my money, I sold my first reservation. I received $17,000 net (after paying a commission to the agent). We used this $17,000 for more deposits, but we decided that from now on we would keep the cash rather than reinvest.

Most of the deposits were for homes not yet under construction or barely started. The market at the time was wild with prices being raised by developers almost on a monthly basis. We ended up selling 33 of our deposits at profits ranging from $3000 to $35,000. Our average profit after costs was $11,500, or $380,000 total. With my original $100,000 I had a half million dollars. The whole operation took less than eight months. For those homes where the value either didn't go up or I could not find a buyer for my reservation, I received my reservation fees back in full.

In retrospect, I made money by my timing. Real estate was booming and I rode the boom period with investments that offered profit and no risk. Since that time I have looked for similar booms. From 1982 to 1987, I purchased and resold lots. I used options to keep my risk down and did nothing but make money. In 1990, I purchased a large apartment complex from a lender. I have recently refinanced this complex so that I have recovered my investment. When the next boom comes, I intend to go with it. I don't know how but I will keep my eyes and ears open.

Note: Beginning in 2001, Robert O. had again started buying and optioning lots, which he is marketing to builders.

Vacation Homes

After their first home, the next step for many investors is a vacation home. Today a vacation home can be for investment as well as enjoyment. As stated, the fact that interest and property taxes are tax deductible helps to offset the cost of keeping a second home.

If you live in a vacation home for 14 days a year or less, you can take depreciation on it. If you use it for more than 14 days, you are not allowed depreciation. Therefore, some owners use their vacation home only a few weekends a year and rent it at other times in order to take depreciation.

The Sunbelt is an excellent area for vacation homes because they can generally be rented more months of the year than in the North and are more readily sold because of the increasing demand for housing in this growing region. However, the sun isn't the only attraction for second-home buyers. There has been phenomenal appreciation in ski-and water-related properties. If there is a recreational interest, there will be second-home buyers.

I own a lakeshore vacation home in northern Wisconsin that I use for five months a year. I do not rent it in the off-season, but the appreciation has far exceeded expenses. In addition, it gives me a great deal of pleasure. My other vacation home was a condominium in Lake Havasu, Arizona, which I rented and later sold at a significant profit.

> My name is Sandra J. I am a schoolteacher in New York. My husband is an ironworker who is collecting a modest pension because of a disability. We purchased a golf course condominium in South Carolina about 10 years ago. We use it for two weeks at Christmas, a week at Easter, and in the summer. The rest of the year it is rented out by a rental office at the development. While the property cost us money for the first three years, we now get enough rent to cover our payments from weekly rentals. We paid less than $40,000 for our unit with $6000 down, and the current value is about $80,000.
>
> We had a dual purpose in our purchase, which was to use it as a vacation home until I retire and then to use it as a permanent retirement home thereafter. I will retire next year when we will move to South Carolina. If we had waited until we had retired, we would never have been able to afford this retirement home. By buying early as a vacation home, we locked in the price of our retirement.

> Note: Sandra J. has retired to her South Carolina property. And while prices have continued to escalate, other investors are doing the same as Sandra J. did; they are locking in their retirement housing costs at today's prices, as their net worth increases with appreciation.

Condominiums

In many areas of the country condominiums, planned unit developments, and cooperatives can be purchased to provide a break-even or a positive cash flow.

Condominiums have the advantage of being relatively easy to rent with fewer problems for the owner (the grounds and exterior are handled by the association). On the negative side, condominiums generally have realized a slower rate of appreciation than other units. In a recessionary period, condo values tend to be softer than those of single-family homes. The reason for these differences is that condominiums are not the purchase of choice of many owners. A condominium is often a compromise dictated by cost for those who might otherwise prefer a single-family home.

Check the restrictive covenants before buying a condominium as an investment. Many condominiums and cooperatives have rental restrictions that could conflict with your plans. Also, obtain a copy of the last operational statement (the seller will be able to obtain this). You want to make certain current assessments are adequate to meet the association's needs. (If not, assessments will need to be raised.) You also want to find out if there have been special assessments for unusual expenses. In some associations, these special assessments seem to be normal rather than special. Because a condominium is governed by an association, an owner has less control over costs and in some cases association fees have dramatically increased.

My name is Seymour T. I am a retired accountant. Because I spent half the year renting in Florida, I decided to buy a condominium. I had a tax purpose in mind. By establishing Florida residency, I would avoid my state income tax, which was running about $5000 per year. I felt this savings would more than pay for my condominium payments and association fees. This would give me a Florida home for free. Because of a depressed market, I purchased a modest two-bedroom, two-bath, west coast condominium in a large development for $38,500 and got the sellers to include the furnishings. I paid $4000 down and assumed the FHA financing. My payments were about $300 a month and association fees were $78 a month. I liked the area, and I had a condominium for free because of state income tax savings.

Then my wife fell in love with a new development in our area. We put a deposit down on a very nice three-bedroom, two-and-one-half-bath single family home. She wanted a big home so the children and grandchildren could visit. Fortunately for us the resale market was still bad. After an unsuccessful attempt to sell our condominium, we advertised it for rent by taking a small classified ad in several Canadian papers. We did this because many of the people renting in our complex were from Canada.

We asked $750 per month rent furnished, and we were astounded at the number of responses. We rented it for six months and received a deposit by mail from one of the first callers. The seasonal rental made my payments for the year.

The first year we also rented the property for three additional months at

$400 per month, so we had a good cash-on-cash return from our investment. In addition, we had the tax benefit of depreciation, which sheltered my income from federal taxes. I began checking on the availability of other units in my development. I placed purchase offers on several other units and was able to buy two furnished units. I let my tenants know of the two additional units and within a week they had found renters for me from among their Canadian friends.

I have continued to put in offers to purchase condominium units, and I now own over 30 units. While I pay a lot more for units today, the rent I now charge has also increased. My criterion is that a single seasonal tenant's rent be sufficient to make my payments for the year plus association dues. The off-season rentals, depreciation, and appreciation were my benefits. Because of increasing costs, I now try to find units that will break even as to cash flow. I expect my reward in tax benefits and value and rent appreciation in the future. My retirement is no longer one of playing cards and lying to my neighbors; it's one of fun and activity and it has become very profitable. Because all my units are in the same development, my management has been fairly easy. While I handle the seasonal rentals, I have a rental agent who now takes care of my off-season rentals. I pay another resident of the development an hourly fee to do any required repairs and/or maintenance. Friends ask me why I don't buy apartments instead. The reasons are that I can get far better financing buying condos, and they are easier to rent than apartments. I can get more rent from condos than apartments because of all the amenities, and I have no aggravation with common-area maintenance.

Many small investors are purchasing condominium units for their children in college. They can frequently purchase units for about a 10 percent down payment. By taking in roommates, the unit can, in many markets, generate enough income to make the payments on the unit. For example, three roommates paying $400 each a month will give you $1200 gross plus a home for your college-age son or daughter. In addition, you will have depreciation on the unit and hopefully appreciation when it is sold. One woman purchased a $60,000 condominium in Santa Barbara, California, for her son while he attended college. She paid 10 percent down. While the appreciation was unusual in this area, she received $165,000 when she sold the unit five years later. That's $105,000 profit on a $6000 cash investment. Appreciation, in her case, ended up more than paying for her son's entire college education. A weak stock market coupled with real estate appreciation has resulted in many thousands of parents looking to buy college housing for their children.

Fixer-Uppers

What I regard as a fixer-upper could be in excellent physical shape. If it is
unattractive or undesirable because of a curable defect, I regard it as a
fixer-upper. If a house has a problem you can solve then it offers fixer-
upper possibilities.

Property that is move-in perfect sells first. When you sell property,
you will generally maximize your net by making a property *stand tall*.
However, the reverse holds true as well. Property in bad condition needing
repair, cleanup, or complete rejuvenation, if not properly marketed, will
often remain on the market for a long period of time. The result is that exceptional opportunities are likely to become available in both price and
terms for this type of *fixer-upper* property.

Generally, the dirtier the property is, the better the deal you can
make. Property in rough shape can often be purchased at a good price with
very attractive owner financing. Often property like this is being foreclosed, is part of an estate, or has been foreclosed and is held by the
lender.

As costs rise, the advantages in renovating property become obvious.
The principle of substitution is that people will not pay more for a property than they would for one offering equal utility and desirability. If you
can buy a run-down or older property and make it equally desirable to
other properties, then your property will have similar worth. This is true
even though your initial cost plus the cost of renovation could be far less
than the value of the comparable properties. For those who can visualize
what can be done to increase property desirability and who have a good
grasp of the expenditures required, the profit potential can be phenomenal
and often is.

Before buying these fixer-uppers, check them out carefully to see
what must be done. In particular check the plumbing, electrical, and heating–cooling systems. Carefully consider what the repairs will cost. Generally, cleaning, painting, and yardwork can make a big difference in value
and salability. Every dollar spent on a fixer-upper can mean many dollars
in profit.

There are a growing number of professional inspection companies
that will evaluate properties for a few hundred dollars. It can be money
well spent to protect you from the unexpected. In addition, defects discovered can be a powerful bargaining tool in determining the purchase price.
In Chapter 9, we will cover qualification and selection of inspectors.

Unless you have had extensive contracting experience, avoid homes that need major structural work. Corrective work is seldom within estimates. Normally, what happens is that additional problems continue to emerge as work progresses.

In addition to necessary repairs, a buyer of fixer-upper property should also consider improvements—additions or amenities the property never had before. The investor should be concerned with the principle of contribution when making improvements. Basically this means an improvement, to be economically feasible, must increase the value of the property by more than the cost of the improvement. Many buyers who purchase fixer-uppers feel that unless the property value increases by at least a two-to-one ratio (a two-dollar increase in value for every dollar spent), then the improvement should not be made.

I recommend carrying this two-for-one-rule a little further. I feel that as an investor in fixer-uppers, you should net after sale costs an amount that at least covers investment costs plus holding costs plus at least $2 for every dollar in repair or renovation plus a trade rate for your own labor plus an additional 10 percent for profit.

Sale price = Sale Cost + holding costs + $2 for $1 out-of-pocket repair costs + your labor at trade rate + 10 percent

Keep in mind that your costs are likely to exceed your estimates, so you need a cushion. If your analysis will not at the least give you the return indicated, I would not recommend it as an investment.

Besides repairs and improvements, buyers of fixer-uppers must consider renovation—the replacement of old amenities with new ones. Money spent in renovating kitchens and baths with new cabinets and fixtures is generally reflected by at least a two-to-one ratio in increased value. The same holds true for new carpeting, paint, and landscaping. While you should always evaluate the effect of the cost to the sale price and plan for an adequate return, things seldom work out exactly as planned. Therefore, you must leave enough room in your estimates to deal with the unexpected.

Fixer-upper buyers not only know how to look for bargains to buy, they also know how to get work done at the lowest cost. Some save by installing used carpeting obtained from carpet layers who redo model homes and from jobs they do for decorators. Quality used carpet can often be obtained for little more than the cost of the pad and laying the carpet.

Today there are fixer-upper operators in every price range. One successful investor buys million-dollar fixer-uppers in Beverly Hills, California, and successfully turns them into $2 million and $3 million homes.

As in any other property, location will affect demand, as will architectural style, view, landscaping, and so forth. You must avoid buying a bargain for bargain's sake. You must consider what the demand will be when the property is ready for resale.

I have a son who restores old automobiles. He recently restored a 1966 Mustang Convertible and an old Toyota Land Cruiser. The 1966 Mustang sold readily at a significant profit, but the Land Cruiser took a long time to sell so the profit was less. While this book is not about cars, it illustrates that the fixer-uppers you should concentrate on are fixer-uppers that will have a strong market demand.

I'm Dennis. I buy new or newer homes in prime areas in the 3000-square-foot category. I buy homes that were foreclosed by lenders, known as REOs (real estate owned). I look for homes that the lender has had on the market for some time.

When the prior owner couldn't sell it and the lender hasn't been able to sell it, it's time for my offer—usually very low and for cash. I don't dicker. There are a lot of opportunities for me, so if a lender won't take my offer, I move on to other opportunities.

My offers are often accepted because lenders have received a dose of reality. There are not many buyers for what they have because what they have usually has problems.

An example of a recent purchase was a custom-designed, four-year-old Spanish-style home. The former owner only lived in it six months and was transferred. He made payments for almost two years before he let it go. He had tried to sell it to break even by asking $695,000. The lenders had the home on the market for six months. While they originally asked $495,000, they reduced the price to $450,000. My offer, the only offer received in three years, was for $310,000. I refused a counteroffer of $390,000 and my offer was eventually accepted.

I ripped out the dark gray ceramic tile in the baths, entry hall, and kitchen and replaced it with 12" by 12" white ceramic tile. I had the dark cabinetry painted white and the cabinet doors stripped and given a white tone finish. The blue carpet was ripped up and replaced with Fleck Berber carpeting. Pink marble was removed from the fireplace and a beehive-style stucco fireplace with Spanish tile gave the room an entirely different look. I tiled the front entrance with Spanish tile and replaced the modern front doors with massive carved doors and appropriate hardware. I upgraded lighting fixtures throughout the house. My total cash outlay was under $60,000. I priced the property at $495,000 and sold it for $485,000. After paying commission my profit was over $80,000. My total holding time: less than four months.

I want my property to offer a competitive advantage over other property in eye appeal as well as price. By pricing right I cut my holding time.

The person who wishes to buy a house, fix it up, move in, and then sell it must be willing to live a nomadic existence and have a spouse willing to go along with it. Moving can be hard on children, who must change schools and friends. Ideally, these ventures are best for individuals or couples without children. Building or renovating is not an easy life. You must be willing to sacrifice present free time and pleasures for future benefits.

Fixer-upper investors can get a sweetheart tax benefit by occupying the fixer-upper for two years. If they do so, then their profit is not taxed as income. This exemption is $250,000 for an individual and $500,000 for a couple. The beauty of this universal exemption is that it is not just a one-time exemption. It can be used every two years. There are many full-and part-time home renovators who move into a house as soon as possible and work around shifting living space. Many of them have found wealth free of taxes. The same procedure holds true for homebuilders. Many now occupy a home for only two years, sell it, paying no taxes on their gain, and then move into another new home.

Building Homes for Resale

Some developers find lots, choose plans, and build homes utilizing a general contractor. By contracting the entire job, they reduce the risk of cost overruns and are able to devote their time to marketing rather than the nuts and bolts of construction.

Instead of building for immediate resale, some developers furnish the home and use it as a model to sell from. They either know of available lots or have tied up lots with a purchase option so they can provide the buyer with a complete package. In most areas, activities like this do not require a real estate license since the developer is acting as a principal and not an agent.

When building a home for resale, don't be too innovative. Look at what is selling in your area. The further you deviate from what others are successfully selling, the greater your risk.

My name is William. After graduating college, I became involved in real estate sales. One of my close friends made a "killing" by buying a lot, contracting with a builder, and then selling the home for a profit. I decided to follow his example.

I found an inexpensive lot, a small builder who gave me a good price, and a bank that gave me an excellent construction loan. My total cash assets at the time were around $500.

Luckily, I sold the house for a profit before it was completed. I say luckily because I had made some serious mistakes. First, I had looked for the cheapest lot. In terms of resale, the cheapest lot is usually the most expensive lot. You should look for a lot in a better area because location sells. It has often been said that the three most important considerations in buying real estate are location, location, and location.

Second, I picked a very contemporary plan—one of those modernistic homes with sharp angles that you see featured in the magazine sections of the Sunday newspapers but which few people build. This type of house is usually difficult to sell although everyone wants to see it. I should have chosen colonial, Cape Cod, Spanish, or standard ranch design.

Since then, I have continued to build one or two homes each year and sell them. But I try to stick with what buyers want. If I had one sentence of advice for would-be builders, "Don't substitute your own likes for the likes of others."

To limit risk some investors build a home, move in, and place it on the market. They live there until the home is sold. They avoid two home payments, which means they can usually afford to hold on until they can make a sale that offers them a reasonable profit. If they live in the house for two years, they will likely avoid any taxes on the gain. The disadvantage of this type of activity is that the investor's family is constantly being uprooted. While it can be a profitable way of life, it is not necessarily a desirable lifestyle.

Some people act as their own general contractor and hire subcontractors for all the work, while others give the entire job to a general contractor. Still others will physically build each house themselves. An advantage of building homes for yourself and living in them until they are sold is that, in most localities, contractor's licenses are not required.

APARTMENTS

Small rental units such as duplexes and fourplexes offer the advantage of your living in one unit and having the tenants help buy the property through their rents. While initial rentals will seldom be sufficient to make the payments, the additional cash needed for the payment will often be less than would be required for a comparable single-family home. Excellent financing is usually available for these smaller units.

Although you cannot take depreciation on your own apartment, you can depreciate the other units in the building. This will often result in a net positive cash flow when income tax liability is considered. Smaller apartments have an advantage in that, because of demand, they are usually more readily salable than larger units would be. Nevertheless, larger apartments can be excellent investments.

> My name is Ed L. After graduating college I took a job as a manual arts teacher at a high school in Washington. Shortly thereafter I married and decided to build my own home during a summer vacation. Because of my relatively low income, I decided on a duplex so that my monthly payment would not be a burden. My bank financed me and by doing almost all the work myself, I was able to finish with money left over. The next summer I built a four-family unit, hiring some student labor, and the following summer I built an eight-unit apartment. After just a few years, by refinancing my units plus having a working wife, I was able to quit my job and devote full-time to building apartments. While I have sold some units that I didn't feel would appreciate in value, I kept most of the units. I retired owning 386 units and have a debt-to-equity ratio of less than 30 percent. Needless to say, I have a healthy positive cash flow. My two sons are now in the business. One son is in charge of property management and my other son handles maintenance and contracting for services. I now spend my time between my farm in Washington and a winter home on a golf course in California. My advice is to have a plan, work it, and repeat it.

Some investors have found another advantage to owning apartments. They buy an apartment building and install one of their children in an apartment as manager, giving the son or daughter an essentially tax-deductible apartment and salary. Though college costs are not deductible expenses, this method also gives a student income plus free housing. (Of course the student pays taxes, but they are likely to be minimal.) Warning: If you pay your child an unjustifiable salary, it could spell trouble with the IRS. Go over any such arrangement in advance with your accountant.

Of course, there are disadvantages to owning apartments, and you must decide if you are willing and able to deal with these problems:

- In many situations the decision to do the maintenance and repairs yourself or hire someone to do it will make the difference between a positive and negative cash flow. If you are unwilling to do menial tasks, you had better be prepared to pay for the work.

- The best apartment management is by the owner who lives on the premises. If you are unwilling to give up the privacy of a single-family home, you will either have to constantly check on the property or have a resident manager.

- If you are the type of person who gets emotionally involved with problems of others, you should obtain professional management. You must be able to deal with your tenants on a professional business basis. Landlords who get involved in their tenants' problems hesitate to increase rents, allow rent arrearages to exist, and are slow to evict tenants. Even when you don't live in the building, residential rentals involve interpersonal relationships. You have likely heard, "If you can't stand the heat, get out of the kitchen." Well, this applies to residential investments.

Generally you can expect the highest return from units that give you the greatest problems. Units in run-down areas or units that have collection or tenant difficulties provide higher rates of return than do quality units. However, problem apartments usually have far less appreciation than the better, more trouble-free units. As a buyer of these more desirable types of units you are substituting present income for later appreciation.

One big advantage of troubled units is that owners frequently are very motivated to sell and often will sell with low and even no down payment or will be so eager to get out that bargain prices will be possible.

To take advantage of these situations, you must have the time, maintenance skills, and interpersonal skills necessary to deal with the tenants.

I'm Tom C. I own apartment buildings. I look for property in older but relatively stable neighborhoods where the owners have problems. I check eviction actions to get purchase leads. I also work with several agents who are always on the alert for something for me. Out-of-town owners are usually the most motivated sellers as are people who have recently inherited the property and are having difficulty dealing with the problems.

I look for buildings where I feel I can obtain a positive cash flow by reducing vacancy factor, raising rents, making minimum renovations and repairs, or a combination of the above. If I don't believe I can achieve a positive cash flow within 90 days, I forget the deal.

How successful am I? I currently own over 300 rental units. Not bad for a retired postman who started out 10 years ago with next to nothing.

There are still many opportunities in buying foreclosed apartments. The Federal Deposit Insurance Corporation (FDIC) and local lenders have REOs (Real Estate Owned) that they want to get rid of, as does HUD and the Department of Veterans Affairs. The inventory of available properties varies as to the area of the country. Many of these properties can be purchased at prices and terms where reasonable management can result in a good positive cash flow. As a point of warning, keep in mind that just because a lender has it for sale does not make a property a bargain. It must make economic sense.

MOBILE HOME PARKS

Mobile homes are not really mobile. When removed from a park, few are ever used as housing again. Buyers of parks, realizing that owners could not readily move, raised rents again and again. Because of what some regarded as abuses by park owners, mobile home park residents tend to be litigious. They have also been instrumental in bringing many parks under rent control ordinances. Nevertheless, mobile home parks can be excellent income producers, although quality parks require a significant investment.

A problem mobile home park is one that has a great many vacant spots, usually an older park with many singlewide units. (Singlewide units are usually 10- to 14-foot wide units that were transported to the site as a single unit. More desirable double- and triple-wide units are transported in sections and joined together at the site.) The problem park could be a purchase opportunity if you can solve the problem. One way is to bring in used units and sell the units in place or use them as rentals.

Recreational Vehicle Parks

Recreational vehicle parks are either destination parks catering to weekend and vacation stays or parks catering to travelers primarily interested in a single-night stop. These parks are located on or near major highways. Sites often have concrete pads, water, sewer, and electrical connections. Parks generally have community recreational facilities and planned activities.

If you are interested in recreational vehicle parks, you should be a people person. Management requires the ability to work with people and get them to like you and each other. You also have to be obsessive about keeping facilities clean.

The future for RV parks looks excellent with double-digit growth expected each year. The permit process for new parks can be costly and time-consuming. It is often less costly to buy an existing park than to start from scratch, although RV parks can be a profitable use of land until land values appreciate enough for other development.

For more information on RV parks, contact the National Association of RV Parks and Campgrounds. Their Web site is *www.gocampingamerica.com/arv/*. The site provides links to instructions about operating an RV park and campground.

COMMERCIAL PROPERTY

Commercial property can be an excellent investment. If property is already well leased, the price and down payment required will probably be substantial. Nevertheless, the demand for these investments is strong. While the economy has resulted in increased vacancies in many areas, it has also resulted in some exceptional purchase opportunities. As the economy strengthens, we can expect higher rents and value appreciation.

If you can locate commercial properties with a high vacancy rate, an owner who is running scared could mean an exceptional purchase opportunity for you if you are imaginative and have faith in your ability to locate tenants and solve problems.

Compared to residential property, commercial property can be a high-risk investment. There are relatively few prospective tenants for commercial property. Because people must have a place to stay, residential vacancies do not decrease at the same rate as commercial vacancies during a recessionary period. During such a period, commercial property owners might have to reduce rents significantly to keep or to obtain tenants. This could result in a negative cash flow situation for many years. Of course, the inability to locate any tenants would mean disaster. In addition, overbuilding in your local area also has a negative effect on both your ability to rent as well as in the amount of rent you can get.

The quality of current tenants, the length and other terms of the lease, and the financial strength of the tenant as well as the local economy all affect the risk of commercial investments. In addition, the larger the structure, the larger the repair costs. The need for a new roof or a new boiler in a large structure could exceed the down payment required to buy the property.

Investors love good commercial buildings with a long-term lease from a major tenant. However, if you are starting with little or no cash, these investments will usually be beyond your reach. But when commercial property has been vacant for a long period of time, owners are often willing to sell with little or no down payment. Even when the owner wants a substantial down payment for a vacant commercial building, it can often be optioned with little cash.

When you have limited capital to invest, consider an option to rent with the right to sublease. You would want an option to lease for one year with renewal options, such as for two periods of five years each. You would want as long a period to exercise the option as you can get. You also want the option to buy the property at an agreed price during at least the first few years of the lease. Your option should be negotiated at what you consider to be a favorable or bargain rental and purchase price based on other rentals and sales.

For a small option price you now have control over a property. If you can sublease the property for more than your lease payment, you will have a positive cash flow. At worst, your downside risk is the price you paid for the option.

If you can find a good tenant and can obtain a long-term sublease (remember you have renewal options), then the value of the building will increase based on the lease. You can now try to sell the building and exercise the option to purchase when you find a buyer.

As an alternative you might be able to exercise the option to purchase without having to sell the property. Based on the lease, if it is to a tenant with financial strength, you could obtain 100 percent financing because the value of the building with the tenant should be far greater than the option price. With a strong tenant, you might even be able to obtain financing in excess of the option price. This would mean not only that you would have purchased a property without a down payment, but that it would also have given you spendable cash.

When you sublease property, it is essential that any obligations under your lease be passed on to your tenant. As an example, if you are to be responsible for maintaining the heating and cooling equipment under a long-term commercial lease, then you would want to pass this obligation on to your tenant. Otherwise, you could find yourself having a significant financial burden without any reimbursement from your tenant.

> Clayton J. worked as an agent in a rental and property management business. He was an excellent rental agent and was able to rent property other agents considered unrentable. He left his office, lured away by the larger commissions offered in sales. Later, he returned to rentals in an unusual way. He would look for problem properties and would negotiate an option to rent them on a one-year lease with several renewal options for longer periods. The leases allowed him to sublease. The type of property he looked for usually offered limited-use possibilities and had therefore been vacant for a long period of time. He would offer really minimum rental terms that were often accepted.
>
> Now his job was to find a tenant. The method he used was quite simple. He would go through the Yellow Pages of the local phone book for business categories he thought might be able to use the property. He would call each firm listed in those categories and make his rental pitch. He simply stayed on the phone day after day until he succeeded. In many cases, the difference between what he was obligated to pay in rent and what he received was substantial. His downside risk was never more than the option price. In just a few years he had become very wealthy. His only complaint was that he had to pay income tax on his profit.

Generally, the bigger the rental problem, the greater the profit potential in solving the problem. You should analyze a property. Ask who could use it. Then use Clayton J.'s method. Go through the Yellow Pages of a local phone book; it will give you all kinds of ideas as to possible tenants.

Office buildings generally require substantial down payments unless they have high vacancies. Older buildings often lose their tenants to newer ones. Some owners panic when they see their vacancy factor increasing dramatically and may be receptive to offers with very low down payments.

> My name is Leroy H. and I rent space that I don't own. What I do is constantly check with the General Services Administration (the real estate arm of the federal government) as well as state, county, and city agencies as to real estate rental needs.
>
> Governmental agencies usually require large square footage but can seldom pay enough for quality buildings. I then look for vacant spaces that I feel from experience and from talking to officials will meet the government requirements. My next step is an option to lease the space at as reasonable a rental as I can negotiate with the specific right to sublease. I then try to rent the space to the government. If I am successful, I make the difference in

rental that I can collect from the government. If not, I have lost the amount paid for the option plus a little time. I have learned government needs to the point where I am right at least 25 percent of the time, and this has resulted in a very nice lifestyle for my family.

With the present glut in office space, I am often able to give the government space in "A" category buildings, which they could not afford just a few years ago.

You should be aware of the Americans with Disabilities Act. An owner has responsibilities to make commercial property accessible to handicapped persons to the extent that is readily achievable. While the language of the act is relatively vague, the penalties are not—$50,000 for the first discriminatory act. "Readily achievable" might include ramping curbs for wheelchairs, providing handicapped parking spaces, handrails on steps not ramped, grab-bars in washrooms, and so on. While it will not remove all owner liability, leases should spell out that tenants shall be responsible for compliance with the act within the space leased.

SELF-STORAGE

Self-storage buildings can offer an excellent return. Land can be leased rather than owned. Some manufacturers of metal storage structures can aid in locating financing. Nationally, occupancy for self-storage structures has been estimated at between 75 and 85 percent but it varies by area. By checking with local self-storage facilities, you will get a good feel for your area vacancy factor as well as local rental rates.

Like any other real estate investment, you will have to evaluate the economic feasibility based on land and improvement costs, management, occupancy factors, zoning, and the like. A major Real Estate Investment Trust has thousands of storage units they have placed on commercial property adjacent to major highways. Their interest is to produce income until the property can be developed for a more productive use. You can do the same, use storage buildings for present income and if the land appreciates sufficiently, redevelop the property for a more productive use.

INDUSTRIAL PROPERTY

Industrial property is difficult to deal in because prospective tenants are far fewer than you would find for commercial or residential property.

While well-leased industrial property is highly salable, vacant industrial property requires problem solving. Many industrial buildings were built for particular uses. If you can find the right tenant for the property, you can make a good profit.

If you wish to get involved in industrial property, you should find out about past tenants who used the property. If toxic substances were released on the property, you as the owner could be held liable for cleanup costs even though you did not cause the problem.

FARMS

A home in the country with several acres sounds idyllic. It can also be a super investment. Besides the house, you have land that should increase in value. Often a home and acreage 30 miles from a city will cost little if any more than a home in the city. But don't expect to make money farming a few acres. Many people who thought they would live off the land have done so but not in the way they expected. They found that their land values had so accelerated that they achieved financial independence by selling the land, not by living on it.

Only a special person should consider the small commuter farm. Generally, purchasers must either bring their jobs with them to the property or be willing to commute an hour or more to and from work. The idyllic existence of the "landed gentry" loses some of its luster when you have to get up at 4:00 a.m. to milk the cow, feed a few animals, and leave for work by 5:30 a.m. When you arrive home each night, the cow will need milking again, and there will be evening chores to do. Weekends are not for ball games on the TV with a bottle of your favorite brew; they are devoted to working on fences, buildings, and a thousand and one other things. Most smaller farms don't have sufficient income to support hired help. It is expensive being a gentleman farmer.

On the positive side, many people love commuter farming. With our increasingly impersonal, technical lifestyles, many people relish the manual labor and feeling of accomplishment that farms provide. The owners of small farms often live vicariously through their children, who are able to have pets, even horses. For many, the sacrifices of a small farm are worthwhile.

Also, a small farm can provide a great deal more than lifestyle. To start with, a farm has the advantages of depreciation of the improvements, equipment, and even the livestock. When a homeowner goes to the hardware store and buys a bucket of paint, it is not deductible, but when the small farmer buys the same paint, it is probably a deductible expense.

While few people go into a small farm for the profit motive, it often works out as the best investment of their lives. Besides development possibilities, there are thousands more city people seeking the same escape and willing to pay for it. We can expect this back-to-basics interest to continue well into the future, driving land prices higher and higher.

> My name is Seymour T. and I'm a city boy who has always been attracted to rural life. I recently purchased a 160-acre farm just three hours from my home for $120,000, which was less than I had anticipated spending for a vacation home.
>
> The property has a 10-room brick Victorian home in good condition, a great barn, 60 acres of tillable land, and 40 acres of pasture. The rest is primarily woodlands. As a farm, it was a loser but as a vacation home it's a winner. I leased the pasture and tillable land to a neighboring farm for more than enough to pay my taxes. I let another neighbor keep her horses in my barn and in return she cares for my horses and watches the property when we are away, but that's not often. We are at our country home most weekends year around, and the day school is out until opening in the fall, my family enjoys the rural life.
>
> We have plenty of room for my children's friends and guests. It's a lifestyle we love. I had several additional reasons for buying my farm. In 30 years when I retire, I intend to sell my city home, which has been appreciating in value at a remarkable rate, and move to my farm. I also expect the value of my farm to rise significantly in the future. While my farm is not for sale, it will make a great legacy for my family.

Large farms today are really big investments. What were once considered just family farms are in many areas worth over a million dollars for agricultural use, not for development. Economical farm size varies depending upon the area and crops. For example, 40 acres in an orchard could be very profitable, but it might take several thousand acres in grazing land to make an equal profit in cattle.

Although large farms are frequently profitable, the profits tend to fluctuate. One year's profit can be followed by a huge loss. Real farming investments should be made only by people able to farm themselves or who have large disposable incomes to cover loss years. While there are many professional farm management firms providing complete service, they are expensive. With the high cost of farm management, a purchaser who is not going to personally farm the land should not expect the income to make the payments. Though there are federal loans to buy farmland, generally farm purchases require substantial down payments. The only exception is marginal farmland or land that is completely raw and has never been under cultivation.

RAW LAND

A significant risk of holding raw land is its illiquidity. It takes time to sell, and during recessionary periods the only way you might be able to sell it is at a giveaway price. This problem in selling makes recessionary periods a good time to buy. When a recovery begins, prices tend to firm up fast. Because of the risks involved, raw land purchases should be only a part of a person's overall investment program and even then it should be purchased with risk capital. While raw land has often had fantastic appreciation, it is still a crapshoot.

Many investors like raw land because it offers excellent appreciation potential plus the advantage of no management problems. If there are no tenants and no structures, there are few things that can go wrong.

The investor should realize that raw land is a long-term investment that involves a negative cash flow. Even if the property is fully paid for, taxes still must be paid. No depreciation benefits are possible because only improvements can be depreciated for tax purposes (see Chapter 3). Your personal income should be sufficient to make your payments. Since most of the payments are applied to interest that is deductible, so the higher your income the less it really costs you to buy raw land. Owners customarily finance the buyers on raw land sales. In many areas 10 percent down is common. Sellers will often carry the balance at interest rates less than market rate.

Raw land sales have attracted many sharp operators who want to sell you small parcels at prices far greater than the land is worth. There have been many fraud convictions for this type of sale. I have advised buyers to contact their sellers to renegotiate their purchases when after several years they still owed more than the land was worth. Actually, they can negotiate from a position of some strength, as the alternative to the seller could be to have the property back.

Don't buy land that is part of a heavily advertised development. Firms that buy wholesale and sell at many times retail value to cover high promotional and sales costs usually make television and glossy mail-order presentations. Often land purchased from these dealers would have to appreciate 500 to 1000 percent in value for you to just break even. While these land dealers offer great terms, terms are meaningless when the value isn't there.

The best time to buy raw land is when new construction is slow. When there is a low demand and many sellers, the negative cash flow element of holding raw land increases the likelihood of an advantageous purchase as to both price and terms.

While raw land in many cases has increased in value several thousand percent in short periods of time, it is more speculative than other investments. Tremendous profits are possible from raw land, however, it takes many years before some parcels show significant appreciation.

One danger to recognize in buying any land is that zoning can be changed. A change in zoning can mean a change in value. A change from residential zoning to commercial zoning could result in a substantial increase in value; conversely, a change from commercial to residential zoning would have serious adverse effects on the value of the land.

Some investors have found ways to get income from land until it is ready for development.

My name is Steve K. I achieved financial success because of recreational vehicles. I purchased a travel trailer in 1966 for our family vacations. I discovered that restrictions in my subdivision would not allow me to keep the trailer in my driveway. I contacted the dealer who sold me the trailer. He suggested I find a friend who has a big yard, or arrange with one of the local ranchers to leave my trailer on the rancher's property. I have a degree in business administration, and my situation seemed to be just like the case analysis method problems we had used at school. Here was a problem that could also be an opportunity.

I checked with the county and found out that a storage yard required industrial-type zoning. I also obtained county zoning information. By checking tax records, I began contacting owners of land. I found 10 acres on a good road about three miles from the city. The owner wanted $5000 per acre for the parcel. While electricity was available, it did not have municipal water or sewer and it would be many years before it did have them. I obtained a 60-day option to buy the property at the full price of $50,000 with 5 percent down ($2500), and the balance at 6 percent interest with payments amortized over 30 years, but all due and payable in 10 years. (This means a balloon payment.) I paid $100 for this option.

My next step was to advertise in our local papers, including the free throwaway papers. My ad indicated secure storage for motor homes, trailers, boats, construction equipment, etc., at $15 per month. Before I carried out my plan, I wanted to see if I had correctly perceived the need. I spent about $400 on ads. From the ads I received 28 deposits (one month's rent).

I then exercised my option to buy. I put up storage yard signs and put cyclone fencing with barbed wire around a section of land large enough to hold about 100 units. I put the fencing up so it could be relocated for expansion. I put up security lights (on a timer) and let two Dobermans run loose when the yard was locked. The yard was open from 7:30 a.m. to 9:30 a.m. and from 4:00 p.m. to 6:00 p.m. For opening at any other time we charged a $5 fee.

At first my wife handled the yard. Within three months we had to increase the size of the yard. Within six months, our income from our storage yard far exceeded my salary, so I quit my job to devote full-time to my storage yard. I eventually expanded my yard and had well over 1000 units, from small trailers to bulldozers, at rates ranging from $15 to $50 per month.

My total cash investment for my yard was less than $6000. (I financed the fencing.) It provided great income for more than 20 years. In the back of my mind was always the thought that the land price would eventually be so great that I would be better off selling. Well, it recently hit that point. I recently sold my highly desirable industrial land for $4.5 million. Actually, I didn't really sell it. We worked out a delayed exchange for new apartment units in order to defer taxes on the sale.

A young person buying raw land might prefer buying larger tracts of land at lower prices. These larger parcels seldom fall significantly in value but can appreciate enormously.

People buying for retirement should be concerned with the quality of the land. They should buy smaller parcels of higher-priced land within 30 miles of large residential centers (in excess of one-half million people) or within 5 miles of cities in the 50,000-population category. I recommend the parcel purchased be in the direction where greatest growth is forecast, even though it will likely cost more than property in other areas.

And there are other possibilities.

My name is Oscar W. I purchased 40 acres about 20 miles outside a city where I lived. I paid $1000 per acre for the parcel of marginal pastureland with large rocks and clumps of trees. I purchased the parcel with $4000 down and monthly payments of $271.92 including interest at 7.75 percent. My idea was to retire at 62 (10 years after I purchased the parcel). I hoped to sell half the acreage then and have enough cash to pay off the other half, as well as cash for a down payment to build a house.

It didn't work out the way I had it planned. I was able to retire at 58 and buy a Florida condominium. Six years after I purchased the property, I was able to sell my 40 acres to a developer for $550,000. My investment gave me the pride of ownership of the land, a feeling of security, and finally almost as much money from this one investment as I had earned in a working career of almost 40 years.

LOTS

Because of the costs of large parcels, some investors buy improved lots. While lots generally offer a lower profit potential than raw land, the profit can nevertheless be substantial. Bargain prices are possible on residential lots in periods of low building activity. In addition, the seller usually finances the buyer with a low down payment. An advantage of improved lots over raw land is that lots are usually more readily salable than raw land.

The easiest residential lots to sell are the best lots in terms of location. Builders realize that a bargain price on a lot will often be regretted when it is time to sell.

Some positive features of good residential lots include:

- Trees and large rocks.
- View.
- Size and shape. Larger lots and rectangular-shaped lots are generally easier to sell than smaller, irregular-shaped lots.
- Slope. In many areas, a sloping lot is desirable because it allows for an open lower level or basement and is suited for an upper level deck. In some cases, a garage can be incorporated into the lower level.

During times when housing is undergoing a rapid appreciation in value, you may find that prices of new homes significantly exceed the cost of a lot plus the cost of construction. This is the time of opportunity. Buy lots. What generally happens is that builders seek to build as many units as they can to take advantage of the marketplace. The result is that the increased demand will cause lot prices to soar.

The opposite of the above is when resale prices of newer homes fall below the cost to build the home plus the value of the lot. It is time to unload your lots quickly.

Some young people can't afford the down payment or the payments on a house. They might, however, be able to purchase a lot. Lots can usually be purchased with low down payments and at below-market seller financing.

Frequently, lot ownership can lead to home ownership. The lot, when paid for, will often give the buyer sufficient equity to qualify for a loan to build a house or provide the trading material to trade for a house. In addition, a lot purchase allows the buyer to tie down the price of a major portion of the total house costs.

REITS AND LIMITED PARTNERSHIPS

You can share in large projects by investing in Real Estate Investment Trusts (REITs) and limited partnerships. These are covered in Chapter 6.

Development

Many investors have found that buying a property from another is not as profitable as building the investment property themselves. While it takes time, the savings can be significant. Some developers started out by simply acting as general contractors or building their own homes and realized they could take the experience gained and transfer it to income properties.

Real estate developers as well as investors get into trouble when they don't do their homework. A flawed plan can mean disaster. Problems can be:

1. Unrealistic development or redevelopment costs.
2. Unrealistic time schedule for renting.
3. Unrealistic operational costs.

It is fine to be optimistic but when evaluating a project, you must be conservative and leave a "fudge" factor to cover the unexpected.

The Opportunities Are Waiting

As you can see, real estate investment covers a wide range of opportunities. You may have discovered that you are already a real estate investor but didn't realize it. Your investment choice should be based on your own needs as well as investments you feel comfortable with. Remember that "under all is the land," so let real estate be the foundation for your future.

3
C H A P T E R

Taxation and Real Estate

The spirit of property doubles a man's strength.

Voltaire, 1764

With our progressive income tax, the more money you make, the more taxes you pay. As wages go up, higher percentages are taken for taxes. It has become extremely difficult to accumulate substantial savings from a salary alone. Even when you are able to save, our tax laws tax the interest you earn as ordinary income, raising you further up in the federal and state tax brackets. Our tax laws really have the net effect of penalizing people who are able to increase their earnings or who are able by thrift to save and earn interest on their savings.

Tax evasion is a federal crime, but tax avoidance is not only legal, it is just good common sense. It is possible for an investor to work within the tax laws, pay little if any income taxes, and have significant spendable income.

PROPERTY TAXES AND INTEREST DEDUCTIONS

Real estate makes tax sense. To start with, property taxes are a tax-deductible expense. (They are a deduction for all real estate.) Interest paid on home purchase loans for a principal residence and for a second home is deductible, providing the loan balance does not exceed the cost of the residence plus improvements and provided the indebtedness on the principal residence (plus secondary residence) does not exceed $1 million. (For debts incurred before October 13, 1987, there is no interest limit.) Interest on home equity loans up to $100,000 is also deductible as long as all combined home loans don't exceed the fair market value of the home(s).

Because interest is a tax-deductible expense, Uncle Sam effectively reduces the rate of interest a taxpayer must pay below the stated rate.

Because of the deductibility of interest, a person can refinance real estate and obtain cash that is not taxed as income and have the interest paid a deductible expense. All interest for business and investment properties is deductible without limit.

Depreciation for Tax Purposes

Many investors look for depreciation because depreciation is treated as an expense for tax purposes. While only a paper expense, since an owner pays nothing out, the expense offsets or shelters other income from taxation.

Unfortunately, some investors buy a tax shelter rather than first analyzing it as an investment. Anyone can get a tax break because he lost money on a venture, and it doesn't take much intelligence to lose an entire investment. Don't buy a tax shelter; buy the total investment. Your first consideration should be: Is it a good investment? Look at the investment from the standpoint of appreciation and income. Depreciation is the frosting on the cake.

As stated, depreciation is a paper expense only. The IRS realizes assets such as an apartment building will not last forever. They therefore allow an owner to deduct an amount as depreciation that allows the owner to recoup the investment. Each year the investor deducts the amount of depreciation taken from the cost basis of the property. *Cost basis* is an owner's cost plus improvements made, less the depreciation that the owner has taken.

Only improvements can be depreciated. Land is never depreciated. Only property held for business and investment purposes can be depreciated. Therefore, a homeowner cannot depreciate his or her own home. It is possible, however, to depreciate portions of a home used solely for business purposes, providing the homeowner has no other office. If an audit would upset you, consider not taking a home-office deduction, since it is one of the red flags that the IRS uses to determine which returns will be audited.

For tax purposes, residential property is depreciated over 27.5 years while nonresidential property is depreciated over 39 years. A straight-line method of depreciation is used for tax purposes, which means that an equal amount is depreciated each year until the asset has been fully depreciated.

For a residential property you would depreciate 1/27.5 per year (27.5-year life), or 3.636 percent per year (100%/27.5 = 3.636%). Therefore, if a depreciable improvement cost $100,000, the owner would show $3636 each year as a depreciation expense until the asset was fully depreciated.

To gain the greatest depreciation, an owner will want to apportion as much of the purchase price as possible to improvements and as little as possible to the land. Remember, land cannot be depreciated. One way to go is to use the same proportion of land to value as the tax assessor does. For example, if the tax assessor has shown 95 percent of the value attributable to improvements and only 5 percent to the land, you can use this apportionment, even though it might not necessarily reflect a proper apportionment. The IRS will generally accept the value apportionment of a tax assessor. While tax assessors tend to place less value on the land than appraisers would, this is not always the case. Should you feel the tax assessment proportions are not realistic, you could have a fee appraisal made and then base the value of your depreciable improvements on your cost and the proportion of value the appraiser placed on the improvements. (Keep in mind that you depreciate from your cost, not from an appraised value.)

TAX SHELTERING

Assume a property has a cash flow of $5000. This means that the cash income exceeds cash expenditures by $5000 for the year. In other words, the investor has $5000 spendable cash in his or her pocket. If the property also had depreciation of $10,000 in that year, it would mean that the property actually suffered a paper loss of $5000. Not only would the $5000 in spendable income not be taxed, but also the $5000 loss could offset $5000 of additional income. The depreciation "shelters" this income from taxation. Real estate is the only real tax shelter left for the average investor.

The 1986 Tax Reform Act has limited this tax shelter. Real estate losses are considered passive losses. Passive losses can still be used to offset passive income (from other real estate) without limit. In other words, if you show a loss on one property of $100,000, it will offset $100,000 in what otherwise would be taxable income from another property. The 1986 Tax Reform Act also limited a taxpayer's ability to shelter active income (income from wages and other activities) with passive losses.

Investors with an adjusted gross income of less than $100,000 can use passive real estate losses to shelter up to $25,000 of income from other sources. For taxpayers having between $100,000 and $150,000 of adjusted gross income, this shelter has been phased out. For each two dollars adjusted gross income over $100,000, the $25,000 limit is reduced by one dollar. Therefore, an investor whose adjusted gross income was $120,000 would be limited to a $15,000 tax shelter. This investor could still use real estate losses to offset $15,000 of active income as well as unlimited gains from other passive real estate investments.

Another limitation imposed by the 1986 Tax Reform Act is that investors who do not actively manage their property cannot use their passive losses to shelter any active income. This means that investors who purchased limited partnership shares or similar investments can no longer use these paper losses from depreciation as a shelter against other income.

If you receive a significant taxable income from real estate rentals, you should contact your accountant to evaluate the possibility of showing the income as self-employment income. While this could be subject to Social Security contributions, it could also allow you to place a portion of the income into a tax-sheltered retirement plan.

CAPITAL GAINS

The 2003 Tax Relief Act benefited real estate investors with lower tax rates on capital gains. *A capital gain* is the gain realized on a sale of capital assets such as real estate. The gain would be the difference between an investor's adjusted cost basis and the price realized at a sale after selling expenses.

As an example, assume an investor purchased a property for $500,000 and put in $300,000 in capital improvements. Also assume the investor depreciated the property $200,000. The investor's adjusted cost basis would be $600,000:

Purchase price	$500,000
Capital improvements	+300,000
	800,000
Depreciation taken	−200,000
Adjusted cost basis	$600,000

In this example, assume the property was sold for $1,000,000 and the seller had selling costs of $50,000. The capital gains would be computed as follows:

Sale price	$1,000,000
Sale costs	− 50,000
Adjusted cost basis	− 600,000
Capital gains	$ 350,000

For property held for one year or less the gain would be taxed as ordinary income for the taxpayer. However, if the asset is held for more than 12 months, it is considered a long-term capital gain and is taxed at a maximum rate of 15 percent. For taxpayers in the 10 and 15 percent tax brackets, the long-term capital gain is taxed at 5 percent. In 2008 the tax for these lower income brackets will be zero.

The tax rate for long-term gains attributable to depreciation deduction remains at 25 percent. (If you are selling property that you have depreciated, check with an accountant as to tax liability.)

LOSSES FROM A SALE

For income and investment property a loss from a sale (capital loss) can be used to offset a gain from another sale. (You suffer a loss when your adjusted cost basis is greater than the sale price.)

If you are going to take a loss on a sale, you want the loss to be worthwhile. You want to be able to fully use it. You should consider selling property that has appreciated in value in the same year as you take your loss. In this way your loss will shelter a gain. If you don't have a gain, then you are able to use your loss to shelter $3000 of other income from taxation. You can carry your excess loss forward and shelter $3000 each year in subsequent years until your loss is used up. (This only applies to income and investment property.)

While gains from the sale of your residence would be taxable, losses from the sale of your residence will not be recognized. Some taxpayers will change the character of their personal residence to income property so they can depreciate it and lower their adjusted cost basis to avoid the loss. By renting your home you might be able to change the character of the home to income property in order to utilize a sale loss, but please see an accountant or tax attorney before you do anything.

Universal Tax Exclusion—Principal Residence

Formerly only elderly persons received an exclusion from capital gains taxes on the sale of their personal residences. This was a one-time exclusion for a lifetime. Well, the rules have changed and now offer significant tax benefits to an investor who has owned a home and used it as a principal residence in two of the five years preceding the sale.

If the investor meets the above residence requirements, the individual investor is entitled to a $250,000 exclusion from capital gains. Couples could therefore have a $500,000 exclusion from capital gains. Both spouses, however, must meet the residency requirement for both to take the exclusion.

Fixer-upper buyers and builders who move into a home they built are now making certain they meet the two-year residency requirement before they sell if they expect a significant capital gain.

The beauty of this exclusion is that it is not just for one-time use. You can use it every two years, have significant gains, and pay no taxes unless the gains exceed the exclusion. In such a case only the excess would be taxed as a capital gain.

The deduction is available for a second home (vacation home) if during your periods of occupancy the second home is your principal residence. If you live in the home five months each year for five years as your principal residence, you would meet the two-year (24-month) occupancy requirement.

If your deduction exceeds your gain, you don't have to report the sale of your principal residence on your income tax return. For more information, contact your tax adviser.

Installment Sales

Because income tax is progressive in nature, the tax rate increases with income. It is possible for some taxpayers to keep their income taxes at a lower rate by spreading the profit from a sale over a number of years. This benefit is available for total obligations under $5 million. Dealers cannot defer income by use of installment sales. *Dealers* are persons in the business of buying and selling property. In answer to a question posed to a CPA as to when a person is a dealer, the CPA replied, "When the IRS says you are one."

TAX-FREE EXCHANGES

Tax-free exchanges allow the taxpayer to get the equity out of his or her property and into another property without paying any tax on the appreciation in value of the property. Tax-free exchanges are covered in detail in Chapter 12.

INVESTMENT TAX INCENTIVES

Federal, state, and local governments offer tax incentives to encourage development in economically distressed areas, as well as to preserve historic structures.

Empowerment Zones

HUD has designated some cities as empowerment zones. Empowerment zone designation allows the total cost of some improvements to be written off as deductions in the year made rather than requiring that the improvements be depreciated over the life of the improvement. Empowerment zones also have a tax incentive for firms that locate into the zones. Federal employee wage credits may be obtained for new hires that are residents of the zone. The wage credits are up to 20 percent for the first $15,000 of salary or training expense. The purpose of these incentives is to make inner city developments more attractive to developers and employers.

Enterprise Zones

States may designate economically distressed areas as enterprise zones and offer state tax credits and other benefits. In some states, firms are credited with sales tax paid on equipment purchased as well as significant tax credits for each new hire.

Community Development Aid

Some states and communities encourage developments that will bring in jobs by offering land at bargain prices, providing low interest development loans, placing a moratorium on property taxes, as well as a variety of other benefits.

Federal Historic Designation

An investor in a property with a National Park's designation as a historic place might be entitled to a 20 percent federal investment tax credit for certified rehabilitation. This means that 20 percent of the cost of the rehabilitation is returned to the investor as credits to taxes owed.

Various benefits offered could make the difference between a poor or marginal investment and one that makes economic sense.

Special Homeowner Property Tax Benefits

A number of states provide property tax benefits for certain homeowners who reside in their homes: veterans, disabled persons, or elderly persons. Generally, the benefits are that a portion of the property value is exempt from taxation. In some states, elderly persons are allowed to defer paying their property taxes until their home is sold or the taxpayer dies.

4

Understanding Financing

The best investment on earth is earth.

Louis Glickman, 1957

It is unusual for a buyer of real estate to pay cash for a purchase. Besides the fact that the amount of cash required is very large, a cash purchase normally is not generally good business. The average sale is generally financed either by an individual, in the case of the seller financing the buyer, or by a lending institution. Lending institutions use money supplied by savers who are satisfied with a comparatively low rate of return coupled with safety. By using financing to buy real estate, you use other people's money (OPM) to make money for yourself.

YOUR CREDIT

Your credit is extremely important; as it affects not only your ability to obtain loans but the price you must pay for the loans (the interest rate charged).

There are three main credit reporting agencies for individuals. They are:

Equifax (800) 685-1111 or *www.equifax.com/*
Experian (TRW) (888) 397-3742 or *www.experian.com/*
Transunion (800) 916-8800 or *www.tuc.com/*

By contacting one or more of these agencies, you can obtain your credit report. If there is incorrect information in the report, notify the reporting agency. The Fair Credit Reporting Act allows you to fill out a credit dispute form, which you can file with the credit agency for investigation. You can also file an explanation to be included with your credit report.

Reporting errors are fairly common so it is a good practice to check your credit report on an annual basis.

Fair Isaac Corporation has developed a credit scoring system (FICO score) used by most lenders, as well as Freddie Mac and Fannie Mae. Credit is scored for an individual from 375 to 900. The higher the score the greater the credit worthiness of the borrower. While lenders apply the scores based on their own criteria, generally scores of 660 and above are considered very good, scores from 620 to 660 are not bad scores but are just not considered as desirable. Scores below 620 generally mean that institutional lenders will not make a loan. There are, however, sub-prime lenders who will take the greater risk but will charge higher loan fees and interest rates to compensate for the increase risk.

Your FICO score is the score at the instant it is computed. It can vary from day to day. While the exact formula for determining your FICO score is known only to Fair Isaac, the score is based on credit payment history, the ratio of debt to credit limits, credit problems such as repossessions and bankruptcy, the number of credit balances, how long you have had credit, applications for new credit, type of credit used, inquiries as to your credit, as well as derogatory creditor information.

Besides sub-prime lenders who charge relatively high interest, persons with credit problems have other investment options such as loan assumptions, owner financing, and use of options. These will be covered in this and subsequent chapters.

METHODS OF FINANCING

The three primary instruments of financing are mortgages, trust deeds, and land contracts.

Mortgages

A mortgage is a two-party instrument in which the mortgagor (borrower) gives a promissory note and a mortgage to a mortgagee (lender).

While the mortgagee is customarily a lending institution such as a savings and loan association, sometimes the seller finances the buyer. When this happens, the seller is the mortgagee and takes a mortgage as security for the balance of the purchase price.

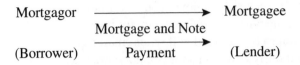

A mortgage is recorded with the county recorder. Once recorded, it gives notice of the mortgagee's interest in the mortgaged property. When the mortgagor pays off the mortgage, the mortgagee gives the mortgagor a satisfaction of the mortgage, which is also recorded. Once the satisfaction of mortgage is on record, the mortgagee's interest in the mortgaged property is terminated.

Should the mortgagor default on the payments or fail to pay the taxes or insurance, the mortgagee can foreclose on the mortgage. In some states, the mortgagor is given a period of redemption in which to pay off the loan after the foreclosure sale.

When a mortgage is foreclosed, the property is sold at auction. If the sale brings less than the amount owing to the mortgagee, in some states it is possible to get a deficiency judgment against the mortgagor for the balance. However, in many states deficiency judgments are either not possible or are very difficult to obtain. I recommend that you check with an attorney in your state to determine your state's laws regarding deficiency judgments so you understand your liability in the event of foreclosure.

Trust Deeds

To avoid the lengthy redemption period allowed in many states for a mortgagor in default, trust deeds have gained favor. More than half of the states allow trust deeds although some of these states also use mortgages.

A trust deed is a three-party instrument by which a borrower (trustor) makes payments on a note to a lender (beneficiary). In order to provide the beneficiary with greater security, the trustor actually gives title (a trust deed) to a third person (trustee) to hold.

Like the mortgage, the trust deed is recorded to show the interest of the beneficiary. When the trustor has paid the beneficiary in full, the beneficiary orders the trustee to return the title to the trustor. This is done with a deed of reconveyance from the trustee to the trustor. Once the deed of reconveyance is recorded, the interest of the beneficiary is terminated. In the event the trustor defaults, foreclosure is relatively quick. After a short notice period, usually several months, the trustee has a sale and the trustor's interest is lost. Generally, no redemption period is allowed after the sale.

Land Contracts

A land contract (contract of sale or contract for deed) is a two-party instrument in which the vendor (seller) retains title and the vendee (buyer) is merely given possession. The vendee does not receive a deed until the vendor has been paid.

Vendor — Seller	Possession	Vendee — Buyer
(Retains Legal Title)	⟶ Payments ⟵	(Has Possession)

Land contracts are normally used in situations in which the seller is financing a buyer who is buying with a relatively low down payment. Since, under a land contract, the seller retains the best possible security, the title, foreclosure is generally relatively quick and simple. However, foreclosure under a land contract in some states can be as time-consuming as for a mortgage. While most states have legislation to protect the vendee, land contracts can still be dangerous. The vendor might be unable to deliver clear title after the vendee has paid for the property. It is now possible for the vendee under a land contract to obtain title insurance for protection. I recommend such insurance very strongly. The vendee should also insist that the land contract be recorded.

Priority of Loans

The priority of mortgages, trust deeds, and land contracts is generally determined by the time and date of recording. A mortgage that is recorded later than another one on the same property is a second mortgage, which makes it a secondary lien. (A lien is a claim or charge against property. A creditor can enforce a lien by foreclosing or forcing the sale of the debtor's property to pay off the claim.) The problem with a secondary (junior) lien such as a second mortgage is that, should a prior lien be foreclosed, the junior lien is wiped out. In order to protect their interests, holders of junior liens can generally step in and make the payments on the foreclosing lien, thus stopping foreclosure. They can then foreclose on their junior liens. In this way they end up owning the property with a prior lien on it. If a junior lienholder waits for the fore-closure sale of a prior lien, he or she then has to bid cash to protect his or her interests. A junior lienholder can generally record a request for no-tice of default so that he or she must be informed of the foreclosure of a prior loan.

PRIMARY FINANCING

Primary financing refers to first mortgages and trust deeds. There are a number of sources for primary financing.

Mortgage Companies

Currently, the largest source of primary financing for home loans is mort-gage companies. Mortgage companies generally make loans using their own funds and then resell packages of loans to banks, insurance compa-nies, pension funds, Fannie Mae, or Freddie Mac. Because loans are resold, the mortgage company will take care to ensure any loans they make meet the loan requirements of the purchaser.

Mortgage companies make money on loan costs and origination fees. If they are able to lend at premium rates, then they can resell the loans at a premium above face value. Besides local mortgage companies, there are literally hundreds of lenders online. As a borrower, you should consider an Internet search for the best combination of interest rates and loan costs for the type of loan you're seeking.

Banks

Banks originate a great many primary loans. Construction loans are likely to be made by banks. Banks like short-term, higher interest loans, al-though almost every bank will make long-term real estate loans.

Like mortgage companies, banks will often resell loans they make to Fannie Mae (Federal National Mortgage Association—FNMA) or Freddie Mac (Federal Home Loan Mortgage Corporation—FHLMC). These or-ganizations buy Federal Housing Authority, Veterans Administration, and conventional loans that conform to their guidelines (conforming loans). Unlike mortgage companies, banks might keep some of the loans that they originate.

Bob Bruss, the syndicated real estate columnist, has come up with a practical classification of lenders as "good guys" and "bad guys."

Good-guy lenders are lenders who keep the loan. Because of this, the loan does not need to conform to the loan standards of Fannie Mae and Freddie Mac. He considers these loan standards unreasonable at times in that they act to constrain what could otherwise be a healthy real estate market. Good-guy lenders are more flexible and are not likely to turn down a loan because the borrower's credit history reveals a late payment three years previously.

Bad-guy lenders are lenders who intend to sell the mortgages they make on the secondary mortgage market. These lenders are at the mercy of Fannie Mae and Freddie Mac. If Fannie Mae or Freddie Mac rejects a loan they originate, then they are stuck with it. In some cases they have to agree to buy back loans that default in order to sell them. Because of this, bad-guy lenders want every *i* dotted and *t* crossed. If they have any doubts at all, they reject the loan.

Some lenders are bad guys on their fixed-rate mortgages but good guys on their adjustable-rate mortgages, which are less risky for them. When shopping for a loan, ask if they are going to keep the loan or if they intend to resell it.

Think twice about advancing significant loan application costs to a lender who is a bad guy unless you are certain you will pass the qualifications with flying colors. Incidentally, if you are self-employed, look for a good guy. Bad guys are tough on self-employed borrowers.

Insurance Companies

Insurance companies prefer larger loans for commercial or large residential projects. They often insist on an equity participation (participation loan). They are generally not much help to small investors.

Insurance companies make loans directly as well as purchase packages of loans from other lenders.

Pension Funds

Pension funds have become a significant investor in real estate loans. They usually buy loans on the secondary mortgage market from other lenders.

Since the decline in stock prices, many pension funds have increased their mortgage portfolios.

Mortgage Brokers

Mortgage brokers are not lenders. They bring together borrowers and lenders. Generally, mortgage brokers deal in loans that other lenders would not make. Borrowers who could obtain loans from banks or mortgage companies usually avoid mortgage brokers because of high loan costs and high interest rates charged. Lenders are likely to be private lenders although some banks will purchase sub-prime loans made by mortgage brokers.

Unscrupulous Lenders

Some lenders engage in unscrupulous tactics. As an example, right before closing the loan transaction, they will indicate a problem, which might mean higher loan origination fees or a slightly higher rate of interest. The loan you thought was "locked in" apparently had a trapdoor for the lender. Lenders who have a reputation of this type of tactic should be avoided. If you feel that a lender has treated you unfairly, document the facts and send the material to the lender's state licensing agency.

SECONDARY FINANCING

Secondary financing refers to second mortgages and trust deeds. In the case of purchase money loans, the seller carries the loans. Otherwise, institutional and noninstitutional lenders make them. Noninstitutional lenders include private individuals, mortgage brokers, union pension funds, and trusts. Because secondary financing involves a greater risk than first mortgages, the interest rate for these loans is higher. As a general rule, the greater the risk, the higher the interest rate the lender will demand.

Both banks and mortgage companies now make home equity loans. Some consumer credit companies have also entered into this lucrative lending area.

Mortgage loan brokers are also active in the secondary financing market. They advertise to the public that it's easy to borrow on a home. They also advertise for investors by emphasizing a high rate of return. The mortgage loan brokers charge significant commissions and fees for putting borrowers and lenders together. They are expensive loan middlemen.

Generally, a primary lender will not want a buyer to obtain the down payment through a second mortgage. The primary lender will require the borrower to verify the source of the funds if the purchase is for a residence, as it will affect the ratios used to qualify the borrower. After a person has purchased a property there is no prohibition or restriction on placing secondary loans on the property.

QUALIFYING FOR A LOAN

To obtain a new loan, you will have to meet lender-qualifying criteria. Lenders are interested in your credit, the collateral for the loan, and the capacity of the borrower to make the loan payments. Lenders typically measure credit by FICO scores and collateral by appraisals. They measure capacity by ratios. They use what are known as *front-end* and *back-end ratios*.

The front-end ratio is the ratio of PITI (monthly principal, interest, taxes, and insurance payments) to the borrower's gross monthly income.

$$\text{PITI} \div \text{gross monthly income} = \text{front-end ratio}$$

Lenders will generally not accept a front-end ratio more than 28 percent. If a loan would result in PITI monthly payments of $1000 and the gross monthly income of the borrower was $4500, then $1000 divided by $4500 would equal 22.2 percent; so the borrower would qualify.

Besides the front-end ratio, lenders also apply a back-end ratio, which considers a borrower's existing long-term debt payments. The back-end ratio is the ratio of monthly PITI (principal, interest, tax, and insurance payments) plus monthly debt payments to gross monthly income.

$$\text{PITI} + \text{debt payment} \div \text{gross monthly income} = \text{back-end ratio}$$

Lenders generally will not accept a back-end ratio of more than 36 percent, so if PITI plus debt service was $1500 and the buyer's gross annual income was $4500, the buyer would have a back-end ratio of 33⅓ percent and would qualify.

Because debt service is an important qualification factor, delay buying a new car or furniture on installments until after a home purchase has been completed, or you will have bought yourself right out of a mortgage.

Ratios are not etched in stone. Lenders who will be keeping a loan for their portfolio might allow higher ratios. Also, certain types of loans such as VA loans allow higher ratios.

Check with local mortgage companies as to special state and federal programs for loan qualifications and down payment requirements. You should check with several companies because some may not wish to tell you about programs with which they do not care to get involved.

Local lenders can also prequalify you for a loan and will tell you how much of a loan you can carry based on the type of loan. Prequalification will save you wasted time in checking on property you cannot qualify for.

Assuming Existing Loans

When you purchase a property that has an existing loan against it, you can either refinance it, which means that the old loan is paid off and a new loan placed against the property, or you can "assume" or "take subject to" the existing loan. A loan can be safely assumed if it does not include a prohibition on assumption (a due-on-sale clause). When you assume a loan, you agree to be liable for it. Depending on the state, you may be liable for a deficiency judgment should you assume a loan that is later foreclosed and the foreclosure sale yields less than is still owing on the loan.

A take-subject-to loan is different. You recognize that there is a loan against the property and that if you wish to keep the property you will have to make the payments on the loan. However, if you don't make the payments and the property is foreclosed, no deficiency judgment is possible against you because you never agreed to be personally obligated for the existing loan.

A buyer, who would not qualify for the loan, can still assume a loan. FHA loans made prior to December 15, 1989, and VA loans made prior to March 1, 1988, can be assumed by anyone regardless of income or credit. FHA loans made after December 15, 1989, can be assumed only by owner-occupants (not investors) who qualify for the loan. VA loans made after March 1, 1988, can be assumed only with approval of the Department of Veterans Affairs.

Some adjustable-rate mortgages allow assumption if the buyer qualifies for the loan being assumed.

Due-on-Sale Clauses

A due-on-sale clause gives the lender the right to accelerate payments on a loan if a property or a beneficial interest is transferred. In other words, the lender can demand that the loan be paid off in full.

During the late 1970s, interest rates rose dramatically to the point where lenders who had large portfolios of real estate loans were losing money since the interest rates they were paying on deposits exceeded the average interest returns on their loan portfolios. At the time, the interest rates for new real estate loans were very high which adversely affected real estate sales. A solution for buyers was to assume existing low-interest loans. Lenders tried to enforce their due-on-sale clauses but in many areas were unable to do so because of state court decisions that rendered the clauses unenforceable. The Garn–St. Germain Depository Institution Act of 1982 basically determined that lending institutions could enforce due-on-sale clauses.

Due-on-sale clauses are not enforceable for every transfer. They cannot be enforced when the transfer is to a spouse or children (divorce) or to an heir (death). There is no acceleration when the transfer is to a surviving joint tenant or when title is given to a living trust.

Many methods have been devised to avoid the acceleration of the due-on-sale clause, most of which involve keeping it a secret from the lender. If a lender doesn't know of a sale, he cannot enforce the due-on-sale clause. However, a buyer will want to be protected as a party on the property insurance policy. Since the lender is going to receive a copy of the policy, the lender will be informed of the transfer.

Many people use leases and lease options to avoid the due-on-sale clause. Because the insurance, taxes, and payments are still made by the lessor, the lender is unlikely to discover that there has been a transfer of interest. However you should realize that the law is specific in that leases exceeding three years and leases containing options do trigger the lenders rights to accelerate the loan under the due-on-sale clause.

Lenders have not been actively looking for violations of the due-on-sale clause. Possibly because interest rates are currently low and there is no strong economic motive to call in loans. While I agree that the likelihood of getting caught might be fairly slim, I do not personally advocate trying to get around the due-on-sale clause. Besides the ethical objection, buyers could find themselves having 30 days to obtain new financing, which could be in a period of tight money. If buyers had access to funds that would pay off the loans, then the danger of acceleration would be removed.

You will find dozens of Web sites offering dozens of approaches to avoid the due-on-sale clause being enforced. Many of the sites promote books and seminars to teach you their "secrets." I have reviewed many of these methods and find them legally questionable at best and, in many cases, bordering on fraud.

Some seminars promote unrecorded land contracts that could place the buyer's interest in jeopardy should liens be filed against the seller who, on the record, is still the owner. Others advise using complicated trust arrangements. Many of the "gurus" offering secret ways to avoid the due-on-sale clause attempt to justify their methods by lambasting lenders as evil blood-sucking corporations. I find this to be an interesting approach to morality.

There are other approaches to financing that you should consider where you won't have to worry about someone finding out what you are doing.

For an in-depth analysis of the due-on-sale clause, I suggest you check John Reed's Web site: *www.JohnTReed.com/dueonsale.html.*

Bargaining with the Lender

If a seller has very little equity in a property and the real estate market is depressed, consider asking the lender to approve a loan assumption. Point out that their alternative is likely to be their owning another piece of real estate that does not pay interest. Lenders want interest not property ownership so your offer may be accepted.

If the current interest rate is the same or lower than the loan to be assumed, lenders will frequently agree to allow a loan assumption or a *novation,* which really is a substitution of parties to the existing loan. One reason you might want to assume a loan at the same or even higher interest rate than you could obtain with a new loan is loan costs. The costs associated with obtaining a new loan might raise the effective rate of the new loan above the rate of the loan to be assumed. In addition, assumption is often quicker than refinancing.

If a lender, after knowing of a prior loan assumption, failed to enforce the due-on-sale clause, the lender could have jeopardized his rights. Failure to enforce a due-on-sale provision could result in a court determination that the lenders had waived their rights to a later enforcement of the due-on-sale clause, even upon a later loan assumption. While you may not want to chance a lawsuit because of both time and expense, you could use the prior waiver as a bargaining tool with a lender. For example, you could agree to a slightly higher interest rate while asking that the loan be increased.

If a below-market-interest-rate loan is assumable, you can also bargain with the lender. You can point out that you could assume the loan and obtain secondary financing, or as an alternative the lender could refinance the property with a new higher interest rate loan at a greater amount. The lender, by advancing additional money will thus clear its books of a low-yield loan.

For example, assume there is an existing $500,000 loan at 5.5 percent interest. You might offer to increase the rate to 7.5 percent if the lender agrees to increase the loan to $750,000. Point out that this really means the lender effectively receives 11.5 percent interest on the $250,000 that the lender advances (2% increase on $500,000 or 4% on $250,000 plus 7.5% on $250,000 = 11.5% for the additional $250,000 advance).

If a loan is not assumable, you could also strive for a new "blended rate" loan—a rate of interest higher than the rate on the current loan, but nevertheless lower than the market rate of interest. If the seller has little equity in the property and the alternative could well be the lender ending up owning the property, the lender might be persuaded to accept less than market interest on a new loan. Again, in a depressed market, a lender does not want to own more real estate. The same is true for problem properties.

Actually, there is no need to worry about due-on-sale clauses when low interest and low down payment loans are readily available. New financing can make more sense than trying to assume an existing loan. Loan assumptions are only desirable when they offer a lower interest rate than new loans, new loans cannot be obtained, or the buyer cannot qualify for a loan.

LOAN TYPES AND TERMS

Amortized and Unamortized Loans

Amortized loans pay off total interest and principal in equal payments over the full term of the loan. Unamortized and partially amortized loans have balloon payments. They have a series of equal payments followed by a last, usually significantly (balloon) larger payment. Customarily such a loan will include a statement like "all due and payable in ___ years."

As a buyer you should be aware of the fact that if a loan has a balloon payment, it means that you will have to make a very large payment—

much more than the regular monthly payment—when the loan comes due. If you are unable to obtain refinancing or otherwise cannot make the balloon payment, you could be foreclosed. Usually you can expect to obtain refinancing because of your increased equity. However, it is wise to arrange new financing well in advance. Often, by agreeing to increase the interest rate before the balloon payment is due, you can persuade the person holding the loan to extend it. But it depends on the market. Lenders tend to be very cooperative in a depressed real estate market, less so in a hot market.

Seller financing and some adjustable-rate loans are often structured with very low payments but negative loan amortization. When there is negative amortization, the amount you owe increases rather than decreases with each payment. Your payments, while low, are not sufficient to pay the interest that is accruing. Before you get yourself into a negative amortization situation, realize that the day of reckoning will come. Eventually, you will have to refinance. The amount of your payment will be significantly more than if you had gone with an amortized loan in the first place.

A *straight loan,* or *term loan,* is a loan with payments of interest only. Because the loan is not amortized, the payments are lower than for a loan that repays the principal as well as the interest. Straight loans are due in full at a set date. Because the entire principal must be paid at a specified date, the owner must generally refinance the property. Payments on an amortized loan are only a few percentage points higher than the payments on a straight loan. Because of this, you would only want a straight loan when you absolutely must keep payments as low as possible or the loan is to be for a very short time period.

Prepayment Penalties

Loans frequently have prepayment penalties. Lenders feel that the agreement is for a long-term loan and that by wanting to pay the loan off early, the borrower is breaching the agreement. They feel that the penalty is justified because it takes time and money to put the money out again to earn interest. Lenders frequently require six months' interest on the loan balance for prepayment.

Lenders will ask for this prepayment penalty even when you wish to prepay a loan that is at a rate of interest below the current market rate. You can very often talk a lender into waiving the prepayment penalty by indicating that you don't have to prepay but will do so only if the penalty is waived. If the lender believes that you are selling the property and it will be refinanced, then the lender will refuse to waive it.

If a loan allows payments of a set dollar amount "or more" per month, there can be no prepayment penalty. The borrower has the right to prepay.

Many states limit both the amount and time period for which a lender can charge a prepayment penalty. These limitations generally only apply to residential loans.

While normally only found in personal property loans, some states allow some real estate loans (generally nonresidential) to have lock-in clauses. These clauses are vicious because while they allow the borrower to prepay a loan, they lock the borrower into paying all interest as if the loan had gone to maturity. Even with a lock-in clause, lenders are frequently willing to negotiate a prepayment penalty much lower than they are entitled to.

Hard Money Loan

A *hard money loan* is a loan in which the lender actually supplies cash. The lender either puts up money for the borrower to buy property or gives an owner money based on the security of the property. Hard money loans bear market rate of interest.

Purchase Money Loan (Soft Money Loan)

A *purchase money loan* is a loan in which the seller finances the buyer. The seller really carries the loan, or paper. Suppose an owner sells a property to a buyer taking a down payment. If the balance of the purchase price were a mortgage given by the purchaser to the seller, then the seller is financing the purchaser.

Sellers will frequently carry the paper on loans at a lower interest rate than would be required for a hard money loan. One reason is that individual sellers cannot usually get a higher rate of interest on a long-term investment. If a seller is only getting 2 percent on a savings account, he or she might be willing to carry paper at 5.5 percent, even though the going mortgage rate is 6.5 percent. Another reason is that the part of the purchase price carried by the seller is usually mostly profit. Sellers are often so interested in the dollars they will receive as profit that they fail to realize that the interest can be a material part of their profit.

Many of the investment gurus will tell you to find motivated owners who will handle the financing at below-market interest with no down payment and sell to you at least 30 percent below market value. Country bumpkins are in short supply. Hoping to find one can be an exercise in futility.

While you're not likely to find below-market seller financing for desirable homes or apartments, seller financing with a low down payment and below-market interest is possible where *it costs the seller money to hold the property*. Prime situations for seller financing would be in buying raw acreage or lots or where there is a problem with the property.

The practical use of seller financing will be covered in Chapter 5.

15-Year Loan versus 30-Year Loan

Because of lower lender risk, lenders are willing to give 15-year loans at from about 0.5 percent lower interest rates than they are asking for 30-year loans.

While a longer amortization period means a lower loan payment, a longer amortization period also means significantly more money spent on interest. Table 4–1 clearly shows you the advantage of paying off a loan with the shortest amortization period possible.

If you can afford a slightly higher payment, consider the following facts:

- The monthly payment to amortize $100,000 for 30 years at 6.5 percent interest is $632.07.

- The monthly payment to amortize $100,000 for 15 years at 6.5 percent is $871.11, or $239.04 more per month. However, let us see the effect of that $239.04 per month:

TABLE 4–1

$100,000 Amortized Loan at 6.5 Percent

Length of Loan (years)	Monthly Payment
10	$1135.48
15	871.11
20	745.58
30	632.07
35	604.16
40	505.46

- $632.07 × 12 = $7584.84 in annual payments × 30 = $227,545.20 total payments on a 6.5 percent, 30-year loan. If we deduct the $100,000 principal payment, we can see that we are paying $127,545.20 in interest.

- On a 15-year loan the payment of $871.11 × 12 = $10,453.32 per year × 15 = $156,799.80. When we deduct the principal we can readily see that at 6.5 percent interest a $100,000, 15-year loan has total interest of only $56,799.80. A 30-year loan for the same amount and interest rate totals more than twice the amount of interest at $127,545.20. If the 15-year loan were at a lower rate (which is usually the case), the difference in interest paid would be even greater. As an example, if a 6.5 percent fixed-rate interest loan were available for 30 years, the chances are that a 15-year loan would be available for 6 percent. Monthly payments on a 15-year loan at 6 percent for $100,000 would be $843.86. Over the 15 years, total payments would amount to $151,894.80 and total interest would be only $51,894.80 (after deducting the $100,000 principal). Therefore, a 15-year, $100,000 loan at 6 percent interest would only cost 40.7 percent of the interest of a $100,000, 30-year loan at 6.5 percent.

On loans that allow the borrower to pay more than the loan payment, a borrower can save considerable interest by making an additional payment each year. The borrower must make certain it is a payment on the principal or a lender could regard it simply as an early payment.

Wraparound Loan

A *wraparound loan* is seller financing where a new loan is written to cover the existing loans plus the seller's equity. This kind of loan enables a seller to keep the benefits of a below-market-rate assumable loan.

As an example, assume there is an existing mortgage for $100,000 at 6 percent interest and the seller will be carrying the financing for $50,000 equity plus the $100,000 owed at an 8 percent rate.

Existing Loan	Seller's Equity
$100,000	$50,000
6%	8%

$150,000   8%

The seller will be receiving the equivalent of 12 percent on the $50,000 equity since the seller receives 2 percent additional interest on $100,000 plus 8 percent on his or her equity.

If, as a buyer, you are offered seller financing with a wraparound loan, land contract, or even just a second mortgage, you will want to find out if the primary loan has a due-on-sale clause so you can assess the risk involved.

If there were a due-on-sale clause in the underlying mortgage, a wraparound loan, land contract, or second mortgage would be dangerous to the buyer as the first mortgage holder could demand payment in full. If the seller could not obtain refinancing, the property would be foreclosed and the equity of the buyer would be wiped out.

The same net effect of a wraparound loan can be obtained by use of a land contract (contract for deed). The land contract would be written at a higher rate of interest than the seller is paying on the existing loan(s). The seller then takes advantage of the interest differential.

Adjustable-Rate Mortgage (ARM)

An adjustable-rate mortgage has an interest rate that can be raised or lowered during the term of the loan. The interest is usually tied to a federal cost-of-funds rate, a Treasury rate, a prime rate, or the LIBOR (London Inter-Banking Offering Rate). When the interest rate increases, the payments increase.

It is very difficult for a borrower to compare adjustable-rate mortgages offered by different lenders because they tend to differ in a number of key areas such as:

- Loan costs (points, appraisal fees, fixed fees, etc.).
- Initial or teaser interest rate.
- Index to which the loan is tied.
- Margin (the amount over the index that the rate is set at).
- Period of time that the initial rate is guaranteed for and period for adjustments.
- Total cap on increases in interest over the life of the loan.
- Cap on periodic or annual increases.
- Negative amortization (allowed or not allowed).
- Assumability of the loan (ARM loans are often assumable).

An adjustable-rate loan has some advantages. The initial interest rate, or teaser rate, is usually below market. Sometimes this rate is guaranteed for one year. This allows buyers to qualify for a loan when they could not qualify at a higher fixed-rate loan. The lower loan cost will allow you to work to raise a property's income so that you will have the income to make the payments when they increase. This is particularly important on property having a high vacancy rate or requiring work to bring it up to its income potential.

The danger of an adjustable-rate loan is that you don't know what your expenses will be. You must ask yourself if you can make the payments if the interest rates rise to the loan ceiling. If not, you should consider a fixed-rate loan.

During tight money periods, lenders will sometimes insist on adjustable-rate loans. The opportunity to raise the interest rate reduces the lender's risk. When there is competition between lenders to get their money out, lenders will offer long-term fixed-rate loans as well as adjustable-rate mortgages. They will, of course, use a low teaser rate to persuade borrowers to take the ARM loan or try to camouflage the adjustable rate nature of the loan by working it into a rollover loan with a fixed rate for a stated period.

Investors who only expect to hold a property for a few years like adjustable-rate loans as opposed to fixed-rate loans. The reason is that they can take advantage of a low initial interest rate. The adjustable-rate loan also is likely to have lower initial loan costs and fees and allow prepayment without penalty. In addition, the loan is likely to be assumable. However, if the investor intends to hold the property for more than around three years, a fixed-rate loan might be preferable.

Rollover Loan (Short-Term Fixed-Rate)

A *rollover loan* is a short-term fixed-rate loan often for 5 to 7 years. The payments are usually based on a long-term (20- to 30-year) amortization schedule. When the loan is due, the loan would likely convert to an adjustable-rate mortgage. As an example, a 5–30 loan might have a fixed rate for 5 years, after which it becomes an adjustable rate loan for the remaining 25 years. Rollover loans reduce lender risk in that they are not tied to what might become a below-market interest rate for a long period of time.

To induce borrowers to accept these short-term loans, lenders offer a lower interest rate and/or eliminate or reduce loan costs. When you expect to have a short holding period, these short-term loans make sense.

Government Loans

Government loans are government-insured by the Federal Housing Authority or guaranteed by the Veterans Administration. FHA loans are only for housing, including homes, apartments, mobile homes, and even mobile parks. VA loans are for homes, farms, or businesses. While VA housing loans are for owner occupancy, FHA loans are available to investors. The Farm Service Agency of the U.S. Department of Agriculture offers a number of loan programs. Since government loans are often made at rates of interest lower than those charged by institutional lenders, they should be considered.

Many different types of federal loans are available. Some programs are limited by insufficient funds, but quite often available loans are without takers. The following is only a partial listing of the special loans available: home improvement, single-family homes, farm labor housing, rental housing, housing for the elderly, housing for military personnel, low-income housing, mobile homes, mobile home parks, housing sites, nursing homes, hospitals, medical office buildings, farms, industrial development, and recreational enterprises. If you are interested in any of these areas, I recommend that you become familiar with available FHA and Rural Economic and Community Development Administration and Farm Service Agency programs. For information on FHA loans, see the Web site *www.hud.gov*.

The Web site *www.hud.gov/sea/infh/seamprog.html* provides information on apartment loans for developers and owners to purchase or refinance apartments with or without Section 8 subsidy. (Section 8 housing is government-assisted rentals for low-income families, that is covered in Chapter 16.)

For information on Farm Service Agency loans, see the Web site *www.fsa.usda.gov/pa5/*. For information on available funding for Rural Economic and Community Development Administration programs, see the Web site *www.rurdev.usda.gov/*.

Federal Housing Authority Loans

Title I FHA loans are for home improvement and Title II loans are for home purchase (one to four residential units). FHA loans have a maximum amount that varies by the area of the country. FHA loans originated prior to December 15, 1989, are assumable. Loans made since then are assumable only by owner-occupants who qualify for the loan.

Because of the very low down payment requirements, you might want to consider an FHA loan when buying a home for your primary residence. FHA loans are made by conventional lenders. Some investors will buy a home, live in it for a year and then rent it out, buying another home with another low down payment FHA loan, and continue to repeat this process.

Veterans Administration Loans

These veteran loans are for a home, farm, or business. Currently, the VA does not require any down payment for loans up to $240,000, although lenders may require down payments. VA loans, which are guaranteed, are also made by conventional lenders. For housing loans the veteran must intend to occupy the premises. Loans originally made prior to March 1, 1988, are assumable by anyone. Loans made after this date are assumable only if the buyer qualifies for the loan. Because of the no or low down payment requirements, VA loans should be considered by eligible veterans for the purchase of one to four units.

State Loans

Many states have loan programs, such as special loans for veterans, first-time buyers, and low-income families. These loans are limited to home purchases for owner occupancy. The loans usually require a very low or no down payment or have a below-market interest rate. If you qualify for such a loan, you should of course apply. One problem is that these loan funds are very limited and every applicant will not be successful.

Community Development Agencies

In many cities, community development agencies will aid you in developing or redeveloping properties. Aid could include land sales at token prices, low cost loans, or property tax incentives.

Conventional Loans

Conventional loans are made by institutional lenders without government guarantees or insurance.

Conforming Loans

Conforming loans are conventional loans that meet Fannie Mae and Freddie Mac purchase standards. Because lenders know they can readily resell these loans, they carry a slightly lower interest rate than nonconforming loans. Conforming loans have borrower-qualification standards and also have dollar limitations. At the time of this writing, the maximum amount for a single-family home loan is $322,700 although this amount is adjusted annually. Loans over $322,700 for a single-family home are known as *jumbo loans* and are nonconforming loans.

The best loan terms are available where the borrower indicates that the home will be the borrower's primary residence.

Private Mortgage Insurance

Conventional lenders want to limit their risk. Lenders want the borrower to pay for private mortgage insurance (PMI) when the buyer's loan to value (LTV) is 80 percent or more. Therefore, a purchase with less than 20 percent down will require PMI. PMI will also be required by some lenders when there is a cash-out refinance resulting in an LTV of 75 percent or more.

The PMI premium is not a tax-deductible expense as is interest. When your loan to value ratio goes below 80 percent, the lender cannot require you to continue to pay for PMI. The lender must automatically cancel PMI insurance when the loan balance reaches 78 percent of the purchase price. For high-risk borrowers the lender can require PMI until the ratio is 50 percent. This is different than the FHA mortgage insurance premium, which continues for the life of the loan.

The charge for PMI varies based upon the amount of the down payment and the size of the loan. Typically, it would amount to an extra one-half percentage point of the loan.

With PMI, lenders can make loans with as low as 5 percent down and for low- and moderate-income buyers the down payment is reduced to 3 percent.

Lenders offer several loans designed to avoid paying PMI:

- *80–10–10*. This is an 80 percent, first loan coupled with a 10 percent second loan, and the buyer pays the remaining 10 percent in cash.
- *80–15–5*. This is an 80 percent, first loan with a 15 percent second loan, and the buyer pays 5 percent down.

While the second loan listed above is at a higher rate of interest, the net effect could be lower payments than paying the PMI premium for the full loan amount.

Participation Loans

Participation loans create a limited partnership between the buyer and the lender. The lender receives an equity position in the property for giving the loan. When the loan plus interest is paid off, the lender still has an ownership interest.

Insurance companies often demand a significant equity position when making large commercial loans. They are successful because of their economic clout. Some private lenders do the same thing. Where a borrower would otherwise have difficulty in obtaining financing, the lender will put up the money if the lender receives a sweetener. The sweetener is ownership up to 50 percent.

This concept is turned around by some investors. In cases where they are seeking 100 percent financing on properties they have lined up, they offer the lender an equity position as a limited partner for a lower interest rate. Investors who use this approach don't look at it as giving away part of an investment. They take a positive approach: They are getting equity in a property that will pay for itself without making any down payment.

Sharing Appreciation Mortgage

A sharing appreciation mortgage (SAM) is a type of participation loan. The lender typically puts up all or part of the down payment, allowing the buyer the chance to own a home.

The home is sold or offered to the buyer (for refinancing) after a set period of time. The appreciation in value during the holding period is then split between lender and homebuyer.

For equity sharing to pay off, there must be appreciation. An investor could find himself or herself with the equivalent of a zero interest loan should the property fail to appreciate. With sales costs, the investor could lose money. This is the danger of setting time limits for selling property. Another danger to the investor is by the owner-occupant. The occupant likely has possession with little or no money down, and since the occupant is a co-owner, a simple eviction might not be possible. There have been horror stories about the occupant retaining possession for over a year without making any payments while the investor owner sought to foreclose the co-owner's interests. To avoid this problem, equity-sharing agreements should clearly indicate that the co-owner takes possession as a tenant, not as an owner.

Equity-sharing percentages of ownership are agreed upon by the parties. The advantage to the buyer-occupant is:

- Little or no down payment
- Tax and interest deduction
- A share of the appreciation

The investor gets:

- Appreciation (share)
- Depreciation
- Taxes and interest deduction (if share in payments)

The best equity sharing is between family members where one member advances the down payment. Equity sharing allows the relative to have a secure loan and an opportunity to share in appreciation.

The typical equity-sharing agreement includes:

- Title ownership with both parties
- Percentage of ownership
- Buyout agreement
- Profit split on refinance or sale
- Arbitration of disputes
- Payments for capital improvements and extraordinary repairs (cost splitting)
- Rental agreement

FINDING MONEY

Besides contacting local lenders and mortgage bankers, there are other sources of funds.

Advertising for Financing

One way to reduce your borrowing cost as well as obtain financing is to advertise for it. Many newspapers have classified sections for loans. The following is an example:

$46,000 Needed
Will pay 12.5% on well-secured second mortgage.

To make the loan attractive, you could offer prospective lenders a due-on-sale clause as well as a balloon payment in five to seven years.

My name is Pat L. I frequently buy property with 100 percent financing and, in some cases, I actually borrow more than my purchase price. This means I am a cash-out buyer.

What I do is look for motivated sellers of income property where I can envision a positive cash flow and/or sales profit by raising rents, improving the property, or changing the use of the property.

I will put in a purchase offer that requires the seller to carry financing. My offers normally call for 80 percent to 90 percent total financing in new loans, loan assumptions, and/or seller financing.

I strive for below-market seller financing. For example, assume I can get 6 percent financing of 80 percent on a $500,000 purchase price when the market interest is around 9 percent. (It is quite easy with motivated sellers—all you need do is ask.)

Then, I would advertise as follows:

12% Interest
I will pay 12% interest on a $100,000 mortgage
on a quality property for a 10-year loan.

If I am able to locate a lender, my total loan cost is 7.2 percent, which might still be an attractive rate.

$$80\% \text{ at } 0.06 \ (6\%) = 4.8\%$$
$$20\% \text{ at } 0.12 \ (12\%) = \underline{2.4\%}$$
$$7.2\% \text{ interest}$$

The lenders for the second mortgage make an above-market mortgage rate from a borrower who consistently has met her commitments, and I get 100 percent financing. I have found that it pays to advertise.

(Note: Make certain that the second mortgage does not violate state usury limitations on private loans.)

Money Finders

If you are unable to find mortgage money, there are professionals who will do so for a fee. Their fees vary with the market, although 10 percent is not unusual for hard-to-obtain loans. Inquiries to bankers, commercial brokers, and industrial brokers could reveal if any money finders are active in your area.

Avoid anyone who wants an advance fee. Chances are you will never hear from that person again unless it is for another advance. During periods of tight money, shady operators appear who claim to be able to find money.

Evaluating Alternatives

As in buying anything else, you should shop the available loans. Differences in interest rates, points, and loan terms can be significant. Look for the loan that best meets your needs.

In evaluating various loan possibilities consider:

- Interest rate
- Loan period
- Fixed rate or adjustable (terms of adjustable)
- Balloon payment or amortized
- Possibility of negative amortization
- Prepayment penalty
- Loan costs (appraisal fees, fixed fees, points, etc.)

Lenders charge points when they feel the rate of interest is insufficient. For example, suppose a lender could make a good, safe, long-term investment at 6.5 percent interest and you want a loan at 6 percent. The lender would be foolish to give you a loan at a lower rate of interest than was available elsewhere. By obtaining points, the lender makes up for this differential. As a rule of thumb, 8 points are considered equal to a 1 percent interest differential. To give you the loan at a 0.5 percent interest advantage, the lender will ask for 4 points. This will give the lender the equivalent of an 6.5 percent return.

The most important thing is to look at the end result of the purchase, not at the interest rate.

Refinancing

While real estate is an illiquid investment, it is possible to pump money out of an investment by refinancing a property. What you are doing is milking your inflation cow by taking out your swollen equity. As a property increases in value with appreciation, further refinancing is possible.

One Los Angeles investor I know has refinanced the same property four times in a little over 12 years. Each time he refinances, he takes more cash out. He uses the cash to "pyramid" by acquiring more properties. He then refinances the new properties as soon as he is able to take out significant cash. He started on his career by refinancing his home to obtain the down payment on a fourplex and has continued ever since.

This process of borrowing on one property to invest in another offering a rate of return greater than must be paid to borrow the money is known as *trading on your equity*. It is an important tool for pyramiding yourself into more and more properties.

The investor I told you about never sells, just refinances to increase his holdings. He is not really concerned that refinancing often turns a positive cash flow into a break-even situation, as long as he can still safely make the payments.

You should consider refinancing when interest rates drop. As a general rule, it makes sense to refinance if your savings in interest within three years will make up for prepayment penalties and new loan costs.

If you intend to refinance a loan that is with a private lender, likely a seller, you should first offer to pay off the loan if the lender will discount it. You should be able to obtain at least a 10 percent discount. This is just like found money.

Loan Workout

If you find yourself in a position where you will have difficulty meeting loan obligations, your best course of action is to contact the lender as soon as possible. Most lenders don't want to be property owners. They want interest. Lenders might agree to interest-only payments or a new payment schedule.

Arbitrage

Arbitrage is the term given to making money on the interest differential when you buy at one interest rate and sell at a higher rate. You can do this when the loan is assumable. By selling using a land contract or wrap-around loan, you take advantage of a low-interest underlying loan rather than giving it to the buyer.

Usury Laws

Real estate investors must be aware of their state usury laws. Generally, individuals are precluded from charging more than a maximum rate of interest. Loans above that rate are regarded as usurious. Depending on state law, usurious interest may be uncollectible or will be set at a legal rate. There may also be severe penalties for usurious interest collected.

Seller financing is generally exempt from usury restrictions, but check with an attorney if you are unsure as to your state usury laws.

Fraudulent Practices

It is fraud to deceive a lender. If the lender were federally insured, the fraud would be a federal crime. Fraudulent methods, some of which have been endorsed by seminar presenters, include using someone else to get the loan and get back an unrecorded deed if your credit will not support the loan; showing a nonexistent down payment made direct to seller; and providing false income statements to obtain a loan.

You can invest, gain wealth, and remain ethical. It is not difficult. You can do this by structuring deals that fulfill the needs of both the buyer and seller.

5

CHAPTER

Creative Financing

> When men have yielded without serious resistance to the tyranny of . . .
> dictators, it is because they have lacked property.
>
> *Walter Lippman,* The Method of Freedom

Creative financing is simply financing other than conventional financing. Some buyers can't qualify for conventional financing. The most common reasons are insufficient funds for a down payment or credit problems. But whatever the reason, if you can't qualify for conventional financing, creative financing is the way to go.

CONVINCING SELLERS TO FINANCE BUYERS

Much of creative financing involves a seller financing the buyer. The buyer may be able to assume an existing loan and give the seller a second mortgage for his or her equity. If a seller has no real need for cash, he or she might be persuaded to sell without any down payment at all if there is faith in the buyer. Just because a seller asks for cash doesn't mean that he or she won't sell and carry the paper. If the seller simply intends to invest the sale proceeds in a savings account or bonds, then he or she can frequently be induced to carry the paper by the offer of higher interest. After all, the seller knows the security value of the property.

    If you ask a real estate agent if a seller will "carry back" financing, you might get a negative response even when the agent isn't certain. Some agents' worry that carryback financing won't leave them enough cash for their commissions. Your best bet, therefore, is to find situations where seller financing offers seller benefits and then ask for seller financing in your offer. If you are using a buyer's agent, your agent will have access to listing information and will be able to pinpoint properties with either assumable loans or properties owned free and clear of encumbrances.

The more difficult a property is to sell (because of market conditions or type of property), the easier it becomes to obtain seller financing.

As an example, if you can find a rental property owned free and clear that has a great many vacant units, you will have an excellent opportunity for very creative owner financing. A structured payment plan with a low down payment and low monthly payments initially, but with increasing payments each year could seem very attractive to an owner. The sweetener to convince the owner to carry the paper would be your agreement to refinance in five to seven years, which is a balloon payment. To make such an offer, you must be convinced from your experience that you can significantly increase revenue by reducing the vacancy factor and/or increasing rents. If you can do so, the value of the property should increase so that refinancing will be possible.

You can offer significant cash with a buyer-financing offer by structuring the offer where you will put a first mortgage against the property but the seller gets the entire proceeds of the loan. The balance of the purchase price would be a second mortgage carried back by the seller.

This technique could be used even when there is a present mortgage against a property. As an example, assume there is an $80,000 mortgage against a property and you intend to offer a $200,000 price. Your offer could be contingent upon a new loan for $120,000 (giving the seller $40,000 cash) and carrying back the remaining $80,000 on a second mortgage.

Once you have worked several of these purchases, you will have a track record and it will be easier to convince sellers that you will honor your agreement and are not trying to rip them off. Since the seller receives all of the loan proceeds, your only profit can be in making the property pay.

You are more likely to obtain seller financing in buying raw land than in any other type of real estate because it is the least liquid of all real estate and is a negative cash flow investment. (It costs an owner taxes even when the land is paid for.) Owners are also more likely to finance profit dollars than equity dollars reflecting actual cash invested. If an owner has owned a property for a number of years, you can assume you are asking the owner to finance profit dollars. In selling an owner on creative financing, you should be promoting the idea for its benefits, not simply as a way for them to sell the property. Benefits include:

1. *Interest rates.* Interest rates on seller carryback financing are usually significantly higher than the owner can get from investing the sales proceeds in a certificate of deposit, government bonds, or a money market account. This is a very strong argument for seller financing.

2. *Annuity value.* Carrying the buyer will often give the owner a greater monthly return than if he or she purchased an insurance annuity package with the proceeds. In addition, the balance due is payable to the heirs upon the deaths of the sellers, while in an annuity returns are only for a lifetime.

3. *Cash.* The owners are receiving more cash back at the sale than they originally invested as their down payment. (This will likely be true if the owners have owned for a significant period and purchased their home with FHA or VA financing.)

4. *Security.* They are receiving profit well secured by their real estate.

If a seller agrees to carry all or part of the financing, you should include in your purchase offer a statement such as "In the event seller wishes to sell (the carryback second mortgage) the buyer shall have a 30-day first right of refusal to meet the price and terms of any sale of the note (and mortgage)."

This simple statement could give you a chance at a price reduction after you have completed the purchase. Assume the seller later needs cash and wishes to sell a $50,000 second mortgage at a 20 percent discount. By exercising your right of first refusal you will have effectively reduced your purchase price by $10,000. If you do not have the means to purchase the note, you could advertise for and likely locate an investor for a $40,000 secured note by offering attractive terms.

Keep in mind that while conventional lenders can be unyielding as to interest rates and terms, rates and terms are usually negotiable when the seller is carrying the loan.

METHODS AND TECHNIQUES

Assuming Loans

Even if you have the cash to meet the seller's down payment requirement or to pay off the seller's equity in full, try to conserve your cash. Liquidity offers you protection in an emergency as well as allowing you to take advantage of additional investment opportunities that come along.

As a buyer, you want to assume or take subject to assumable favorable loans. An astute seller will want to sell on a land contract or with a wraparound loan in order to take advantage of the lower interest rate rather than pass on the benefits to the purchaser. This is not of great importance when interest rates on new loans are lower than on loans that can be assumed (as it was in 2003). However, in a recovering economy, interest rates will rise and the lower rates will appear as bargains.

If you have a private lender that is willing to let the loan be assumed it means the lender wants to keep that income flow. This creates an opportunity to renegotiate the existing loan at better terms or even increase the loan amount and take cash out.

Balloon Payment

To induce a seller to carry a loan, you might have to agree to refinance the loan and to pay the seller off within a relatively short period of time, say, five to seven years. It can be difficult to get an average seller to carry the paper for any longer than this, although when yields on certificates of deposit are significantly lower than the interest rate you are proposing, owners are more willing to carry paper for long periods of time.

When a balloon payment is due, you might want to offer to extend the loan. Offering to boost the interest rate by 1 percent might interest the seller, especially if you have made your payments in a timely manner.

The Real Estate Commission

If a property is listed through a real estate broker and an ad indicates owner financing with a low down payment such as 10 percent, it is obvious that the seller is really only asking for enough cash to pay the real estate commission. Ask the broker to accept a commission in the form of a personal note or second mortgage. While some will not agree, many sophisticated brokers will go along with such an arrangement. Your offer to purchase might then state that you are offering a particular price and that you will pay the commission. The seller and the broker together can end up financing you for the entire purchase price.

Many investors who have real estate licenses earn commissions on their own purchases. In this way, they reduce their cash requirements for the purchases. If you have a real estate license and want to share in the commission, just keep in mind "full disclosure." If the information is of the type a seller would want to know, then disclose it.

Free Rent

When a seller has not yet purchased another property or does not have firm plans, a low-down-payment–seller-financing offer can be sweetened in an unusual manner. Offer the owner rent-free use of the premises for a stated period of time, such as three or six months after the closing. Such a provision will make you appear in a better light and will increase the chance of a low-down-payment offer being accepted.

Giving a Life Tenancy

Offers should be tailored to the seller's needs. The following case explains how one buyer did just that.

> My name is Russell L., and I'm 50 years old. I work for a large manufacturer as a purchasing agent. Sending my two children through college had decimated what I had thought were sizable savings. I still had $14,000 in cash plus my home equity, which was only around $30,000. I could see a retirement of eating tube steak (hot dogs) and beans. Though my employer had a retirement plan, it was anything but generous. When I was ready to retire, I would probably have to sell my home and move into an apartment, the thought of which I hated.
>
> Out of necessity, I actively sought a way to protect my future. I had 15 years to do it. I decided my best bet would be to buy a modest apartment building. It would provide a hedge against inflation, and if it would break even now, in 15 years it should provide a significant cash return to supplement my company retirement plan plus Social Security.
>
> I began reading everything our county library system had available on real estate investing. I also visited several dozen apartments that were for rent in order to get a feel for rental value. I attended meetings of a local apartment owners' association. I also talked to brokers who were having open houses for rentals. I pumped them for sales information, taking all my preparation very seriously.
>
> I then began a search for a building to buy. A few agents were not interested in working with me when they found I had rather meager capital to invest, but several agents did show me smaller units.
>
> On the third Saturday of my weekend hunts, an agent who had shown me several units asked if I could do him a favor. He had a 24-unit apartment building that had been on the market for six months without an offer. He

wanted me to look at it because he wanted to show the owner he was working on the property.

The apartment complex consisted of three, two-story brick structures, each with eight units. The owners wanted $800,000 cash. The property had not sold because of a tight money situation. The price actually was reasonable for the area based on comparable sales. It was about eight times the gross income. After going through several units, I realized the price was really a bargain. Tenants paid all their own utilities, and the apartments, which were all two-bedroom units, were renting at least $100 less than comparable units.

The elderly owners indicated that they were selling because maintenance was getting to be too much for them and they did not want the sale to be a burden on their estate, since their children did not live in the state. The owners indicated that they would like to rent their present apartment from the new owners. There was no mortgage against the property. After reading all those investment books, my mind was racing to figure out how I could take advantage of this bargain.

When the agent and I returned to the real estate office, I told him I was interested in the 24 units and would get back to him. I am sure he thought I was crazy because with $14,000 in cash, I was just $786,000 short of the owner's asking price. I arrived home around 3 p.m. and from then until 2 a.m. on Sunday morning I worked at the kitchen table figuring out how I could present an offer that would interest the owners. Some of my ideas were far-out, but I finally came up with what I thought would make sense to the seller:

1. Purchaser to give sellers a rent-free life tenancy in their present unit (to end upon the death of the last survivor).

2. Purchaser to pay all closing costs, including escrow fees, title insurance, etc.

3. Purchaser price to be $750,000. Price to be paid as follows:

   a. $100,000 at closing. This sum to be obtained from a $100,000 first mortgage to be placed on the property by the purchaser.

   b. Buyer to assume owner's obligation to pay the agent's commission in the amount of $45,000.

   c. Seller to take back a second mortgage on the amount of $605,000 with payments of $4439.31 per month based on a 30-year amortization and 8 percent interest. The entire loan balance shall be due in full 10 years from the date of closing.

I contacted the real estate agent on Sunday morning and met with him and his broker. I told them that if they would agree to carry their commission on a note, I would make my offer. After some discussion, it was agreed that I would pay them $5000 in cash and the balance of the commission on a $40,000 note secured by a third mortgage. The agreement was to be an 8 percent note amortized over five years. The broker indicated that normally he wouldn't carry paper but because the listing was close to expiration, he would.

Well, my offer was accepted. The broker indicated that the owners liked the rent-free life tenancy and felt the 10-year payoff really would meet their needs and their children's needs. That's how I purchased a prime building with less than 1.5 percent as a down payment. By raising rents, I immediately achieved a positive cash flow.

My payments were:

$100,000 1st mortgage 10% (25 years)	$ 908.71
$605,000 2nd mortgage 8% (30 years)	4,39.31
$40,000 3rd mortgage 8% (5 years)	811.06
Monthly payments	$ 6,159.08
Estimated Maintenance	$ 1,000.00
Taxes and Insurance	1,600.00
Utilities (common areas)	100.00
Total monthly outgo	$ 8,859.08

My monthly income is:

23 units (based on new rents)	$10,345.00
less estimated 5% vacancy factor	− 517.25
Effective gross income	$ 9,827.75

While I have to spend my Saturdays at the apartment building making repairs, cleaning, etc., I have an additional $1000 each month to spend or save.

If rents go up just 3 percent per year, I should have an additional $1600 plus per month in income within five years. I will also have paid off the agents in five years, so I will have another $800 in my pocket.

While I love the sellers dearly for giving me this opportunity, eventually their apartment will be available for me to rent. Right now, I think it would rent for at least $600.

I don't envision having a problem refinancing the loans in 10 years. With just moderate inflation in rents, the cash flow should justify a loan in excess of what I will require.

Right now my intentions are to take an early retirement in five years. While I won't get much from my company plan, my cash flow from the apartments should more than meet my needs.

Note: Russell L. has retired. His present rental gross is over $19,000 per month and his debt service has been significantly reduced since he was able to pay off the third mortgage and refinance the balance owed at 7.5 percent interest. He has indicated that this single investment is giving him a six-figure annual cash flow (cash flow is the difference between actual income received and out of pocket cash expenses).

Sweat Equity

Some owners will accept "sweat equity" down payments. Often purchasers of new homes are credited by the builder for tasks such as painting. It reduces the cash down payment required.

One of my former students buys "fixer-uppers." He purchased a house with no down payment from a seller who did not need the cash. The seller nevertheless wanted additional security. The seller agreed to the no-downpayment sale providing the buyer painted the exterior of the house and put in a sprinkler system and lawn. The escrow did not close until the work was completed. With the labor and money the buyer invested in repairs, the seller felt secure with no down payment. The chances of the seller defaulting were greatly reduced. In addition, the improvements and repairs increased the value of the security.

Borrowing Based on the Lease

Suppose you have an option to buy a lot for $100,000, a contractor who will put up a building for $400,000, and you have found a national tenant who has signed a long-term net lease for the premises to be built for $60,000 per year. Because of this lease, the property is really worth more than the $500,000 it would take to buy the lot and build the building. A lender might set a value of $800,000 on the property and agree to give you permanent financing of $550,000, which would mean a loan for $50,000 more than your total cost. (They are really loaning on the lease.)

There are investors who seek to meet the needs of franchisors and large chain store operators. The investors are often able to borrow 100 percent and more because the rental and financial strength of the tenants have a tremendous influence on value. Most large franchisors and chain operations have employees responsible for leasing. They generally are very responsive to inquiries concerning their future needs. One reason many firms don't want to own property is that they don't want their balance sheets to show long-term debt. If they show the debt, their net worth appears to be reduced even though, over the long-term they would be better off owning their property.

Payments in Advance

To make a relatively low down payment appear more substantial to an owner, consider adjusting your purchase offer to reflect that part of your down payment is really the first year's payments made in advance. This is to your advantage for a number of reasons:

1. Interest is a tax-deductible expense, but a down payment is not. Most of the monthly payments would be interest, so most of the first year's advance payments would be a tax-deductible expense. If you are in the 40 percent tax bracket (both federal and state combined), the government pays almost 40 percent of your advance payment.

2. Since you have made one year's payments in advance, you have no payments for one year.

This technique is likely to be acceptable to sellers only if they own the property free and clear or have existing loans that are being assumed. If the sellers must make monthly payments, they would be unlikely to accept this arrangement.

Graduated Interest

Owners can often be induced to carry back loans with a low-down buyer by using greed as a tool. For example, an offer that provides 6 percent interest the first year, 7 percent interest the second year, 8 percent interest the third year, and 9 percent the fourth year up to a limit such as 15 percent will often excite a seller. What you gain in such a purchase is a short-term, high-leveraged loan. It is short-term because it would not be economical for you to keep such a loan very long. By waving the prospect of an almost obscene interest rate in front of them, owners can sometimes be induced to finance you with little or no down payment. Be certain such an arrangement does not violate your state usury laws. (In most states, seller financing is exempt from usury.)

I acted as a consultant for a group who wished to purchase a large ranch for a polo club. The owners, the heirs of the original ranch owner, had been adamant that they wanted all cash, which was several million dollars. Since the group did not, at the time, have the cash, I tailored an offer with graduating interest rates that was accepted. The loan was paid off in only a couple of years and the ranch is now one of America's premier polo clubs.

Graduated Payments

A seller can be induced to give you low initial payments on a property by offering a graduated payment schedule with payments increasing each year. The payment for the first year may result in negative amortization (the interest actually exceeds the payments, resulting in the loan principal increasing). Such an arrangement will allow you to make repairs and renovations and could give you a positive initial cash flow when you need it that otherwise might have been impossible.

Insured Mortgage

Mortgage insurance really doesn't insure that a mortgage will be paid. In reality, it is a declining policy of term life insurance. The cost of mortgage insurance is based on your age, so the offer of an insured mortgage is best for younger buyers who would pay a lower premium. Your estate would benefit by having a property free and clear in the event of your death. The seller benefits from your death because the loan would be immediately paid off. The lender would not be faced with collecting payments from a widow who might be financially pressed, or worse yet, having to foreclose on the family of the deceased buyer.

That little extra bit that can tip the scale in your favor when an owner is considering financing your purchase is when you include in your offer to purchase the requirement that you will carry mortgage insurance to pay off the mortgage holder in the event of your death.

Unsecured Notes

An unsecured personal note can be used as part of a down payment. Including the note with the down payment might serve to magnify the down payment in the eyes of the seller. For example, assume a seller wants a $10,000 down payment for a property but will carry the balance. Your purchase offer could read:

> Purchaser shall make a down payment of $10,000 upon closing in the following manner: $5000 cash upon closing, $5000 in the form of a promissory note bearing interest at the rate of 7 percent. Said note shall be due in full one year from date of closing.

The $5000 note is really a deferred down payment, but to show it as such would result in stating that the down payment was only $5000.

In the case above, the note does not call for payments, so the property's cash flow is not negatively affected. If the seller objects to the unsecured note, then you can provide security by adding the $5000 to the amount of financing to be carried back by the seller and provide for a partial balloon payment of $5000 in one year.

Price versus Terms

An owner can be induced to sell for a low or no down payment by an offer to pay the full purchase price or even more. Often the seller doesn't really expect to get that much. You should couple the offer with a reduced interest rate.

While bargains in price are seldom available in a seller's market, a purchaser can nevertheless often obtain favorable terms equivalent to a bargain price. For example, assume the going mortgage rate for the type of property is 8 percent. If savings and loan institutions are paying depositors 4 percent, an owner might be persuaded to carry the paper on the transaction at 6 percent interest if the full asking price is paid. If the loan is $100,000 at 6 percent, the monthly payment on a 20-year amortized loan will be $716.44. This amount at a 8 percent rate would only make the payment on an $86,000 loan. In this case, by getting a favorable interest rate, the purchaser has obtained an advantage equivalent to a $14,000 reduction in price. There is more than one way to get a bargain. (An amortization booklet is an important tool for a real estate investor.)

Actually, there is some disadvantage for the buyer in raising the price and cutting the interest. Since interest is a deductible expense while payment on the principal is not, you do lose tax deductions by this method. If you are the seller, check with a CPA before accepting a below-market interest rate. If the rate set is too low, the IRS may impute a higher interest rate and tax the seller as if it had been received.

There are other possible benefits besides lower interest when paying full price.

> My name is Carol P. In the mid-1960s I purchased a home in a new subdivision in Utah. The developer had a number of unsold homes. He turned down my original offer of $2000 below his listed price. He told me that he had lived in the area all his life and if he gave me a bargain, other purchasers in the development would be unhappy. He said that someone at the savings and loan would talk about his cutting his prices and soon everyone would know.
>
> I therefore presented a new offer for the full price contingent upon the seller agreeing to finish the basement and pour a patio slab at a price that was acceptable to me. I signed a separate agreement for this work at a price of $10. This really amounted to more than the $2000 price reduction I had originally asked for, but the seller was pleased.

Note: While this case is almost 40 years old it is still applicable. In 1999 I purchased a home in a large development that supposedly was "one price" in that there were no price exceptions. While I paid the advertised price for my lot and home, I did negotiate the inclusion of $21,000 in upgrades at no additional cost.

Using Mortgages

If you are holding a mortgage or trust deed on property you sold, you can use that existing loan in three ways to buy other property:

1. Offer the mortgage or trust deed as the down payment (or part of the down payment) on another property.
2. Sell the mortgage or trust deed and use the cash for purchase purposes. This might involve having to accept less than face value (discounting the loan).
3. Borrow from a lender using your mortgage or trust deed as security.

The first alternative is often the best approach because you receive full credit for your paper. When using existing mortgages you hold to buy property, you effectively convert them to a cash equivalent without suffering a discount.

If you sell the mortgage, the price you receive will be based on the security for the mortgage, the credit of the borrower as well as the mortgage terms. If the buyer judges any of these three as less than adequate, a sale will likely be at a discount from face value.

Cash can be added as a sweetener. A package of cash and a mortgage can be used to buy property and/or pay commissions. A sweetener increases the chance of acceptance.

Manufacturing Mortgages

Some sellers want a substantial down payment more as a matter of security than necessity. In such cases it is possible to supply additional security by manufacturing paper. While it might be difficult or very expensive to borrow on your equity, you can use this equity as down payment material for acquiring more property. The seller not only has the security of the property you have purchased but also the additional security of the property mortgaged for the down payment.

By putting a mortgage on your own property to use as a down payment, you can in effect obtain 100 percent financing. The property you buy can now be used to create another mortgage for a down payment on yet another property. An endless chain becomes possible limited only by your sales ability and the available properties.

If you own undeveloped land, creating mortgages on such land is one of a very few ways you can use your equity. Most lenders will not loan on such property. If you don't have other property, you may still be able to use property of others to buy property for yourself. If you have relatives or close friends who would help you if they had the cash, you might be able to borrow their paper. I know of a father who put a lien on his home, which his son used as a down payment on a house. The son pays the lien on his father's home as well as the lien on his own. You should realize that you are asking a great deal when you ask to use someone else's property to buy property. There has to be a great deal of trust or love before a person is willing to do this.

One investor has pyramided herself to great wealth. She used her paper equity in property by giving second mortgages as down payments. As values increase, she gives second mortgages on her most recent acquisitions as well as additional mortgages on other property. She claims she has had as many as five outstanding mortgages on one property. To understand this concept, suppose you owe $80,000 on a house worth $100,000. You give a $10,000 second mortgage on that property as a down payment on another property. If the value of the original property rises to $120,000, you can then take another mortgage to use as a down payment on a third property, since you have a $30,000 equity. You would now owe $90,000 on a property worth $120,000.

Even though it is possible to borrow on your property to get cash, you are better off giving the loan directly as a down payment. Not only can you significantly reduce the interest rates, but also you can save the substantial loan costs and commission necessary to arrange a cash loan.

Mortgages not only can be used as your down payment, they can also be used for fees to real estate brokers. You should structure your offer so you will pay the real estate commission. You should have the broker agree in writing that if the offer is accepted, he or she will accept your mortgage in total or part payment of the commission.

Separating the Land from the Building

William Zeckendorf, a renowned real estate investor of the 1950s and 1960s, was one of the first investors to separate land from buildings as a technique to maximize his leverage and his sale price. He went even further in some cases and created a master lease separate from the building. For example, the land would be separate from the building and the building owner would pay a ground rent to the owner of the land. The building owner would lease the entire structure to an operator under a master lease. The master leaseholder would then lease the space to the users. Mr. Zeckendorf found he could borrow on and sell the land separately, the building being subject to the ground lease and the master lease.

By separating the land from the building, you could create very interesting investment opportunities. You should be able to reduce the sales price by the land value, and the seller will usually like the idea and security of retaining title to the land. Owners who otherwise would not consider a low or no down payment find this type of offer very tempting. As part of the purchase agreement you should try to negotiate an option to buy the land for cash within a stated period of time (as long a period as possible). The seller may require that the building be paid off when the option is exercised. This would mean that you would have to refinance the property to include land and building. If values increase, you will be able to refinance and buy the land and end up in the same position as if you had purchased the land and building together.

While you might cringe at the thought of buying the improvements without the land and having only an option to buy the land, this is really better situation than having to make a balloon payment five to seven years after purchase. With this usual method of seller financing, you must refinance to pay the balloon payment. When buying the building without the land but with an option to buy the land, you are actually better off because you don't really have to refinance. If you fail to exercise the option, you still have the building and a lease. If you fail to obtain financing to pay a balloon payment, you would probably be foreclosed.

My name is Ronald D. I am an investor who strives to understand sellers' needs and to prepare offers to purchase that sellers will find difficult to reject. In other words, my offers to purchase really look good. As an example, let me explain a purchase I made.

An owner owned a commercial property free and clear and wished to sell it for $1 million. The building, which had four tenants with relatively short-term leases, was generating $75,000 income after expenses. Assuming the building was purchased at $1 million with $200,000 down, there would still be a negative cash flow with 10 percent interest.

Because the building was in a very desirable area and had good strong local tenants, I was still interested, even though the owner appeared tight on price and terms.

I decided on an end run, an offer that would catch the owner off-guard but would nevertheless make a lot of sense.

I offered to buy the building alone for $400,000 with 25 percent down ($100,000). I would lease the land for 20 years on a triple net lease at $30,000 per year (triple net means I pay taxes, insurance, and all other costs.) At the end of the 20-year lease the owner would get the building back and own the land and building again. The owner was getting $400,000 for a building he would get back plus a 20-year annuity of $30,000 each year. It sounded pretty darned good.

What I received for my $100,000 down payment was a $75,000 cash flow from which I needed to pay debt service on the $300,000 due plus the ground rent:

After expense income	$	75,000
Debt service	−	35,000
Ground rent		30,000
Spendable income	$	10,000

For the first year I would have a 10 percent cash-on-cash-invested cash flow, but I didn't buy the property for just a 10 percent return. (Even though it would be tax-sheltered income because of depreciation.)

The gross rent was $100,000 and expenses were figured at $25,000. If the rent and expenses would each increase just 5 percent each year, at the end of five years my gross rent would be $127,627 and my expenses would be $31,907 leaving $95,720 but my land rent and debt service cost would only be $65,000. This would mean a 30 percent cash return on cash invested.

At the end of 10 years, I would have a spendable cash flow of $57,165 and by the end of the 20th year my annual cash flow would be $133,994.

Now, 5 percent per year for increases in rent and expenses is a relatively conservative figure, but you can see what happens with the magic of compounding. (Each year it is a 5 percent increase from a higher number.)

I added a twist to my offer: I paid $5000 additional for an option to buy the land anytime during the lease for $1,200,000 (in addition to the $400,000 I paid for the building). Anyway, my offer was accepted and if history is any indication of the future, I will be exercising my option in the twentieth year and my purchase price will be a bargain.

I have been separating land from structures for some time now. It makes for offers they can't refuse and gives me positive cash flows right from the start.

Moving a Mortgage

Many people, especially retirees on pensions, like mortgages. After they have been receiving steady payments to supplement their income, they often don't want the loans paid off. Chances are they will not like having to invest the money in certificates of deposit or Treasury notes, as the interest will be significantly less than you are paying them.

If because of a sale or refinance, you will be paying off a loan on which you have been faithfully making payments to an individual lender, consider asking the mortgage holders if they would like to transfer the mortgage to another property you own or are buying.

The mortgage holders continue to get the payments to supplement their pensions and/or Social Security and you get additional financing at a relatively low cost.

Don't offer to increase the interest rate as an inducement, as the mortgage holder will likely think the security is less than the other property. You should convey to the mortgage holder that you are giving them first opportunity at the mortgage so they can keep their payments.

I have learned from experience that younger working mortgage holders are far less likely to agree to transferring a mortgage than are retirees.

Subordination

When you look through ads for lots, you will often see the words "owner will subordinate." In a subordination, the seller not only finances the buyer but agrees that his or her lien will be secondary or subordinate to another loan. To illustrate, assume that an owner agrees to sell you a lot for $100,000 with $10,000 down and to subordinate a mortgage for $90,000. You could now go to a conventional lender and ask to borrow to build a $200,000 structure. As far as the lender is concerned, you would be asking for a two-thirds loan because the lot, to the lender's way of thinking, is free and clear. The lender, by giving a $200,000 loan, would have both the land and building as security under a first mortgage. You have really used the lot seller's equity to finance your loan, even though you have not paid for the lot.

Why would a seller agree to such a deal? If the lender foreclosed, the lot seller would either lose his or her equity or be forced to step in and make the borrower's payments and foreclose on his or her second liens; however, some sellers are very motivated. If they are having difficulty making tax payments, they may be willing to subordinate. When there are few sales being made, a seller who has faith in a buyer might agree to subordinate. A buyer with a good reputation in the community or a buyer who has previously purchased property from sellers who subordinated their loans without problems could influence a seller to subordinate.

Often sellers who subordinate are owners of a large number of lots. They want to see some of the lots developed, so as to increase the desirability and value of their other lots. To obtain development, they take a calculated risk by subordinating. As an example, several high-priced homes built in a new subdivision will increase the value and desirability of the other lots. Many speculative builders look for subordination opportunities to keep from having their capital tied up in land. Also, by agreeing to subordinate, a seller will often be able to obtain a premium price.

If a seller agrees to subordinate for a particular loan, such as a short-term construction loan, then when the construction loan is repaid the seller's loan becomes the primary loan. It would be foolish for a seller to agree to just subordinate without reference to a particular loan, since in such a case the subordinated loan would always be the last in terms of priority.

The word *subordination* is now a dirty word to many people. Unethical purchasers inserted the word in seller-financing purchases. They were then able to borrow on the seller's equity by refinancing the first mortgage. They thus became "cash-out buyers" who then walked away and defaulted on the loans. An example of this was a California purchaser who agreed to sell a home for $550,000. The home had a $200,000 trust deed against it. The buyers gave the sellers $50,000 cash and gave a $300,000 second "subordinate" trust deed that was due in full in six months. The sellers thought they had a good deal, but what the buyers did was to refinance the first trust deed. They obtained a $350,000 loan. This not only reimbursed them for their $50,000 cash investment, it left them with $100,000 cash. Of course they defaulted on all of the loans and the sellers had to bid in at the foreclosure sale to save their remaining equity.

Be on the alert as sellers if a buyer uses the word *subordination*. Others may view you as targets.

RAISING CASH

If you are buying an apartment building in which the tenants have made large security deposits or prepaid the last month's rent, you should realize that these deposits are turned over to the buyer at the closing of the transaction. They may reduce the amount of cash you need to complete the transaction. (In states where tenant deposits must be kept in trust accounts, buyers cannot utilize these deposits as part of the purchase funds required.)

Most rents are due on the first of the month. An excellent time to schedule a closing is on the second of the month. In this way, as buyer, you will be credited with practically the entire month's rent receipts. This amount will reduce your cash requirements as of the closing date. The net effect of taking over security deposits and the prorating of rents could reduce your cash needs considerably when you are buying with a relatively low down payment.

If you don't have enough ready cash to complete a transaction, you should consider the following possibilities:

1. Insurance policies. It you have a whole life insurance policy, you can borrow up to your loan value. The loan value is usually shown on a table on the policy.

An advantage of borrowing on your insurance is that loans are at a very low rate of interest. I borrowed on my GI policy to finance my honeymoon. I borrowed on it again to buy real estate. Since I am paying 5 percent interest, I cannot imagine ever paying it back.

2. Retirement accounts. It is theoretically possible to buy and sell real estate within a self-directed IRA account. There must, however, be a third-party custodian. A small number of IRA plan administrators allow real estate purchases—most do not.

Until recently, most 401K retirement plans did not allow investment in REITs (real estate investment trusts). With the drop in stock and mutual fund values, plan administrators have come to realize that REIT mutual funds are an appropriate investment because they are asset based and provide exceptional income. If you have a 401K plan, check if you now have the choice of REIT funds for your retirement monies.

3. Personal property. You can borrow on your personal property such as furniture. This is a high-interest loan and should only be used when funds are required for a short period of time.

4. Family loans. Relatives are an excellent source of money. I recommend that family loans be in writing and bear interest. All payments should be by check. Avoid any possibility of a misunderstanding about the obligations and repayments. If you would rather not take money directly from relatives, you can borrow their credit instead. By having relatives cosign for you, you may be able to qualify for a loan. Be aware, it is a lot to ask as the cosigner could end up making the payments.

5. A line of credit. Approach the bank where you do business as to a line of credit. A line of credit allows you to borrow on your signature only up to the line of credit limit. The effect of having a line of credit provides instant cash for deposits with offers, as well as money for short-term loans until other financing can be arranged. A line of credit may be tied in with a home equity loan.

If you have a strong financial partner, you could arrange for a significant line of credit requiring both signatures. You really don't always need a partner's investment; his or her credit will often do.

6. Credit cards. You have probably received letters from banks offering you cash credit lines on their credit cards. Apply for those where there are no fees. Having the option of immediate credit card money gives you the ability to rapidly respond to opportunities. You can use your credit card as a type of swing loan until more permanent financing can be arranged.

While the interest rate for credit card borrowing is high, the cost for a short borrowing period will likely be acceptable. In many cases, interest will be less than an interim bank loan because of the absence of loan costs.

7. Redevelopment funds. Redevelopment grants and loans are available within designated areas of many communities. Loans are usually at below-market interest, and generally grants require the owner to expend his or her own funds as well, such as in matching grants. These funds are primarily available for exterior renovation, but they could be given to demolish and rebuild. Check your local redevelopment agencies. The availability of these funds could significantly increase the desirability of many investment opportunities.

Your ability to buy real estate depends directly on your credit. If you fail to meet obligations, you cannot expect others to trust you in dealings involving many thousands of dollars. In business, we measure a person by his or her past actions. You must therefore be zealous in protecting your credit, for in business your credit is your honor.

6
CHAPTER

Partnerships, Syndicates, and Real Estate Investment Trusts

The natural tendency of every society in which property enjoys tolerable security is to increase in wealth.

T. B. Macaulay, 1835
Edinburgh Review

PARTNERSHIPS

An often-quoted definition of a partnership is "two people getting together for a business or investment, one of whom has the money and the other the experience, after which whose positions become reversed." This cynical definition has unfortunately been true in too many cases. Many partnerships don't work out.

Why Some Partnerships Go Sour

Whatever the reason, most partnerships are relatively short-lived, even when the business or investment is profitable. It also seems that the more partners there are, the more partnership problems there are. Don't form a partnership for a fixer-upper property. It will more often than not end in a disastrous relationship between parties. A partnership, like a marriage, requires total dedication if it is going to succeed.

Four friends asked me for advice on a real estate investment. I told them of the problems of partnerships, but they said I didn't understand. They were very close friends, almost family. They would not have any problems in that area but just wanted an opinion on a six-unit building in which they were interested.

The four friends purchased the building, which was well-located but in bad shape. They were going to fix it up, get better tenants, and sell it. Well, only two partners showed up to start work on the weekend after the purchase. One of the other two partners had a family affair he "had" to attend and the other one had to work at his job. The second weekend it was the same. It turned out that two partners carried the burden of work while the other two helped only on rare occasions. One of these men was completely incapable of performing the simplest mechanical task.

During the renovating period, the property had a negative cash flow because the units were vacant for the renovation. In addition to the payments on the loans, materials had to be purchased. One of the partners who performed the largest share of the work refused to contribute additional money for the payments. He argued that if everyone had worked as he had, the job would have been done; he would not pay for their laziness. The other three had to make the payments to avoid foreclosure. The building was put on the market for sale "as is" before the work was completed and while it was vacant. The four former friends sold the property and luckily got their money back, but they now won't have anything to do with each other.

Partnerships don't have to end this way. I have a partner in some of my investments. We get along great and have for years. We have agreed to a division of responsibility and we stick to it. Our teamwork has been fun as well as profitable; our different backgrounds complement each other.

Partnership agreements need not be in writing to be enforceable; nevertheless, I recommend putting them in writing. It is not so much a matter of trust as business. To avoid misunderstandings, write down rights and duties. Having it in writing can help a partnership to work.

ADVANTAGES TO PARTNERSHIPS

A big advantage a partnership offers to an investor is courage. Many people will not move to invest alone but will invest with a partner. Another person who agrees that an investment is good reinforces a person's convictions. Without the psychological crutch of a partner, many investors would not have made their first real estate investment.

Another advantage of a partnership is that it can provide greater capital, thus allowing the investors to buy higher-quality investments. Occasionally, you will see a "partner wanted" ad. Though the investment may be excellent, don't jump at it. Don't enter a partnership with a stranger.

Financial Partners

Many successful investors take financial partners who put up the money in exchange for interest and/or equity in the purchase.

The problem with partners is that many people will indicate an interest, but most will hesitate to actually commit to the deal when it is before them. Nevertheless, partners can be used in many ways. For example, parties could agree to the following:

- Partner puts up entire purchase price (or down payment) secured by a mortgage providing for a fair rate of return.
- Partner has an equity position as a limited partner. Partner receives his or her percentage of the operating and/or sale profit.

This arrangement is similar to the participation loans insurance companies made to developers during the 1970s and 1980s. The lender put up the money for the loan, which was secured by a first mortgage. As a sweetener to make the large loan, the lender was given an equity position as a limited partner, often up to 50 percent. When the loan was paid off, the insurance company was still part owner in the property (usually office buildings or shopping centers).

If you have locked in a deal such as an option on the land, have bids on construction costs, and a prime tenant but are still unable to obtain financing, you should consider a venture capital firm; they are really just another financial partner. The firm will either agree or decline to supply capital after evaluating your project. In addition to interest, they will want an equity position if they supply the money. You should be able to find the venture capital firms active in your area by checking with local redevelopment agencies and industrial development agencies.

Limited Partnerships/Syndicates

A limited partner is an inactive partner who contributes only money to an investment. While in a general partnership a partner has unlimited personal liability for the partnership debts, in a limited partnership the limited partner's liability is limited to his or her investment. If the partnership fails, the limited partner is not personally liable to unpaid creditors.

Because a limited partner cannot utilize any tax loss from an investment, investments should be made based upon income and/or likely appreciation. On the plus side, the limited partner has none of the landlord's hassles. They are taken care of for him or her by a general partner.

> A schoolteacher became quite well off because of limited partnerships. This young man was a native of a developing area and had an excellent knowledge of real estate and agriculture in the area. With a wife and three small children, he didn't have money to invest. He saw what he considered to be "steals" go by because he couldn't put together even a modest down payment.
>
> The young man heard of a ranch for sale and thought it was a terrific opportunity. He went to see the owner, who agreed verbally to give him a 10-day option to buy the property. This option was not legally enforceable because it was not in writing and no consideration was given for it. Nevertheless, this young man felt that it would be honored.
>
> He contacted quite a few of his friends and acquaintances, including his doctor, dentist, and attorney, and had a meeting at his home. With maps of the area, he explained why it was a good investment. He told them about the depreciation possibilities on the citrus trees (at the time depreciation was allowed to pass through to syndicate investors) and why he felt that a quick resale for profit was possible if desired. The terms were $400,000 with a $50,000 down payment. The young man told his audience he wanted five investors as limited partners. Each would put up $15,000, which would give them some money for payments. The groves could be leased to another grower, but the property would still have a negative cash flow and the investors would each have to plan on coming up with at least another $5000 every year. For acting as the general partner he asked for one-sixth of the investment to be paid out of profits after a sale. His share was not to be computed until all monies invested by the limited partners were repaid. He found his five investors that night, and within a few months the property was resold for $600,000.
>
> The teacher found other properties, and his partners rolled over their profits into his new ventures. Several of those who failed to get into the first venture now wanted in. Friends of investors became interested as well.

Once you have demonstrated success, investors tend to find you. While this young teacher succeeded without a cash investment, limited partners are more willing to invest if the general partner has a cash position in the investment. Investors prefer the general partner to have a very positive interest in the success of the group.

This young man has quit his job teaching and spends all of his time on his partnership business and is still riding a wave of success. His latest partnerships have been to buy distressed property at bargain prices.

Not all limited partnerships are successful. In striving for great profits, limited partnerships are usually highly leveraged. That is, they are financed as much as possible. Many early limited partnerships were so heavily leveraged that real estate market fluctuations resulted in lower rents, a negative cash flow, and eventual foreclosure and total loss of investment. General partners milked some early limited partnerships and were the only ones who saw a profit.

Many stock brokerage firms sold limited partnerships in the 1970s. Advantages of these investments were no management responsibilities, limited liability for losses, as well as the primary benefit, a tax shelter. Depreciation from investments was passed through to the investors who could then show a large paper loss that sheltered or exempted other income from taxation. Many limited partnerships were set up that made little economic sense except for the tax shelter aspects. Changes in the tax laws that no longer allow these "passive" losses to be passed through to investors have taken the allure of these investments away.

Some limited partnerships are set up to buy specific properties. Where the properties have not been selected it is known as a *blind pool*. Many people will invest in blind pools when they have faith in the general partner who has had a record of success. Most limited partnerships today have a goal of dissolution within a specified time period so that investors will hopefully gain the return of their investment plus a capital gain. A major disadvantage of limited partnerships compared to real estate investment trusts (REITs) is the fact that there is much less of a market for partnership interests, and if a sale is necessary, the interest might have to be discounted less than the value attributable to the interest if the partnership were dissolved.

A *syndication* is simply a group investment. While syndications can take many forms, they are usually limited partnerships set up by a general partner. Buying shares in new syndications is generally not a good investment. Many syndicators add on high costs and profits so that property usually must appreciate a minimum of 20 percent before the value of the property equals the purchase price of the shares. Instead of buying wholesale, investors in new real estate syndicates generally pay above-retail prices.

Before you buy a syndicate interest, check with the general partner and with other purchasers; evaluate financial statements and the contract with the general partner; and most important, evaluate the assets. The track record of the general partner is very important. Find out what else he or she has done in the past. Get the names of previous investors, and call them to verify profits and the relationship. Ask if they know of other investments the general partner has been involved in. The general partner might neglect to tell you of investments that didn't work out well.

There are real bargains in established limited partnerships. Many offer returns far in excess of what would be possible from government bonds. However, in evaluating distribution, be careful to ascertain that part of the distribution is not return of capital rather than earnings. If the limited partnership is selling assets, future yields will decline.

If you are interested in a major syndicate, check with a stockbroker who has access to the National Partnership Exchange (NAPEX). This computerized system has about 25,000 members and allows you to find what the asking and bid prices are for 1400 listed partnership interests. For information on NAPEX, you can call 1-800-356-2739.

The American Partnership Board (800) 272-6273, *www.apboard.com*, provides an online auction site for limited partnerships. They have data on several thousand limited partnerships.

The New York Asset Exchange provides information on how they price limited partnership interests as well as handle resales of such interests. The Web site is *Nyaex.com/ltdpart.htm*.

While there are ways to purchase and resell limited partnerships, researching their underlying value can be difficult. Because they are out of favor with most investors, they are seldom written about in financial magazines and newspapers. If you are interested in a particular firm, I recommend an online search.

If you are interested in setting up a limited partnership for real estate investments, have an attorney draw up the papers. An attorney can also advise you as to any state regulations and securities laws governing small syndicates.

Tenancy in Common

Tenancy in common is fractionalized ownership. Interests need not be equal. The market for tenancy in common ownership has been expanding in commercial real estate. They can be used for 1031 tax-deferred exchanges or just as investments (1031 exchanges are covered in Chapter 12). A number of firms are offering individuals a chance to participate in ownership of investment-grade properties. Disenchantment with the stock market has fueled the demand. Major firms such as CB Richard Ellis Investors LLC, Triple Net Properties LLC of Santa Ana, CA, TIC Properties LLC of Greenville, SC, and Inland Real Estate Group Inc. of Oak Brook, IL offer programs of fractionalized ownerships. Some investments are blind pools and others are for specific property ownership. The advantage of tenancy in common over limited partnership investments is the ability to conduct like-kind exchanges when an investor wishes to sell. Investments generally are for persons having a significant net worth. Like any other real estate investment, I recommend that the property be evaluated and that the investor considers facts, not salesperson hype in making a decision. While a fractionalized ownership may offer quality property, some offerings benefit the investment seller more than the investor.

REAL ESTATE INVESTMENT TRUSTS

Organized under federal law, REITs must consist of at least 100 members, and at least 95 percent of the income must be distributed to investors each year. The shares in these trusts are freely transferable and are treated as partnerships rather than corporations for tax purposes.

A corporation was formerly subject to double taxation in that the profit was taxed to the corporation and the remainder was again taxed to the individual stockholders if it was paid out as dividends. In a partnership, profit is simply taxed once to the partners. With a REIT, only the earnings retained by the trust are taxed to the trust.

REITs offer the small investor an opportunity to have ownership interests in multimillion-dollar properties. Shares of REITs are listed on stock exchanges and can be purchased through any stock brokerage office. There are three basic types of REITs, *equity REITs* that own property, *mortgage REITs* that invest in mortgages, and *hybrid REITs* that own real estate and also hold mortgages. Over 300 REITs hold assets of more than $300 billion dollars. As properties appreciate in value, rents and dividends increase, which tends to increase the value of the shares. While values fluctuate, REIT values tend to hold relatively stable in large stock market declines. However, when the stock market soars, REITs tend to be left behind as investors seek far greater returns.

When interest rates are low, residential renters are often able to become buyers. The result is a higher vacancy rate for residential REITs and lower earnings, which might be reflected in dividends and the stock price. However, when interest rates are high, fewer renters can become owners so rental demand becomes greater. Vacancy rates decline and residential REIT income increases. The results are usually favorable as to both the price of residential REITs and their dividends.

I personally hold stock in 26 separate REITs. The advantages of REITs are that they pay large dividends (they must distribute at least 95 percent of earnings). I evaluate REITs using the following criteria:

1. **Type of property.** Most REITs specialize. While most of my REITs are apartment communities, I am pleased with several REITs that I hold in warehouse facilities, personal storage, net leased commercial, and mobile home parks.

2. **Debt to equity ratio.** The higher the debt to equity ratio, the greater risk there is of default. Many early REITs had a high debt to equity ratio and a weak rental market led to a number of bankruptcies, leaving investors with worthless shares.

3. **REIT history.** A history of dividend growth over the years is an indication of good management.

4. **Dividends.** A comparison of dividends to price is important but not if the dividends are not justified by other factors. A number of REITs have cut dividends and witnessed a tumble in stock prices.

5. **Funds from operation (FFO).** This figure is the amount of income in excess of operating expense and debt service. It does not deduct for depreciation or include gains from sale of property.

6. **Cash available for distribution (CAD).** I feel this is a better indicator of performance than FFO. The CAD is an adjusted FFO that deducts capitalized expenses (depreciation) necessary to maintain income.

7. **Occupancy rate**. The occupancy rate and changes in the rate can indicate future dividend changes.

8. **Tenants.** When a commercial REIT has just a few tenants such as national chains, the REIT risk becomes related to the financial well-being of the tenants. The more concentrated the leases, the greater the risk.

9. **Area.** REITs that own property in highly competitive rental areas will have less appreciation and greater risk than REITs where properties are in areas of high demand.

10. **Self-dealing management.** Just like other major corporations, some officers have treated a REIT as a private piggy bank. I try to steer away from REITs where officers and directors sell or buy property from the REIT or control a firm that contracts with the REIT.

11. **Institutional holding.** I like REITs where institutions hold a significant percentage of stock. It tends to reinforce my evaluation because "experts" are in agreement with me.

12. **Net asset value (NAV).** I don't like to pay much of a premium over the per-share asset value of a REIT. However, don't use asset value as your only criterion. Some REITs trade at prices less than the underlying per-share asset value of the REIT, since price is more closely aligned to income than to asset value.

While your stockbroker and stock market research Web sites can provide information about REITs, you can also check the major reporting services such as Standard and Poor's at your local library. Also check the Web site for the National Association of Real Estate Investment Trusts at *www.NAREIT.com/aboutreits/faqtext.cfm*. Value Line Investment Service (800) 833-0046 has information on established REITs and provides expectations as to continued dividends. The Realty Stock Review (908) 389-8700 covers REITs as well as mutual funds and some limited partnerships.

INVESTMENT CLUBS

Many stock market investors first got involved in the market as a member of an investment club. Each member put up a set amount of money each week. Members were given assignments to research stocks and report on them. They also had brokers talk at their meetings. The group decided what to buy and what to sell and usually developed a diverse portfolio.

I have been told about a real estate investment club similar to the stock clubs of the past. The eight members all work in the same area. They meet once a week for lunch plus one Saturday morning a month to visit properties. The group has now purchased and resold several lots and made over 100 percent profit in their first year on their cash investment ($5000 each).

This particular group intends to dissolve in another two years. The group will have accomplished its purpose, which was to educate its members in real estate investments. Acting as a group also gave the members the courage to make financial decisions. Profit on each individual's $5000 investment will just be an additional benefit. Land is probably the best investment for clubs, since it does not involve the problems of renovation and division of physical work.

7
CHAPTER

Locating Property

If you want to make money in real estate, find out where the people are going and get there first.

Will Rogers

Anyone can find property to buy. The papers are full of ads and the streets are full of "For Sale" signs. What is difficult is finding property that makes economic sense.

Many individuals, as well as families, have found that looking for investment property can be fun. Just as many families enjoy flea markets and garage sales, looking for the overlooked treasure, searching for the right property at the right price can be emotionally and financially rewarding. If they find a property with problems and can solve them, they will have turned the problem into an opportunity. They will achieve an emotional high that will be further enforced if reality meets or exceeds their expectations.

LOCATION VALUE

The old axiom "The three most important factors for real estate investment are location, location, and location" is still true. The best location offers the greatest liquidity (shortest sale time) and the greatest appreciation during periods of growth. It is also easiest to obtain loans for well-located property, and lenders are more willing to lend to their maximum loan-to-value ratio for such properties. And the downside of such property is less severe.

During periods of economic recession, well-located real estate will suffer a much lower percentage of decline in value than less desirable locations.

The best location, therefore, offers a real estate investor the least risk even though the initial cost will be higher than a similar property in a less desirable location. For example, two college professors came to the same California college in 1971. One purchased a 2000-square-foot, eight-year-old home in a prestigious subdivision for $40,000. The other professor wanted a brand-new home. He purchased a 2200-square-foot home on a large lot in a small subdivision with many smaller homes. He felt he had a great bargain at $40,000 because he definitely got more house for the money. Today, the home in the better subdivision has a value in excess of $300,000, or about a 700 percent increase in value. The larger home, which is a better structure, has a value of only $120,000 at most. The walled subdivision it's in sits in a high-crime area. Now who has the bargain?

Stick to Your Own Backyard

Learn the values of property in your particular area. It's easy to get a good understanding of value in a limited area for a particular type of property, but no one can know values for all types of property over a broad area.

Many investors are able to achieve a value insight more accurate than values arrived at by many professional appraisers.

Working with a broker will provide data on list and selling prices, as will visiting open houses. Viewing vacant apartments will help you understand rental value.

Avoid investments outside your geographical area unless there is a strong reason for the investment.

Property advertised outside its normal market area should generally be avoided. It is either overpriced or has a problem, which is why it hasn't sold to a local buyer. You should avoid property outside the United States because of high risk. Political turmoil, outright government appropriation of your property, and other factors make it impossible to monitor your investment. The less familiar you are with the country, the more this is true.

USING REAL ESTATE AGENTS

The easiest way to find property is through real estate professionals—the real estate brokers and salespeople active in your area. They know what is available and frequently what isn't available but could be. A knowledgeable real estate agent can also give you a good perspective on price and current market conditions. In a few hours an agent can often present many properties for consideration. What could have taken months might be accomplished in a few days. Most active brokers belong to multiple listing services (MLS), so they have access not just to their own office listings but also to the listings of many other offices.

To get the maximum benefit of a real estate agent's time and expertise, tell the agent how much cash or other assets you have available for a down payment and for monthly payments. You may find some unimaginative real estate agents who are not interested in working with you if you can't make a substantial down payment. This type of agent usually lacks the ability to structure purchases with little or no down payment.

In selecting real estate agents, look for success. A successful agent is usually better informed about available property. Actually, you want more than just a successful agent, you want an agent who is successful in the area and type of property that you are interested in. He or she will have the skills necessary to match your needs with appropriate property in a professional manner. If you feel an agent is not really interested in working for you, don't hesitate to contact another agent. Many successful investors have developed a close working relationship with a single real estate agent they trust and respect. An agent who fully understands your needs and is willing to expend effort to meet those needs in an expeditious manner is a valuable asset.

You must keep in mind that, though the real estate agent may try to find property that meets your needs, in a normal sales transaction the agent represents the seller and not you, the buyer. You want what is called a *buyer's agent* whose first allegiance is to you and your best interests and not to finding a buyer for a seller.

You will likely be asked to sign an authorization to locate property. The authorization may be an open agreement where you can also use other agents or it may be an exclusive agency agreement. If you have faith in the agent, I recommend an exclusive agency agreement. This means that the agent will be your only agent and if you use another agent, the exclusive agent will still be entitled to a fee. The agreement should provide that if you locate a property yourself, without the agent's help, no fee shall be paid.

I don't recommend an "exclusive right to locate property" that obligates you to a fee if you locate a property yourself without the agent's help.

Even though you signed an agreement to pay a fee, the agreement probably will allow the broker to cooperate with the seller's broker and receive the fee from the seller. As buyer, you would be responsible for the fee if there were no fee being paid by the seller. This would be in the case of a for-sale-by-owner situation, property held by lenders but not listed for sale, auction situations, etc. The advantage to you is that a buyer's broker will show you these opportunities but a seller's broker will not because there is no financial incentive to do so. Brokers who only represent buyers are likely to be aware of many opportunities that seller brokers have no knowledge of.

Why a Third Person Can Make a Difference

A third person often has a greater chance of getting your offer accepted than you would have in dealing directly with the owner. Owners tend to be calmer and more objective when they are dealing through an agent. They are less likely to let emotions affect their judgment. Third parties are able to work with sellers as well as help you tailor an offer to overcome objections.

Working without an Agent

While real estate agents can lead you to many distressed properties, some of the best deals will be found by searching on your own. Because most real estate agents have a background as sellers' agents, they tend to avoid many situations because of the lack of funds available for commissions. This is often the case in sheriff's sales as well as foreclosure and tax sales, where the total property indebtedness might exceed the property value. In these cases, purchases must be made at the sale or arranged with the foreclosing lienholder or high bidder after the sale.

Owners Who Don't Use Agents

Often owners try to sell without an agent because they feel they can save a commission. Occasionally, an unsophisticated owner does not have a good idea of values and will ask a bargain price. Usually, however, if the property has been on the market for any period of time, the owner has been contacted by many real estate agents and will have a good idea or possibly an inflated idea of values.

An owner will often place an unrealistically high value on property. The price may be based on what the owner believes some other house sold for or on what a real estate agent said the property could bring. Often the sole basis of the pricing is simply because they will sell at that price. It is a price they want that may be unjustified by any data. Unfortunately, some real estate agents will try to "buy a listing" by appealing to an owner's greed and promising a sale at an unrealistic price. When an owner is given this sort of misinformation, it becomes difficult to purchase the property at a fair price.

Beware of the sophisticated seller looking for an unsophisticated buyer. These owners may attempt either to hide something detrimental about the property or to obtain a price much higher than the market will justify. They may use deceiving ads. I have come across some shrewd operators who posed as "bumpkins" in hopes of snaring a buyer. Be on your guard when dealing directly with owners.

ADVERTISING LEADS

You should get in the habit of reading classified ads for both property for sale and property for lease. Even though you should concentrate on sale ads, when an owner sounds desperate to lease (because of rental concessions offered), he or she is also likely to be motivated to sell.

While you will quickly find out that appearances on paper are often far different from the physical property, you are more likely to find property represented as it actually is in for-sale-by-owner ads.

Look for ads that indicate a seller is under pressure to sell such as divorce, relocation, pending foreclosure, and the like. By making up a list of questions based on the ad, when you call you will be able to find out if it is worth taking the time to physically inspect it. Keep in mind at all times that the more motivated an owner is to sell, the greater likelihood of a purchase that makes economic sense.

Whenever you see a neighborhood bulletin board, such as those frequently found at supermarkets and laundromats, take a few minutes to scan the ads. You will find real estate listed for sale that frequently is not advertised in newspapers. This will give you the opportunity to contact owners before they have been bombarded with calls from agents.

Advertising for Property

Besides looking for the ads of others, you can effectively advertise for property to buy. You will be amazed at the variety of responses you will receive from your own ads.

Figures 7–1, 7–2, and 7–3 are examples of classified ads successfully used by real estate investors who buy and resell single-family homes.
Some investors use a direct-mail approach with flyers similar to the above
ads. They mail to owners likely to be highly motivated, such as owners in
foreclosure, divorce, owners' delinquent in taxes, and even owners who
have tenant problems evidenced by evictions. A great many leads are
available from legal notices. A little time spent at the courthouse should
reward you with a number of good leads.

Some buyers prefer postcards to letters. An advantage of using postcards is that they must be read. Owners in default are often besieged by
creditors and might otherwise assume your letter is just another collection
letter.

FIGURE 7–1

Sell Me Your Home
$ for Cash $
Highest Prices — Fast Close
Call Tom Jones at 555-7133

FIGURE 7–2

I pay cash
for your real estate equity even if
you are delinquent or in foreclosure.
Call me for my evaluation. No fees — No cost.
Tom Jones 555-7133

FIGURE 7–3

I will buy your home
Cash in 7 days
Tom Jones 555-7133

FINDING THE BARGAINS

Your first opportunity to make money in real estate will be at the time of purchase. If you can buy a property for 20 percent less than fair market value, you have made a profit at the time of purchase. This is possible in a number of circumstances. Strong seller motivation, problems with the property the owner is unable or unwilling to rectify, or faulty owner evaluation will all help you to buy right.

Don't dismiss property from consideration because the asking price is too high. Keep in mind that the majority of real estate sales are made at prices lower than the asking price. The only way you can find out if an owner will accept your offer is to make it.

While a significant reduction from the list price might not appeal to a seller who has recently placed a property on the market, the longer it has been on the market, the more likely the owner will be receptive to a low offer.

As a prospective purchaser you should bear in mind that when an owner has owned a property for a long period of time, even offers that slash the owner's asking price usually provide the owner with a profit. If the seller has held his or her property more than 10 years, chances are that, with inflation, the asking price is considerably more than the owner paid for the property. Properties that have been vacant for long periods and on which owners have been making large mortgage payments are ideal candidates for a low offer. To purchase this type of property, you should have the means to make the payments and faith in your ability to find a buyer or a qualified tenant. Out-of-the-area owners are also often more receptive to low offers than area owners would be.

Some investors consider "What could I net from the resale of this property within a reasonable period of time if I had to?" They use this evaluation even if they don't intend to sell. Since a sale commission plus all sales associated costs would likely approach 10 percent, to break even, they would need to gross 10 percent over what they would pay. While this should not be the only criteria to use to make a real estate investment, it will indicate if it is a bargain. Keep in mind that buying below market value is just one way to increase your advantage and even property priced at fair market value and sometimes even over fair market value can be an advantageous purchase.

Don't be concerned that a property is dirty or needs maintenance. This helps you as an informed buyer, since many other buyers would be turned off by such conditions. When there is little competition to buy, a bargain is more likely. A house that needs painting and yardwork might be available for $160,000, even though it would be worth $200,000 or more when properly maintained. You can buy a lot of paint and lawn seed for $40,000.

The longer a property has been on the market without an offer, the greater the chance that you can obtain a bargain in price or terms. When a property has been for sale for a long period without buyer interest, any offer is likely to receive serious consideration. Ask your real estate agent which listings have been on the market for an unusually long time.

In a rising market, new homes can actually be a bargain. Builders often set prices based on their costs rather than the market. When a project has exceptional sales activity, it generally indicates that the prices were set too low based on market demand.

I know of a successful investor who became wealthy doing nothing but buying new homes and condominiums that he resold, usually at a profit. His criterion for buying was the public acceptance of a project. When sales are greater than expected for a subdivision, he will wait until they are almost sold out and then buy several units. When a desirable project is completed, the resales are usually significantly higher than the original sale price.

He has another formula for really large projects being developed in phases. If the first-phase sales are exceptionally good, he will buy several units before they are sold out. When a developer has exceptional sales on the first phase of a project, the developer can be expected to raise prices significantly for later phases of the project.

There will be some bargains available regardless of the real estate market. You just have to look for them.

Evictions

Owners of single-family homes who have to evict tenants for nonpayment of rent are usually very motivated to sell. Often they rented their homes, hoping for a trouble-free income only to discover they are living a nightmare. Evictions, therefore, often can lead you to unusually attractive opportunities.

> My name is John N. and I am a 37-year-old jack-of-all-trades. I found my niche in buying fixer-upper property, making necessary repairs and selling it for a profit.

While working on one of my properties, I met the property owner next door. He was very upset because he had just evicted a tenant who not only didn't pay rent but also had left the premises in a shambles. The owner, who lived out of the area, asked what I would charge to make required repairs to his property. Instead of offering to do the work, I purchased the property on the spot.

Since that time the bulk of my purchases have been made by using public records. My wife checks eviction notices filed in the county courthouse. She looks for owners living outside the area who are evicting tenants for nonpayment of rent. From the addresses we determine if we are interested. (I want property in desirable areas because it usually means quick and profitable resale.) We then call the owners and ask if they are interested in selling their property. Usually they are unsure, so we tell them we will call back the next day after they have talked it over with their spouses. The second telephone call often results in a positive response; in fact, after talking it over, they often are eager to sell. After I inquire about loan details, I tell the owners I will prepare an offer.

Often I buy property before the tenant has vacated. By going to the door and being polite, I usually can get to see the interior of the property. If I am unable to get inside, I ask questions of the neighbors. If I have not seen the interior of the property, my offers reflect a worst-case scenario. Of course, if the property has been vacated, I arrange with the owner to enter the property.

I present my offer, which is usually highly leveraged, in person. What I like about buying from evictions is that I am not in a competitive environment with other buyers. I have reached the owners first and they are mine to negotiate with.

Divorce Records

While divorce agreements might mean that one spouse gets the real estate, today the real estate is more likely to be sold and divided because the couple's real estate equity is likely to be their only significant asset and will therefore usually be split between them.

In a divorce, the spouses are often very eager to get their cash and get on with their lives. The owner motivation can be such that I have included divorce property under the category of distressed property. Letters, similar to the ads shown in Figures 7–1, 7–2, and 7–3, are an effective way to find possible sellers. Your mailing list is readily available from courthouse records and/or legal newspapers.

Probate

Information on property in probate can be obtained from legal newspapers, as well as by checking the filings in probate court. This is public information.

Heirs often can't use the property, don't want it, or want the money more than they want estate property. This is especially true when heirs live outside the area where the estate property is located or the number of heirs requires a division of the property.

In looking to buy probate property, you might be in competition with real estate agents who will be seeking to list such property for sale.

Probate sales can be at auction or by private sale. Sales usually require court approval and in some states, courts will consider late bids; therefore, a property you thought you had purchased could be lost to another bidder.

If your state allows late bids at the approval hearing, it might be advantageous to check with an attorney as to the requirements of making a late bid in court. This tactic can catch the previous high bidder by surprise.

Notices of Abatement and Code Violations

Owners who are not sophisticated investors tend to get agitated when confronted with problems. Owners who have received notices to abate a public nuisance (such as noxious weeds or acts of tenants) as well as of code or fire violations are usually a bit disgusted. The timing could be right for a sale. The owner is likely highly motivated if he or she responds positively, so advantageous price and terms might be possible.

The notices are matters of public record and information can be obtained from the applicable department at your county courthouse or city hall.

Before you put in an offer on such a property, be certain you have a fairly accurate knowledge as to the costs of corrective action. You might also want to find out if time extensions as to completion of the work are possible.

Neglected Property

While not always the case, financial difficulties often seem to go hand-in-hand with failure to properly maintain the exterior of a property. Many investors look for neglected property even though there is no for-sale sign.

They then contact the owners, who they find are quite often in financial distress and motivated to sell.

Friends

Let friends and acquaintances know what you are looking for. Many sales are made because a friend knows someone who is considering selling his or her property. In this manner, many sales are made without property ever being officially on the market.

Networking

Communicating with other investors will provide you with a source of properties as well as sale opportunities. Many investors will find properties that, while attractive, do not meet their specific needs. By knowing each other's interests, the relationship can be mutually beneficial.

There are many real estate investment clubs. You can find clubs by using an Internet search engine, type in "real estate investment club" and your city or state. Many clubs have regular monthly meetings and even newsletters. Membership in a club can be a valuable learning as well as networking forum.

You should also consider membership in Building Owners and Managers Association (BOMA) International. While the organization focuses on building management, many investors are members. BOMA provides personal development programs as well as pertinent information for building owners. There are over 16,000 members and local chapters in most major cities. You can contact the organization at *www.boma.org*. You might also consider membership in the Association of Independent Real Estate Owners (AIREO). AIREO offers investor meetings, educational opportunities, an investor bulletin board and other benefits. To learn more go to *www.aireo.com*.

Earning Finder's Fees

In many states you can legally accept a finder's fee for introducing a person to a property even though you are not a licensed real estate salesperson or broker.

In your search for property, you will likely come across other investors and learn what they are looking for. You will likely have to pass up great opportunities because they aren't right for you.

You don't have to waste these opportunities. There are just so many properties one person can effectively handle. Obtain a written finder's fee agreement from another investor or from the agent involved before disclosing particulars about a property or investor. If the investor buys it, you get a fee.

TURNING DOWN BARGAINS

You have heard the expression "Don't bite off more than you can chew." Well, it applies to real estate investments. In evaluating an investment, consider the holding costs. Consider different scenarios. If you would be in trouble unless you could sell quickly, avoid the purchase. There are plenty of other opportunities around.

8

Foreclosures, IRS Sales, and Tax Sales

The moment the idea is admitted into society that property is not as sacred as the laws of God . . . anarchy and tyranny commence.

John Adams

In foreclosures, IRS sales, and tax sales there is generally no place for an agent. There are a few buyer agents who keep track of these sales and work with foreclosure buyers. Buyer agents can be very helpful but they expect a fee. Most foreclosure buyers find the deals for themselves. If foreclosures interest you, I can help. If there is no sales listing, most agents don't even want to know of these sales.

FORECLOSURES

Why is there such great interest in foreclosure property? Why do we see foreclosure seminars with standing room only? The reason is very simple: Foreclosure provides an opportunity to buy at wholesale rather than retail. A resale at market price will yield a profit.

But don't look at foreclosure buyers as vultures. The simple truth is that someone is going to make a profit from a foreclosure. Foreclosures are caused by a number of reasons. They might result from personal problems having to do with alcohol, divorce, or employment difficulties. On the other hand, some are the result of simply spending beyond one's income.

There actually are three separate types of "foreclosure" opportunities:

1. Buying from an owner prior to a foreclosure sale.
2. Buying a property at a foreclosure sale.
3. Buying from a lender after foreclosure.

Foreclosure publication notices required by your state laws might be in special legal newspapers or in newspapers of general circulation. In larger metropolitan areas there are frequently legal papers published strictly to meet the statutory publication requirements of foreclosures and other notices. See if your community or county is served by such a paper. If so, you will want to subscribe if you are going to be dealing in foreclosures.

Many people don't even know of the existence of these legal papers. Therefore, default and foreclosure notices published in such papers are likely to mean fewer preforeclosure buyers as well as fewer bidders than if the notices had been published in a general newspaper.

There are a number of Web sites that offer nationwide foreclosure information. Some charge for services or offer to sell you courses on buying foreclosure properties. A couple of sites to check are *www.foreclosure.com* and *www.foreclosurefreesearch.com*.

In some areas foreclosure notices are posted in public places, usually on a bulletin board at a county courthouse. You will also find foreclosure opportunities as well as other distress property by advertising that you buy property (see Figures 7–1, 7–2, and 7–3).

In some areas, private newsletters provide information on distressed property (property in foreclosure). These newsletters can save you a great deal of time if you are interested in buying at the foreclosure sale or from the lender after the sale. However, you will want the information as soon as possible if you want to buy from the owner prior to the sale. Because of the newsletter delay, you are better off scanning the legal notices in your local and legal newspapers.

Foreclosures involve more than homes. No matter what kind of property you are looking for, purchases are possible in the foreclosure market.

Not all foreclosures are by lenders. Any lienholder can foreclose on his or her lien. As an example, property owner associations, can foreclose on a lien filed for association dues and assessments.

BUYING BEFORE FORECLOSURE SALE

An advantage of buying a home from an owner before a foreclosure sale is that you are able to avoid a competitive auction.

Contact the owner in foreclosure with a phone call emphasizing that you are looking for properties in a particular area and that you buy homes fast for cash without real estate fees. Do not mention foreclosure during these contacts. Don't claim to be a foreclosure consultant. You are dealing for yourself as a potential buyer. Don't claim to be anything else.

If you get a positive response from an owner, you want a property profile from a title insurance company to check the indebtedness against the property. Although you should also ask the owner, because they expect it, don't take the owner's word for what they owe. They forget, they don't actually know, they lie—or a combination of these.

Never buy from an owner before you have checked out the owner's equity situation. Jumping too fast to buy a property could land you in the fire. It is far better to miss an opportunity because you didn't act fast enough than to be burned. You won't run out of opportunities.

The customer service department of a local title insurance company can give you information on ownership, liens, and encumbrances at no cost.

You will need the assessor's parcel number or the legal description. They will give you a property profile. This is not a policy of insurance. If they make an error, you have no recourse unless you actually purchase a title policy. Ask the title company to search the files for IRS liens, bankruptcy filings, tax liens, and judgment liens. These may be in separate files, and they might otherwise not check for them unless asked.

A cooperative title company expects you to give them your business. You can expect future cooperation if you do. Because a property profile is a no-cost service, don't give the title company long lists of properties. Don't ask for a property profile until you talk with the owner or have otherwise decided you will pursue a property. If you ask too much from a title company, you will overwork their courtesy.

When a property is not overly encumbered, a purchase before foreclosure should be considered. As the time for the foreclosure sale approaches, owners' expectations tend to decline.

As a point of beginning for purchase negotiations, ask the owner to name a "walking-away price," a price to be received in cash over and above all encumbrances.

When an owner is in default, you could consider a package offering such as:

1. A small amount of cash.
2. A note.
3. Several months free rent and a rental agreement thereafter (if desired by the owner).

Don't give the seller an option to buy back a property without checking with an attorney. In many states, a transaction such as this is regarded as a mortgage, not as a sale. The seller could still have redemption rights, and your anticipated sale profit could place you in the position of charging a usurious rate of interest, which could result in severe penalties.

In making any purchase offer prior to foreclosure you must find out if existing mortgages or trust deeds are assumable. If they are not, then new financing will be required. Make certain you can obtain such financing before you make your offer. Loans that include a due-on-sale clause (alienation clause) cannot be assumed without risk (see Chapter 4).

If you intend to reinstate an assumable loan, you also must make certain that it can be reinstated. In many states, the reinstatement period ends a specified number of days after publication of the sale notice or during a specified period prior to the foreclosure sale.

If you are working to arrange financing to purchase a property from an owner where a foreclosure sale is imminent, consider contacting the lender for a postponement of the sale. Most conventional lenders don't want to go through with foreclosure because they know they will have security problems with the foreclosed property, as well as expenses to prepare the property for sale. In addition, the lender will not be earning interest on the investment during the period of holding the property. For these reasons, lenders will often agree to one postponement if you can show you will be able to buy the property and either refinance or cure the current default.

Of course, if the seller owes too much, you should be looking beyond—to the foreclosure sale or after it. You should be honest with the owner. Don't let on that you are interested when you know you cannot buy before the foreclosure sale.

Keep in mind that most foreclosures don't reach the point of sale. Generally, foreclosure actions end in reinstatement. Some states allow a homeowner in default the right of rescission from any contract to sell their equity. Other states offer a rescission and/or criminal penalties for taking unconscionable advantage of an owner in default. If your state offers a rescission period, don't pay consideration or accept the deed while the owner can still rescind. If your state provides a penalty for taking unconscionable advantage of an owner in default, it is strongly suggested that an attorney represent the owner. You don't want even a hint of impropriety.

Another approach is to buy the interest of the foreclosing lienholder. When a property is in foreclosure and the foreclosing lienholder is a private party who holds the first mortgage, you should consider contacting that party and offering to buy the mortgage. Besides a cash offer you could offer to exchange mortgages you hold on other properties that have a history of prompt payment. Generally, an individual foreclosing is a prior owner who wants payments, not aggravation.

If you offer cash for the loan, consider asking the owner to discount it. By buying at less than face value, you can end up getting an exceptional return on your money should the buyer redeem the property in foreclosure. If the property is not redeemed, you end up with a purchase at less than the amount of the first mortgage. You can also make a quick profit of the amount of discount you were able to obtain should the price be bid up at the foreclosure sale. Discounts of 10 percent and 20 percent are common when purchasing first mortgages held by private parties in foreclosure.

You can advertise that you buy real estate loans that are in default. Many owners who have financed buyers will hesitate to foreclose because they do not really want the property back and would like to get out of a stressful situation. With such owners, a steep discount is possible.

When a property that interests you is in foreclosure, keep track of it. If a purchase is not feasible prior to the foreclosure, then consider the foreclosure sale. If you will not be able to cash out the foreclosing lienholder, contact the foreclosing lienholder prior to the sale and try to arrange a purchase agreement contingent on the lienholder being the successful bidder. You want to arrange a purchase prior to the lender having to incur management and/or fix-up costs as well as additional interest expense.

One danger of purchasing a property before foreclosure is that the seller could go bankrupt. If the bankruptcy court determines that the sale was for less than market value, the court could take back the property, upon the return of the consideration that you paid.

Upside-Down Opportunities

An upside-down situation exists when the indebtedness against a property (mortgage) exceeds the value of the property. This situation was prevalent in areas such as Southern California, where values soared in the late

1980s, resulting in high loans, but experienced a significant reduction in value in the early 1990s. Many owners simply walked away from their homes while others continued to meet loan obligations. At first glance, these situations appear hopeless from a buyer's view, but they actually offered unique opportunities.

The last thing lenders wanted was to own the property they loaned on. They were willing to wheel and deal if they had a firm proposal. There were thousands of "short sales" where lenders agreed to accept less than they were owed in full settlement of their mortgages or trust deeds.

The owners of upside-down properties were not really concerned with the sale price if they could extinguish their debt without a loan default on their credit report.

Should "the real estate bubble" break, these opportunities will again be available. While I personally do not believe the real estate market will suffer a significant decline, should it happen a paragraph such as the following could be included in any purchase offer:

> This offer is contingent upon (lender) providing the seller with written confirmation by (date) that they will reduce their loan balance and accept a short payoff equal to the seller's proceeds from this sale less all seller closing costs, commission, and any seller-required corrective work.

BUYING AT THE FORECLOSURE SALE

In addition to won't-sell owners, we have can't-sell owners where total indebtedness against the property exceeds its value. Because the foreclosure of a priority lien wipes out junior liens, such a property could be advantageously purchased at the foreclosure sale while it could not be economically purchased prior to the sale.

Foreclosure sales notices specify where the foreclosure sale will take place. If you are unsure, contact the attorney (or other party) handling the sale. Often it is on the courthouse steps and a crier announces the sale. In other areas, it is just inside the courthouse doors. In some areas of the country it is the county recorder's office. You have to be alert because unless you know what is happening, the foreclosure sale could be over before you realize it has even begun.

Before a foreclosure sale, call the person who advertised the sale to make certain the sale is still on. The property may have been redeemed, the owner could have declared bankruptcy, which serves to delay foreclosure, or the sale could have been postponed for some other reason.

One reason there generally are few bidders at foreclosure sales is that bidders other than the foreclosing lienholder must bid cash (depending upon the state), which they must have with them or be able to obtain quickly. By arranging a line of credit with your bank, you can bid at foreclosure sales using your credit line to obtain cashier's checks.

Another reason that there are few bidders at many foreclosure sales is that most people are afraid of what they don't understand. Foreclosures are an unknown to most people, even most real estate professionals. Not understanding a foreclosure makes it something to be avoided.

While most conventional lenders would prefer to have a loan paid off than to foreclose on the property, some finance companies and merchants look at foreclosures as a separate profit center of their business. They don't want the owner to redeem at the sale, nor do they want other bidders to buy at the sale. For example, a major carpet dealer reportedly made as much or more on real estate foreclosures as he made in selling carpet. They advertised no money down if you own your own home. They were not concerned if carpet buyers were unemployed or had poor credit, as long as they had sufficient equity in their home.

To encourage borrowing, carpet dealers as well as some other home improvement companies often advertise before Christmas that the dealer will give a gift to the family and no payments for periods as long as six months. The salespeople secure their sales by taking a mortgage on buyers' homes. If the payments are not made, the dealers will foreclose and resell properties through their own property sales organization.

These types of lenders often go to great lengths to avoid competing bidders at their foreclosure sales. Quite a few San Diego County foreclosure sales are scheduled in Borrego Springs, California, at about 8:00 a.m. Borrego Springs is a remote desert town about two hours from any significant population center. Even then, when competing bidders show up, the sale is often ordered to be postponed. In California, and in many other states, the lender is allowed to postpone the sale. Statutes generally limit the number of postponements to no more than two. This tactic is used by some of these lenders to tire out the competition. If you hang in there, you can prevail.

Never bid at a foreclosure sale without personally ascertaining the position of the foreclosing lienholder. There could be prior recorded liens, in which case, as buyer you would take title with those obligations intact.

The purchaser at a foreclosure sale only takes the priority of the foreclosing lender. While junior loans (recorded at a later date) are generally wiped out, the purchaser takes title subject to prior liens (there is some difference as to lien priority among the states). Keep in mind that property tax liens and liens for special assessments are generally priority liens.

Most bidders at foreclosure sales have not seen the interior of the property. Often buyers discover a total disaster area when they finally open the doors. Because of this possibility, a great many investors assume that they will need new floor and window coverings, paint, cabinet repair and refinishing, as well as 10 days' work from a general handyman. In expecting a worst-case scenario, bidders aren't in shock when they see what they have purchased.

If you have contacted the owner to see if purchase is possible prior to the foreclosure sale, you are likely to be the only bidder who has seen the property's interior. Knowing the condition of the interior will allow you to bid from a position of knowledge rather than total ignorance. Some prospective bidders will approach an owner in foreclosure and explain that a sale price in excess of the liens against a property will go to the owner— and be allowed to inspect the property in order to bid intelligently.

In cases where you are unable to obtain permission to enter a property in foreclosure, consider knocking on a few neighborhood doors in the immediate area. Explain that you will be bidding on the property and ask the neighbors if they had been in the house and when, as well as the general condition at the time of their visit. Also, ask if the owners have mentioned any problems with the house. By questioning a neighbor, a foreclosure buyer I know discovered that an owner had just removed and sold the built-in appliances as well as the central air-conditioning unit.

While a house might be in excellent shape a week before foreclosure, this may not be the condition you'll find the house in after the sale. Though rare, some owners will actually trash the interior of the house when they finally realize that they have lost their home. Because of this possibility, some foreclosure buyers drive by the house early on the day of foreclosure in order to detect any outward signs of damage. If it is vacant, they will walk around the house and look in windows. While unlikely to be prosecuted, this technically is trespassing.

Notify your insurance agent that you might require coverage before you bid at a foreclosure sale. Let the agent know that you will be calling for a binder if you are the successful bidder. You don't want to be in the position of having taken title and then suffering a loss for which you were not insured.

Title insurance is not always obtainable on foreclosed property since the title insurer cannot ascertain if the sale was properly conducted. Therefore, it is important to have checked the records for liens and/or obtained a property profile from a title company. Bear in mind that if a policy of title insurance is not issued, the title insurer has no liability even though you may have relied on incomplete or false information they supplied.

You should also make certain the sale met all statutory notice requirements. You can do this by questioning the person conducting the sale. If there is an IRS lien, ask the person conducting the sale if they have a copy of the IRS notification. The IRS must be notified at least 30 days in advance.

Before you bid at foreclosure sales, attend a few sales to familiarize yourself with the procedures in your state. In some states, you need to qualify yourself for bidding at a foreclosure sale by showing your cash or cashier's checks. Certified checks may be unacceptable because it is possible to stop payment on them. Even though you must have all cash (or cashier's checks) in some states, in others you need to have only a percentage of the sale price, such as 10 percent in cash or cashier's checks. You will then have a period of time (such as 30 days) to pay the balance.

If you are bidding at a foreclosure sale, you will want to have a cashier's check for the amount of the foreclosing lien or required percentage as well as additional cashier's checks in $1000 increments (or larger) up to the amount you have preset as your maximum bidding limit.

By use of a line of credit you can obtain these cashier's checks and, if you are not the successful bidder, you can return them to the bank so that you will be charged minimum interest. While cash can be brought to a foreclosure sale, don't do it. It serves no purpose other than to subject you to a risk of loss and even bodily harm. Use cashier's checks. In a foreclosure sale, cash has no emotional effect. It is the highest bid, not the show of greenbacks, that decides who is the buyer.

If you attend a number of foreclosure sales, chances are other bidders who might be regulars will approach you. You could be offered cash not to bid, a bidding partnership (where several of you will bid as one and then either draw straws to see who gets the property or agree to share in the profits), or a rotation agreement whereby you will take turns in buying property where there are no other bidders. Don't make any agreement that restricts bidding. These actions, known as *bid chilling,* are felonies punishable by fines and/or imprisonment. It could be ignorance of the law on the part of the offeror or an offer with criminal intent. It might even be a government sting operation.

If there are a number of other bidders, a tactic used by some bidders is to qualify at a price far more than a property's value. The purpose is to intimidate other bidders and keep them from competing. Normally, you should qualify for the maximum for which you have cash or cashier's checks.

Many foreclosure bidders will not bid more than 75 percent of what they believe the quick turnaround value to be. In this way, they are protected against unexpected problems.

It isn't just dollars that determines the successful bidder. Understanding bidding tactics can mean purchases at lower prices. Some of these tactics are discussed under Auctions (see Chapter 10).

One of my friends was recently at a foreclosure sale where an unusual and unethical tactic was used. Two men were talking before the sale (within hearing of most of the other bidders) about the problems with the interior of the home and what it would take to put it in a salable condition. This was a pure scare tactic. My friend had been invited into the house by the owner on the day prior to the sale and the house was in generally good condition. What these men were trying to do was to cast doubts in the minds of their competition as to how high they should bid and even if they should bid at all.

If you buy a property with a recorded IRS income tax lien against it at a foreclosure sale, the IRS has a 120-day redemption period after the foreclosure sale. They only need to pay you your high bid plus expenses and interest. Therefore, don't spend money on property until IRS rights have expired. If the IRS was not properly notified of the sale, then the IRS lien will remain intact against the property after the foreclosure sale. You could find yourself owning a property with a lien against it that exceeds the property's value.

Similarly, some states give the foreclosed owner a redemption right for a period of time after the foreclosure sale. These periods are as long as one year. You should check with a real estate attorney as to redemption rights in your state. You wouldn't want to have invested a considerable sum in improving a property and then have the former owner redeem the property.

If there is a Small Business Administration (SBA) lien against a property, be aware that the SBA has a one-year redemption period after a foreclosure sale, even though the foreclosure was a prior lien. While the chance of SBA redemption is probably slight, consider this possibility before expending considerable funds on the property.

In some states, you can get quick possession after foreclosure sale by an ejectment action. In other states, the former owners have a redemption right after foreclosure sale and are entitled to remain in possession. However, you are entitled to a fair rental. If the foreclosed property is tenant occupied, go to the tenants after the sale and either give them legal notice to vacate or ask them to sign a new lease. Generally, the foreclosure of a prior recorded lien wipes out tenants' rights under a later lease. If you can't work it out, see an attorney.

It is difficult to logically comprehend why some properties are foreclosed for relatively small liens compared to their value. Sometimes this is the result of marital problems where both parties walk away from the property. A similar situation can happen with partners who have a falling out where neither partner is willing to pay property indebtedness.

> A California homeowners association foreclosed on a condominium because the owners had failed to pay $5412 in association fees. There were only two bidders at the sale and they bid together and purchased the property for $5412. The condominium, which was free and clear of debt, had a fair market value of between $150,000 and $160,000. The buyers were both professional foreclosure buyers who had attended hundreds of sales. While this would have been a tremendous bargain for them, a California court set aside the sale in 2001 because of the conduct of the buyers. The court held that by joining together before the sale, the bidders eliminated competition. The court held that this was "bid chilling" which is illegal. While every joint bid would likely not be considered illegal, in this case the buyers had previously competed with each other and their association for this purchase was based on the idea that they could benefit with a lower price by bidding together.

BUYING AFTER THE FORECLOSURE SALE

When the lender is the successful bidder at the foreclosure sale, the property becomes known as a *real estate owned* (REO) property. This is your third opportunity to buy foreclosure property.

Actually, the best time to buy REO property is before it becomes such. One tactic is to send an offer by registered mail or special messenger to the president of a foreclosing lender prior to the foreclosure sale. The offer, which has an acceptance period that expires 24 hours after the sale, includes a check for at least $5000 made out to the closing agent. If the lender is the successful bidder, the lender is now in the position of being able to immediately flip the property without the problems associated with taking it over. By only giving 24 hours after the sale and giving a sizable deposit, the lender must take the offer seriously and make a quick decision.

When you buy after foreclosure from a lender, the property is usually vacant. If it isn't, your offer to buy can be contingent upon the property being vacated. However, a lender would be more responsive to an offer where you save them the problem of evicting tenants or holdover owners.

Some lenders are reluctant to provide information on their REO property. If you can't get it from a loan officer, send a registered letter to the president of the institution. Some employees act as if they will be without a job if the bank gets rid of their inventory of foreclosed real estate.

Though some lenders just want to get their money out of foreclosures, others will try for a profit and mark up the property. Therefore, don't take what a lender says as to a fixed-dollar amount or as to "all-cash sale" as gospel. The best approach is "listen, then ignore." The lender must dispose of property so you are helping the lender. Make your own offer. Don't let the lender make it for you. If a property is in bad condition, don't be afraid to offer less than the amount the lender bid at the foreclosure sale. Whenever you make an offer on a lender-owned property that is in bad condition, consider taking some Polaroid photographs depicting the problems. Attach these photos to the offer. Chances are the officers of the lending institution have never seen the property, so such a graphic display can be valuable in inducing a lender to rid themselves of an obvious problem.

If a lender refuses an offer, ask the lender about other REO property. For that matter, if the lender accepts your offer, you are in a position to build up a working relationship with that lender. Many lenders offer properties immediately upon foreclosure to one or more investors who have proved to be people of their word. Thus, they are able to quickly rid themselves of what they regard as problems.

Lower-level employees who are given little flexibility often turn down bids. Should a lender turn down an offer made shortly after the foreclosure sale that is at or over the sale amount, send a registered letter (as well as a copy of your offer) to the president of the lending institution, asking why the institution turns down offers that allow it to dispose of foreclosed properties without a loss. By going to the top you have a chance to reverse this refusal.

You should ask the lender to finance your purchase. If you didn't need seller financing, you would have bid at the foreclosure sale. Lenders often say they must have all cash, but what they say and what they will accept can be vastly different. When lenders finance the sale of their foreclosures, they are generally not as particular as to the credit of the buyer as they would be if they were making a cash loan. Keep in mind that the lender doesn't have to give you 100 percent financing to buy with nothing down. A second mortgage from another lender can make up the difference. Check the availability of secondary financing before you make your offer.

Lenders often trade loans to sell REO property. Two lenders might be financing each other's REO sales. The reason they do this is so they are not financing their own sales. It is less likely to be viewed negatively by bank regulators.

There are additional ways to persuade lenders to finance buyers of their foreclosure inventory.

> I'm Robert R. I am just getting into foreclosures (a little over two years). I attended a foreclosure seminar, but I felt uncomfortable about approaching owners in foreclosure and didn't have the cash to bid at foreclosure sales. Therefore, I contacted lenders prior to foreclosure sales with purchase offers.
>
> My first offer was to buy a home being foreclosed by an $81,000-plus first mortgage. There were also several judgments against the owner that would be wiped out by the sale. My offer was for the full amount of the foreclosure, $81,326, in cash. The offer was contingent upon the foreclosing lender being the successful bidder and the lender giving me a $90,000 home equity loan on my personal residence. (I had sufficient equity to justify such a loan.)
>
> After the foreclosure sale (the lender was the only bidder), the lender contacted me. After an appraisal of my home, they made a new loan to me, a person with a good credit rating, and they disposed of their foreclosure property for cash. This is the type of transaction that looks good on the lender's books.
>
> My next step was an offer to another lender to buy a similar home in foreclosure. My offer was again for cash but conditioned on the lender making a loan on the first home, which was free of encumbrances. Well, I have been working this back and forth between lenders. I have found two lenders who will work with me. I solve their problems and I make money. I have enough cash to pay off the home equity loan on my residence if I want to. I own my last purchase free and clear, plus I have purchased a new Mercedes. I still hold my full-time job, but it won't be long before I contemplate an early retirement. My formula is really six words, "Borrow from Peter to pay Paul."

Foreclosing lenders in many areas are faced with a multitude of problems including high vacancy factors, rent collection problems, neglected maintenance, and even vandalism. In many cases, foreclosure has resulted in administrative nightmares. Even though lenders understand money, they seldom have people with both the real property skills and authority needed to turn their problem properties around. As I have said, lender problems create unique opportunities for investors who know what needs to be done and who have faith in their ability to do it. Lenders under pressure to unload inventories of property are open to creative offers.

Moratoriums

Some of the most creative offers I have seen made to lenders for their foreclosures involve the use of moratoriums.

A *moratorium* is a cessation. A moratorium on payments means a buyer need not make loan payments for the period of the moratorium. A moratorium on payments could include a moratorium on interest so the amount due does not increase during the moratorium period. You can see that the effect of a moratorium is a significant reduction in price. Lenders in some cases have accepted moratoriums when they were reluctant to cut the price. When they cut the price, they immediately show a book loss on their loan. A moratorium, on the other hand is simply a delay in recovering the investment.

A moratorium can frequently be obtained from other sellers where the seller is financing the purchase; owners will often agree to a six-month moratorium of interest and principal payments. The six-month period is short enough to be acceptable to many sellers and it gives the buyers cash flow to make improvements.

> My name is Thomas T., and I am a real estate investor. I particularly like turnaround property. I learned from a loan officer I had previously done business with of a 200-unit, six-year-old apartment complex in Texas. The units had a 60 percent vacancy factor and were poorly maintained. The local economy was severely depressed. The former corporate owner had lost all of its property and neglected maintenance for some time prior to foreclosure. The units needed cosmetic work, but several units had serious problems because of vandalism, and the management was next to nonexistent.
>
> After careful evaluation of the property and the area, I offered the lender $3 million for the complex with 10 percent down. This came to $15,000 for each of the two-bedroom, two-bath apartments. My offer, which was accompanied by a cashier's check for $300,000 (full down payment), required the lender to carry the balance on an 8.5 percent loan, all due and payable 7 years from date of closing with payments based on a 30-year amortization. I included an unusual provision in my offer: I asked for a 2-year morato-

rium on payments and interest. The offer was accepted after my agreeing to increase the interest rate to 9 percent and to be personally liable for specified repairs. I then relocated by leasing a home in Texas in order to work with this property.

The moratorium gave me an immediate positive cash flow that I used to rehabilitate the property and to do extensive landscape work. Within one year, I had over an 85 percent occupancy rate. My net spendable for my second year was in excess of $500,000, which not only returned my cash investment but a profit as well. The value of the property has also significantly increased.

When my payments began, I still had a significant spendable cash income, much of which was tax sheltered. I will likely refinance the property when the balloon payment becomes due. I intend to milk cash out of the property because I anticipate the property will support a new loan of at least $5 million.

> Note: Not only did Thomas T. refinance the property and take cash out, he later sold it for $7 million to a real estate investment trust using a tax-deferred exchange.

Hazardous Material

If a property has been foreclosed by a lender, the one thing a lender would not want to hear about is hazardous material or waste on the property. For legal liability, they would prefer total ignorance.

An offer to purchase property that refers to the property's hazardous material or waste problem in the offer or cover letter would likely upset the lender because the lender now has notice of a problem. Having notice, the lender now would have a duty to disclose the problem to other potential buyers.

My name is Charles C. I am a mechanical engineer and work for a large engineering firm. Several colleagues and I have made money buying and selling foreclosure property. We recently made a rather unusual investment.

A local lender recently foreclosed on a nearby 12,500-square-foot, light industrial building on a 1.5-acre site. The firm that owned the building went bankrupt. An officer of a bank from whom we had previously purchased a property asked me if we were interested in it. One of my investment partners knew the building and thought it would be easy to rent if we could keep the rental competitive. While it wasn't the type of investment we had been making, we got the keys and made an inspection of the premises.

Inspection revealed there was asbestos in the floor and ceiling tile. Asbestos wallboard was used extensively around the heating plant and in a former welding area. The boiler had asbestos cement insulation and the exposed heating pipes were wrapped with asbestos. There had been a poor attempt to encapsulate much of the asbestos with a spray-on coating.

We also discovered there was an underground fuel tank on the premises. Inquiry revealed that it had been used for diesel fuel since its installation in the late 1970s.

We did not feel the fuel tank would be a problem because it was relatively new. We did realize that there was a serious asbestos problem indicating an opportunity.

We contacted a firm with extensive experience in asbestos removal. Because of the open nature of the asbestos, removal costs were estimated at slightly under $50,000, which included the disposal of the material in an approved dumpsite.

The bank was asking $750,000, which included the amount of their loan plus accumulated interest. The bank officer had given the impression the bank would be receptive to offers. The $750,000 was probably a little high, but was still within a reasonable price range.

We never intended to offer a reasonable price. After we realized there were asbestos problems, we decided to take a relatively unreasonable approach. While we had hoped to locate a tenant before we put in any offer, we decided to put in an immediate offer at a price where we could give a tenant a bargain rent if necessary and still be in good shape.

We had our attorney set up a corporation for us. The attorney also prepared the offer from the corporation (to reduce personal liability). Our offer was for $420,000 with no down payment. Our offer provided that we would remove the asbestos from the structure within six months of closing and prior to any tenant occupancy. The lender was to carry back a first mortgage in the amount of $420,000 at 8.5 percent interest. The lender was also to pay the first $50,000 toward the removal of asbestos and other hazardous substances presently located in the structure or soil.

Our offer included a hold harmless clause whereby we agreed that we would not hold the seller liable for any asbestos or other hazardous waste removal beyond the $50,000 agreed liability. We sent the offer by messenger to the president of the bank.

An agitated loan officer called me. She wanted to know about the hazardous material on the property. I explained where we had discovered asbestos and also that there was a possible problem with the underground fuel tank on the premises. I also pointed out that we had not taken soil samples so we did not have direct knowledge of other chemicals that may have been discharged on the property by the previous owners. Three days later, we were notified that our offer had been accepted.

The net effect is that we obtained 100 percent financing from a very worried lender. In addition, they agreed to give us the $50,000 needed to remove the asbestos. We leased the property to a very strong tenant on a triple net 15-year lease at 38 cents per square foot (which was a below-market rent for the area). The lease payments, which are tied to the Consumer Price Index, give us $4750 per month. Since the tenant pays taxes, insurance, and all maintenance costs (triple net lease), we have $1100 spendable after our loan payments of $3645 per month.

We have a tenant who will actually buy our building for us, give us cash in our pockets each month (which will increase with inflation), and our only expenses were attorney's and filing fees totaling less than $3000.

FANNIE MAE, HUD, AND VA FORECLOSURES

Fannie Mae (FNMA) is the Federal National Mortgage Association. While formerly a government organization, it is now a private corporation that buys and sells FHA, VA, and conventional mortgages. They designate brokers who are given the sale listing of their foreclosures and who also renovate the properties for resale. Properties are listed on local multiple listing services. Properties offered for sale are vacant and generally in good condition, although FNMA does not warrant the condition of the property. Sales are by offer (sometimes auction) and offers are accepted or rejected in just a few days. In some cases, FNMA will counteroffer and the final price will be negotiated.

FNMA brokers will inform you of any low-down financing available for both owner occupants and investors through a FNMA lender. Since FNMA appraises their foreclosures and tries to set a fair price for a relatively quick sale, real bargains are seldom available unless you feel that the appraiser had underestimated the value. Nevertheless, many investors deal exclusively in buying and renting or selling FNMA foreclosures.

Freddie Mac (FHLMC) is the Federal Home Loan Mortgage Corporation. Now a government chartered private corporation that buys loans from other lenders. Freddie Mac will repair their foreclosed property and will usually sell with 5 percent down, waiving mortgage insurance requirements.

The Department of Housing and Urban Development (HUD) resells mortgage-company foreclosures where the FHA insured the loan. Any broker who qualifies as a HUD broker can offer HUD foreclosures. Minimum work is done to rehabilitate property. Sometimes these properties are boarded up and may even have been vandalized. HUD homes are sold as is.

A list price (appraisal) is advertised, and the general method for sale is by sealed bid. Bids are submitted through HUD brokers.

There is a bidding period, at the end of which all bids will be opened. During this initial bidding period homes will generally only be sold to owner occupants. If no bid is accepted, bids will continue to be sought and investors can submit their bids.

High bids below the appraisal will be accepted within limits. Your HUD broker will tell you the minimum percentage for the type of sale. Buyers must have their own financing, so buyers should prequalify for a loan before bidding. There is an FHA Section 2031(k) loan that may be available for investors to rehabilitate and sell property.

If the home is vandalized between the time of the offer and closing the sale, investors who back out are unlikely to get their deposits returned.

Because of the condition of many of the properties, HUD foreclosures can be a good investment as a fixer-upper.

Since bids are competitive, you may have to bid for a number of properties before you become a buyer. Some more desirable properties may sell for significantly more than the appraisal.

Besides HUD-approved brokers, you can obtain information on locally owned HUD properties by searching links through HUD's Web site: *www.hud.gov/buying/index.cfm.*

The Department of Veterans Affairs (still commonly referred to as the Veterans Administration) handles the resale of loans by mortgage companies that had VA loan guarantees. It is very easy for a broker to qualify as a VA broker to resell these properties. The homes are frequently in poor condition and are sold without renovation. You can bid for properties through a VA broker. The VA will accept less than the price advertised, but will have a minimum. A broker who deals extensively in VA foreclosures can inform you as to the likely minimum based on recent sales. VA low-down financing is available for investors (see your VA broker). Like HUD foreclosures, you may have to submit a number of bids before you are able to make a purchase.

There are other government-related sales such as property seized by the U.S. Marshal.

OTHER DISTRESSED PROPERTY SITUATIONS

IRS Sales

Some foreclosure-type buyers prefer IRS sales to foreclosure sales because there are usually fewer bidders. One reason for this is the sales are not as well publicized as other foreclosures. Usually, there is just one publication and a posting on the property.

IRS tax liens are general liens against real estate. They do not have the priority of property tax liens. Therefore, when property is sold by the IRS for unpaid income taxes, the purchaser takes the property subject to all priority liens, so a careful title check is imperative. The IRS gives no guarantees as to the property or fitness for use.

Realize that taxpayers have a period of 180 days to redeem their property after an IRS sale. While the redeeming taxpayer must pay interest at the rate of 20 percent per annum, it would be wise for the purchaser not to invest much money in the property during the redemption period. For further information on IRS tax sales, you should go to the Web site *www.ustreas.gov/auctions/irs*.

Tax Sales

Tax sales offer some exceptional opportunities. While some property sold for taxes has no redeeming value, some properties are lost for taxes that represent only a small proportion of the value of the properties. In some cases, owners have died and their estates or heirs have no knowledge of the ownership. Tax collectors are not detectives. It is not their job to determine if an owner is dead and, if so, who is the heir or heirs. In some cases of marital problems, both spouses have at times gone their separate ways each leaving the property to the other.

Tax sale purchases differ from normal foreclosure sales. Real estate taxes and special assessments for property improvements are priority liens. Foreclosure of these liens generally wipes out junior liens, which would even include any mortgages recorded prior to the taxes even becoming a lien. While buyers at a mortgage foreclosure must worry about priority liens, this is not the case with tax sales. In almost every instance, taxes would be the priority lien. Before you bid at tax sales, check with an attorney to ascertain tax-lien priority in your state.

Some investors contact owners who are delinquent in taxes and offer them cash, notes, or a combination of the two for their equity prior to the tax sale. To buy property from an owner prior to the tax sale, you should realize that you will be taking the property with all liens fully intact, including the lien for unpaid taxes. It is therefore essential that you obtain title insurance.

Most investors wait for the tax sale. When you go to your first sale, you will find that what you considered the good properties (single-family homes in desirable areas) are not being sold. What has happened is that the owners redeemed them by paying the back taxes. I have been to sales where more than two-thirds of the properties advertised were redeemed prior to sale. Delinquent taxpayers are assessed interest on their unpaid taxes. Interest rates are relatively low in some states. The result is that, in periods of high interest rates, some sophisticated property owners will leave their taxes unpaid, but will pay the delinquent taxes and interest prior to any tax sale to redeem their property. They are in effect really borrowing from the tax collector at a below-market rate of interest. When interest rates are high, tax delinquencies increase.

In larger counties, thousands of properties may be listed for tax sale. No bidder can possibly check out every property. Generally, bidders have only checked out a few properties. Even with several hundred bidders, there will be properties up for bid that none of the bidders have actually seen.

For raw land and for lots, some bidders will make their bids from subdivision maps and plat books that show the parcel size and access. If you are interested in raw land and lots, you should also check both zoning maps and government geological survey maps. The geological maps will show the contour of the land and could indicate a flood problem or land so steep it is suitable only for mountain goats. Though use of these maps will reduce your risk in bidding on land, maps can be a poor substitute for actually physically checking the land. There could be neighboring use or change that has reduced the value or rendered the land practically worthless or there could be serious access problems.

If there are agents' or owners' for-sale signs for similar property in an area, call the advertisers and find out what they are asking. You should look for a pattern as to prices in an area. Keep in mind that what others are asking for their properties does not determine value. Selling prices are far more valuable in this regard. If there is a local real estate broker with whom you have done business, contact the broker and ask for computer comparables in the area. Do not call attention to the particular property you are interested in.

Buying at tax sales is frustrating work, since proper research takes a great deal of time, and much of the research will be wasted when properties are redeemed prior to sale. To be successful at tax sales and reduce your property inspection and research efforts, pick particular areas and work them. Try to check properties of many different owners rather than a single owner of many properties. In this manner, there is a greater likelihood of the number of those properties being available at the time of sale.

For single-family homes, drive by and check the exteriors of the homes. If a particular house is vacant, consider walking around the property and looking in the windows. While it is technically trespassing, you are unlikely to be prosecuted for doing this.

You should also knock on neighborhood doors to inquire about the vacant property. Do not mention that the property is being sold for taxes. Instead, ask why it is vacant. Is it for sale? What is the condition of the property? Do they know of any problem with the property?

Don't be a crapshooter like some tax sale bidders. They bid without knowledge. They feel at a few thousand dollars, they can't go wrong. You can go wrong at any price if you can't resell the property for more than you paid.

In some counties, tax certificates for unpaid taxes can be purchased from the tax collectors office The investors get the interest on the tax certificates and the county, by selling the certificates, get the tax money right away.

After a redemption period, which varies by state, the certificate holder could foreclose on the property. The tax certificate is a priority lien so the holder would bid the amount of this lien at the foreclosure sale. If someone bids higher the certificate holder receives the amount of his or her lien, which would include interest. If not, the certificate holder would gain title to the property.

Some states allow a redemption period after the sale. The owner must pay the sale costs plus a statutory interest. In some cases, the interest is sufficient to make the tax purchase a good investment even if the owner redeems the property. (It is generally around 10 percent but in Texas it is 25 percent.) In some states the redemption period is as long as one year. This would preclude a buyer from reselling the property and would also discourage any major expenditure of time and/or money. Check with your local tax assessor's office. They can tell you if your state allows redemption after the tax sale and about the rights of the buyer.

For some desirable properties, there can be heated bidding that can result in sale prices approaching or even exceeding market value. Again, buying property at a tax sale does not guarantee you a bargain.

WHEN YOU ARE IN FORECLOSURE

If you are having financial difficulties in paying a loan, don't wait for the lender to contact you. Instead, contact the lender and explain your problem. Let the lender know that you want to meet your obligations and would like to work with him to arrange a plan to accomplish this. Keep in mind the one thing most lenders want least is your property. They may be loaded with foreclosures and will prefer to avoid foreclosing whenever possible.

Solutions to consider are:

1. Moratorium on payments for a stated period of time.
2. Partial moratorium with a reduced payment for a stated period. (Keep in mind that this, as well as the prior solution, would result in negative amortization, which means you will owe more after the amortization period than you did before.)
3. Moratorium on both principal and interest payments for a stated period. (Some lenders have agreed when they have large numbers of foreclosures and/or the resale market is slow.)
4. Interest-only payments for a set period of time. The reduction in payment will vary based on the age of the loan. Older loans would have significant reductions.
5. Restructuring a loan for lower payments. Extending the loan for a longer period or reducing the interest rate.

If you are going to be foreclosed, go to the lender prior to foreclosure and ask for a lease on the property (if they are the successful bidder, plus an option to buy the property back). This arrangement will enable the lender to avoid major renovation that would raise the sale price and also avoid management problems. After foreclosure, when you are in possession under a lease, and have been making rent payments on time give the lender your offer to buy with a small down payment. Lenders who say they must have cash often accept leveraged offers.

CHAPTER

Analyzing Property

Every man who invests in well selected real estate in a growing section of
a prosperous community adopts the surest method of becoming independent, for real estate is the basis of wealth.

Theodore Roosevelt

Don't count on a broker to tell you what you should buy. The broker generally represents the owner, who wants a sale at the best price and terms
possible. Even when the broker represents you as a buyer's agent, the broker does not earn a fee until you have made a purchase. The agent's interest, therefore, might not be identical with yours.

Since you are the one putting up the money or accepting financial
obligations, purchase decisions must be yours, based on your understanding of the property, the area, and the economy.

At times you will find a property that appears to be an excellent investment opportunity but find yourself uncomfortable with the idea of
buying it. Though not always right, I have turned down properties for reasons I couldn't really explain at the time only to see a purchaser burned by
the investment. I have learned to trust my instincts.

An exception to the above are first-time investors, who often are so
nervous that they will always be uneasy with a purchase. First-timers must
overcome this fear of the water and dive in with the rest of us. You can't
learn to swim if you are unwilling to get wet.

The degree of risk you are willing to accept must be based on your
personal needs, goals, and guts. It takes guts to invest, but it doesn't mean
a willingness to gamble; guts refers to your self-esteem, your belief in

your ability to evaluate a property and in your ability to work to make the investment successful.

LOCATION

The first thing to consider for any purchase is location. When weighing several alternatives for long-term investment, you must use all available information in making your decisions. Chamber of commerce information is very valuable in this regard. They will have information on planned future developments of private and public nature and will likely have studies as to future growth as well.

People generally make money in dealing in areas where they understand values as well as trends in the marketplace. Investors usually suffer large losses because they have gone outside their area of expertise. Because values vary so much by locality, don't assume anything or base a decision on opinions provided by anyone who will realize a financial gain from your purchase. Ask yourself, "What will be the desirability of the area in 20 years?" If you don't think desirability will remain the same or improve, it is not an investment for appreciation. However, it could still offer opportunities as a "flipper"—a property to be purchased and resold.

Property tends to go through three distinct stages: integration, equilibrium, and disintegration. During integration the area is being developed. Early users often determine the character of future development. After being developed, an area generally goes through an equilibrium stage in which the character and use of the area remain relatively unchanged. Finally, the area will start to disintegrate or go downhill. It will become less desirable. Occasionally, an area is rescued and is revitalized from this stage.

Exceptional appreciation opportunities exist in older communities that are beginning to experience gentrification. *Gentrification* is the conversion of an area by the entrance of younger, affluent residents into the neighborhood.

Positive signs are buyers renovating properties for their own use. The gentrification process is most likely happening where there are larger homes of distinctive architectural styles.

The stages of development hold true for individual properties as well as areas. They illustrate the principle of change, which means that use and values do not remain constant; change must always be expected. To find what stage a property is in, check the area. What is happening? You should consider what has happened to an area in the last year, the last 5 years, and the last 10 years. These changes will give you an excellent indication of what will happen to the area in the future. The study of trends and changes is invaluable in deciding when and what to purchase, as well as when to sell.

Positive signs would be low vacancy factors, evidence of remodeling or expansion of existing structures, or the replacement of existing buildings with new structures. In areas where commercial tenants are doing well, there will be few changes in businesses or ownership. On the other hand, a high turnover in a commercial location, as well as frequent changes in ownership, normally indicates marginal or loss operations. When people in an area are not doing well economically, maintenance often gets deferred. Because of rent collection problems, owners tend to reduce expenditures to a minimum.

Other negative signs are a decrease in retail volume and a decrease in the percentage of owner-occupied housing. An increasing crime rate is often accompanied by higher fire insurance rates for an area. The following are also unfavorable indicators of declining values:

- Conversions of large homes to apartments generally is a negative indicator.
- Abandoned buildings or unrepaired, fire-gutted buildings usually indicate very severe problems for an area.
- Graffiti, especially gang symbols, are a sign of decline in an area.

Such factors as income, age, family size, ethnic background, and even religion can affect spending habits of the residents, which in turn have a bearing on commercial values. New factories, golf courses, schools, and so forth will tend to raise values in nearby areas.

In most urban centers the greatest residential growth tends to be in just a few areas. Within general areas, specific pockets generally have greater growth potential and/or greater desirability. These are the areas of preference for investing simply because the application of the law of supply and demand causes values to increase with increased demand. A forward-looking investor will, therefore, realize that what appears to be a bargain investment at present could be a poor long-term choice. Appreciation in value and income might be far less than an investment that does not pencil out as well in the present but will be positively influenced by demand increases. Consider the following general rules in making area decisions:

1. Better homes tend to be built outward from a community in the same direction, especially if toward higher ground.
2. Commercial property tends to grow outward along major transportation routes.
3. Small service industries tend to gather around major industries.
4. One early major development in an area will affect the character of later area developments.
5. Desirable recreational facilities (such as parks and golf courses) will increase the desirability for housing.
6. The close presence of colleges, universities, and medical facilities will increase the desirability of an area for housing.

Blight is contagious. In what direction are blighted areas growing? Because of natural or artificial barriers, blight is often channeled in specific directions. You should consider the fact that the existence of present or former chemical dumps in an area adversely affects value.

Also, the presence of an atomic energy plant or even a large chemical plant can reduce values and might affect them more radically in the future. Enterprises that emit dust or unpleasant odors, such as stockyards, have a negative effect on residential values as do businesses that cause noise or heavy truck traffic near residential areas.

As to residential property, you should consider the location in relationship to jobs, public transportation, freeways, schools, shopping, and recreational facilities. Transportation, traffic count, and the population within the purchasing area of the property as well as its purchasing power and purchasing habits also affect commercial property. Industrial property is concerned with location in relationship to a labor supply, suppliers, as well as transportation and availability of utilities.

PROGRESSION AND REGRESSION

Generally, it is best to buy the least expensive property in a good area. The value of the other property will actually pull the value of your property up. This is known as the principle of progression.

The opposite is the principle of regression. It is not a wise investment to have the most valuable property in an area. The surrounding lower values will tend to pull the value of your property down. We can understand these principles if we consider a builder who builds a $500,000 home in an area of $200,000 homes. The lower values in the area will make the property difficult to sell at that price. If the house had been built in an area of $1,000,000 homes, it would probably be readily salable even at a higher price.

Zoning

After evaluating the area, consider the zoning of the specific property. Will it allow the present or contemplated use? Is the zoning in the area consistent with the zoning of this particular parcel? Consider area zoning as well as individual property rezoning because zoning patterns can affect future zoning changes. Many people have more than doubled the value of their properties by simply applying for and receiving zoning changes. The feasibility of rezoning to a more productive use makes a property a much more attractive investment.

Look for evidence of downzoning, a change in zoning to more restrictive uses, such as a change from commercial to residential zoning. A number of instances of downzoning in an area might indicate that other property might also be downzoned. If an undeveloped property is downzoned to a more restrictive use, it tends to lower the value of the parcel.

It is also possible for zoning to be changed to make property more productive. For example, the value of a single-family home zoned for residential use could materially increase if it is rezoned for offices.

Just because a vacant property is zoned for a particular number of units does not mean that the maximum number of units under a zoning classification can be built on the parcel. When minimum square footages of each unit, parking requirements, height, and side yard limits are all considered, it might be physically impossible to build the number of units allowed by the zoning.

Frequently, properties have nonconforming uses. The current use could have preceded the zoning. In these cases the use is allowed to continue but should it cease for some reason, the use cannot be started again. Generally, you can expect a property with a nonconforming use to have a lower value than if the use was consistent with the zoning.

Some property has been used for years in violation of the zoning. Just because someone else got away with a zoning violation in the past does not mean that you will be able to do so in the future. For example, in the past many people remodeled to create a separate apartment for relatives, such as an in-law unit. Later owners may have rented the extra unit in violation of the zoning.

If a unit has been remodeled for a change in use, such as an apartment split into more units or a large house broken up into apartments, you should be concerned with the zoning as well as with whether or not the work was done with a building permit. Many people have "bootlegged" units. If units contrary to either the building codes or zoning are discovered, the result could be an order to tear out the work.

Covenants, Conditions, and Restrictions

Besides zoning, consider covenants, conditions, and restrictions (also known as *restrictive covenants*). These CC&Rs are private restrictions on the use of a property placed on it by a subdivider or by agreement of all the property owners subject to them. The restrictions may apply to use, size, height, building setbacks, architectural styles, and even such things as colors. Even though zoning may allow a use, if the use violates the CC&Rs, it would be possible for any other person subject to the same CC&Rs to obtain an injunction prohibiting the intended use. When CC&Rs and zoning disagree, the more restrictive use governs. Since the CC&Rs are recorded, they are available. A title company can obtain a copy for you.

Political Climate

Property developed in an area where the supply of new property is being restricted will show exceptional appreciation in value. It is simply the principle of supply and demand in action. On the other hand, undeveloped property in such an area would likely be a poor investment. Restrictions on development would keep the value down until or unless you received approval for development.

Growth control might be based on the "I'm aboard! Now let's raise the drawbridge" syndrome, or a basic lack of resources, such as water, or the inability of the community to supply needed services. Pressure from environmental organizations has restricted and even halted growth in many areas. The local building inspector will be able to tell you if there are any current or planned limitations on the number of building permits issued.

Similarly, the presence or likelihood of restrictive rent-control legislation will serve to dampen future appreciation of rental structures and lower the value of apartment sites.

Rent control protects tenants from the market forces of supply and demand at the expense of the property owners. While a property in a rent-control area might offer a reasonable return on the investment, future growth in income and appreciation in value might be severely restricted.

Under rent control, the tenant gets a great deal of the benefit from appreciation, not the landlord. In some rent-controlled areas, tenants are able to sublet their rent-controlled units as "furnished" apartments at significantly greater rent than they are paying. In New York, where rent-controlled apartments rent at bargain prices when compared with property without imposed rent restrictions, many renters own other homes but use their bargain apartments as city homes for the workweek. They refuse to give up the apartments that cost them so little.

A property in a nonrent-control area with lesser return would be a better investment than a property at the same price with greater return but subject to rent control. There are, however, various degrees of rent control. Where ballot initiatives and referendums are possible, tenants can be expected to vote their pocketbooks, which means restricting their landlords from raising rents based on market forces.

In some communities increases in rent are based on the Consumer Price Index. In other areas, owners are limited to increases in their costs. Similarly, some communities allow rents to be reset when units become vacant. Other communities require the landlord to keep the same rent base. The more severe the rent control, the further you should stay away from the property as an investment. Consider the likelihood of rent control in making a purchase. The more renters in an area, the greater the possibility of rent controls.

PHYSICAL ASPECTS

Sewer, Water, Electricity, Natural Gas, and Cable

If you are buying undeveloped land, you will want to have information as to the availability of sewers, water, electricity, natural gas, and even high-speed Internet access. Some utilities can be relatively close to a property, but the cost to bring them out to the property can be considerable if the property is prematurely developed.

If municipal sewers are not available but septic systems are allowed, you will want to know if the property can pass a percolation test. If it cannot, a building permit might not be issued, or an expensive mound system or holding tanks will be required. Many people have invested their savings in land that cannot be developed because of poor percolation. Percolation is a problem where the water table is either close to the surface or where there is a great deal of clay in the soil.

Recently, a young man purchased three lakefront lots at a very good price. The lots were served by sewer and water and were at the end of a street that sloped to the lake. The buyer did almost everything right; he cleared the lots of brush so the view was opened, added sand fill where needed, and generally made the lots very attractive. He intended to build his own home on one lot and to sell the others. When he applied for his building permit, he discovered that he had to install a sewage lift station costing $18,000.

Check with the building department prior to purchase to avoid unpleasant surprises. Just because a natural gas line is in place does not mean it is available for use. In the past, some, utility companies were limiting taking on new customers because they were afraid they might not be able to supply their needs. We can expect similar limitations in the future.

Compaction

Some land has a compaction problem, which means that the land cannot properly support structures. Usually this land has been reclaimed by drainage or is filled land. In some cases, expensive pilings must be driven to support a structure. Excessive construction costs will reduce value. If you feel that a parcel of land may not be able to support a structure, hire a civil engineer to check the property.

Topography and Drainage

If you are buying undeveloped land, walk the boundaries of the land. If it is large, you should also walk through the parcel so you fully understand its topography. Frequently such a walk will discover problems such as drainage, which is an important factor on raw land. A little time spent can save you from a mistake.

I recently volunteered to help find a new location for a workshop for developmentally disabled citizens. I found a location that appeared excellent and the price seemed extremely low. While the fact was not visible from the ground, I discovered by checking a U.S. Geodetic Survey Map that the property was in the center of a natural drainage area (these maps show elevations and contours of the land). Further checking with local residents revealed that the roads in the vicinity of the parcel and most of the parcel itself had been under as much as two feet of water on several occasions in the past 20 years.

Many communities will deny a building permit for a property in an area prone to floods.

Roads

Roads that show on maps as nice straight lines can in reality be nothing more than a pair of tire ruts in the earth. What appears to be a public road to a property could very well be a private road over which you would not have rights. You can check with the county department of roads about a specific road.

Undeveloped property on a major road, or on what looks like it could become a major route, can show dramatic appreciation. Roads that lie on section lines (government survey lines located every mile) often develop as major roads. Generally, land fronting on a section line road sells at a premium to investors.

About 20 years ago I was offered eight acres of land for $30,000. The seller didn't think the road the parcel was on would ever be a major traffic artery or that the land would be desirable to others. The road developed as a major artery and the parcel next to the one I was offered recently sold for $50,000 per acre. This would have been more than a 1200 percent profit if I had acted. At the time the parcel was offered to me, the state highway department had extensive plans for widening the road and diverting other traffic to it. I had not bothered to check with them. I have learned that you can't win them all, but it's hard to lose a good one.

A visit to the county or state highway department should be a must for you whenever you are interested in any highway frontage property.

Vehicular and Pedestrian Traffic

For commercial property, the traffic count, the hours of peak vehicle traffic, traffic speed, and foot traffic all affect value. If traffic is primarily during relatively short periods in the morning and late afternoon, then the property is probably on a route to a major employment area. Most of these drivers are in a hurry to get to and from work. Property on such a route probably will not be as valuable for commercial purposes as a location with the same traffic count spread over a longer period of the business day.

Traffic moving on a street at 50 miles per hour is much more difficult to stop than that moving at 25 miles per hour. Slower traffic is more desirable for retail businesses. Foot traffic is of course important for retail locations with window displays. An ideal location for foot traffic is between two major stores.

Parking is extremely important today for commercial, industrial, and even residential properties. A 12,000-square-foot commercial building was for sale. It was in a congested area with poor access and had only 10 parking spaces. I own a much older building of the same size and use in the same general area. The street my building is on has half the traffic count of the other building. In addition, the building I own is quite plain, while the building up for sale was very deluxe. Nevertheless, my building was receiving almost twice the rent per square foot as the building that was for sale. The difference was that my building has more than 50 parking spaces in a large paved lot readily accessible from two streets.

Property Shape

Even the shape of a parcel can affect its value. A triangular lot will generally sell for less per square foot than a rectangular parcel since the rectangular parcel can be developed for greater utilization of the lot at a lower price.

Highest and Best Use

In your analysis of a property, you should consider its highest and best use. The highest and best use of a property is that use that provides the greatest net income to a property. As an example, assume that you are comparing three possible uses for a lot: (1) as an apartment site, (2) as an auto repair shop, or (3) as a parking lot. Assume the following costs:

Apartment
Value of property when developed	$1,000,000
Development costs	−900,000
Value of land for apartment use	$ 100,000

Auto Repair Shop
Value of property when developed	$ 300,000
Development costs	−175,000
Value of land for auto repair use	$ 125,000

Parking Lot

Value of property when developed	$ 275,000
Development costs	−125,000
Value of land for parking lot use	$ 150,000

The highest and best use of the property in this analysis would be the parking lot.

If your analysis of a property is at a higher and better use than the seller envisions, the price you pay could be a bargain. As an example, in some areas of Los Angeles there formerly were many light industrial locations. Investors began buying up these properties at prices consistent with industrial use and developed them into office space for advertising, high tech, and film tenants who liked the high ceilings, skylights, exposed beams, ducts, and block walls. The loft-like offices brought rents several times greater than was formerly possible. With minimum renovation what had been shop spaces renting for about 50 cents per square foot became desirable office space renting upwards of $1.35 per square foot. Early investors discovered a higher and better use resulting in exceptional profits. Incidentally, the conversion of shop space to offices had a ripple effect in that displaced tenants were competing for available shop space in outlying areas, driving up rental prices.

Highest and best use could mean that a structure should be demolished, as the land is more valuable for another use. As an example, an older 40-story hotel in Chicago was purchased and demolished to make room for an office tower. Even though the hotel was profitable, the economics indicated that the highest and best use was for offices, even considering demolition and construction costs.

FINANCIAL HISTORY

In evaluating investments, keep in mind the expenses and income of the past are merely history. While history will help you in predicting future income and expenses, these figures should not be the basis of your investment. Your investment should be based on your estimate of the income and expenses that you will have with the property.

Income

The rent schedules owners provide cannot always be believed. An owner may fail to inform you that one tenant has a reduced rent for some management duties. One owner neglected to tell me that 3 of his 12 tenants had given him notice when he notified the tenants of the new higher rent schedule. He just told me that this was his current rent schedule and gave information on how long each tenant had been there. From the facts given, it looked good. While the facts were all true, the intent was to deceive.

An owner might rent a unit for $800 per month when the market would justify only $650 per month. The owner might have given the tenant several months' free rent to sign a one-year lease. If this were the case, the tenant can be expected to leave at the end of the lease. The best way to verify rents is to talk with the tenants. You may find that things are not always as indicated in the leases.

When you request rental figures or operational costs from an agent or owner, always ask that the figures be verified in writing by the owner's accountant. You will find the attractive verbal figures given are seldom the same as those put down in writing. Check rentals with the tenants themselves. You want to verify rents, find out how long the present rental rate has been in effect, and whether any concessions were given to rent the unit. Some prospective buyers want to see the owner's tax returns for the previous two or three years. These will show trends in income as well as trends in expenses. It is excellent information for helping with projections of income and expenses. However, some sellers have been known to prepare false returns for buyers and lenders. If things look a little too good to be true, verify—verify—verify.

Even though a particular building is fully rented, realistically consider a vacancy factor. By checking with local apartment owners' organizations or with large property management firms, you can get a good idea of the vacancy rate for the area. Tenants do move, and even when units are rented quickly, there is usually a period when rent is not collected. The period can be from a few days to several months. In addition, sooner or later you will have a tenant who moves out owing money that will never be collected. You cannot realistically expect 100 percent occupancy and 100 percent collections.

When inquiring about a property, be on the alert for terms such as *scheduled rents*. This does not mean that the rents are actually being collected. Another term frequently used is *broker's net income*. This is not a net figure because it does not consider either a vacancy factor or any collection loss. It represents the ideal, not the actual, situation.

In situations where there is not a good rental history, such as in the case of new buildings, real estate agents prepare a *pro forma statement*.

This is not a statement of current income or expense but rather an estimate as to what they will be. Brokers, in preparing these statements, are sometimes overly optimistic. The figures given should not be accepted without your own independent analysis. I have seldom seen a pro forma statement in which the actual income exceeded what was estimated or in which expenses were less than contemplated. If you doubt figures provided by an owner, use your own estimates instead.

In evaluating property, be skeptical of the rent schedule when the property is vacant (or a number of units are vacant). If you feel the current rents are too high, make your investment decision based on what you consider to be a realistic rent. Otherwise you will probably either have to reduce rental rates or offer sweeteners such as free rent with leases.

There are actually many instances when rents are too low. Sometimes an owner has become a friend of the tenants and hesitates to increase rents. Other times it is simply poor management. Often when property is held in a trust or estate, there is no real incentive for the administrator to increase rents. The administrator is more concerned with avoiding problems. Sometimes out-of-the-area owners are unaware of the rental potential of their properties. I know one commercial tenant who scared the out-of-state landlord into giving an extremely low-rent, long-term lease with the threat of leaving, despite the fact that the property was highly rentable. In analyzing a property's income, consider the feasible income, not necessarily what is actually received. In larger buildings income from parking revenues and receipts from coin-operated laundry equipment are frequently overlooked.

Be particularly leery of projected income in sale-leaseback opportunities when sellers have weak credit ratings. The likely reason they want to sell and lease back the premises is that they need the capital. Often sellers will offer to lease back property at rental terms that make the sale price appear a bargain. In these cases, all too often sellers end up defaulting on a lease. Buyers then discover they cannot rent the premises for the rental the sellers agreed to pay. What begins as a positive cash flow investment might turn into a negative one.

Therefore, in sale-leaseback situations, base your purchase on what your research of the area indicates is the fair rental value of the property. Also get a credit report on the seller-lessee. Be particularly leery of sale-leasebacks where the building was constructed for a special purpose and would be desirable for a very limited number of possible tenants.

Sheila F. purchased a large frozen food processing plant in a small town and leased it back to the seller. After about one year, the tenant told Sheila that if she didn't agree to rewrite the lease at significantly lower rent, he would default on the lease and go bankrupt. Sheila was unable to find another tenant for the special-purpose structure and ended up agreeing to the tenant's demands. The tenant's financial weakness and the limited use for the property served to give the tenant tremendous bargaining power.

If a tenant leaves a special-purpose building, it could be vacant for a long time. Some special-purpose buildings have had vacancy periods measured in years rather than months. You must learn to look a gift horse in the mouth. Too good a bargain from a sophisticated real estate investor or through an agent who also buys and sells would indicate that something is wrong.

The problem could be a major tenant leaving the property or the area, a change taking place because of highway changes, and the like. While you should always look before you leap, when the sale seems incongruous to the seller and/or the agents involved, be extra careful. Check with neighbors, the city for building and fire code violations, the leases, and even the tenants. Generally, I have found that deals that appear too good to be true are exactly that.

Expenses

In evaluating an owner's claimed expenses, understand that owners who do the management and repairs themselves do not include their labor as an expense. As a buyer in evaluating a property for purchase, add the estimated value of your labor to the expenses. Management expense is the most often omitted cost, and you must consider it even if you will do it yourself. Ask yourself, "What would it cost me for these services if I could not do the work myself?" Anyone buying the property from you will consider it an expense. You had better do the same or you will end up overpaying for the property.

A very unethical tactic used by some sellers has been to show average expenses for the past 5 or 10 years. While on the surface it seems very reasonable, you must consider that taxes, utilities, supplies, and services have all been increasing. The net effect is that the average figures are unrealistically low, and you will find actual expenses will be significantly higher than the average.

In evaluating operating statements make certain that the property manager's apartment is shown as a fixed expense when it is provided to the manager. I have consistently seen creative pro forma statements that "inadvertently" show it as income only.

When analyzing insurance costs, obtain a copy of the current policy to determine coverage and costs. Often an owner's coverage is closer to the price the owner paid than to the current value. This means coverage may be inadequate and proper coverage would increase the insurance costs far beyond the figure shown.

Coverage is very important. You should consider smoke and water damage as well as fire and lightning. Losses from vandalism and from nature should be considered. If a property has plate-glass windows, you should consider coverage. Rental interruption insurance might be a consideration. It reimburses the owner for rent loss because of damage and destruction. If personal property is included with the property, it should also be covered. In this lawsuit-happy world it is essential that you carry substantial liability coverage. Flood and earthquake insurance should also be considered in areas prone to either of these. Your actual insurance costs could end up several times higher than the present owner's costs.

Tax figures provided by the owner are usually of little value in predicting your own tax obligations. Property is often reassessed when sold. The new assessment is likely to be materially higher than the figure used for the previous owner. A better estimate of taxes can be based on the recent reassessment of similar properties.

When analyzing developed property you should be very concerned about whether the owner pays utilities and whether the utility rate increases are passed on to the tenant. In the past decade utility costs have increased more than the Consumer Price Index. Some properties have operated at losses because they were leased under long-term leases to tenants who were not obligated to cover these increases. When you check on a property, you will be given figures on utility costs. Ask to see actual utility bills, not just figures. Make your own estimate of current and anticipated utility costs based on the actual utility consumption in the past. The only thing that is meaningful in old bills is the actual cubic feet of gas, gallons of oil, and kilowatts of electricity used when the premises were fully occupied. Be careful, some sellers might neglect to tell you that the annual figures include a period of several months when the premises were not occupied. To avoid surprises, I recommend that you estimate that utility costs will increase at least 150 percent of the annual Consumer Price Index increase.

ASSESSING PHYSICAL STRUCTURE

Paint

In checking a structure, don't let a coat of paint fool you. Cosmetic repairs can hide serious problems. In the same manner, remember that paint is cheap; don't let the need of paint negatively affect your purchase decisions.

Electrical Wiring

Many older buildings are not wired adequately for today's living. Age isn't the only potential problem. In the late 1960s and early 1970s, aluminum wiring was used in many homes and apartment buildings because it was cheaper than copper wiring. Because this wiring creates a serious fire danger (it tends to arc where joined to copper), aluminum wiring might have to be removed, which can be expensive. By removing a wall plate, you can ascertain if aluminum wiring was used in your property. If a structure has any aluminum wiring, you should use this fact to obtain seller concessions.

Roofing

Check the roof, especially if it is flat. Flat roofs have a shorter life and need more frequent repairs than pitched roofs. Get on the roof. It will generally be easy to see if the roof has been patched. Discolored water spots on the ceilings indicate leaks. If the roof has a pitched area and a flat area, the likely place for leaks is where these areas join. If an owner indicates that a roof was repaired, ask who did the work, and check with the roofer about the condition of the roof. He should give you an honest assessment, since misinformation will only alienate you as far as future work is concerned.

Plumbing

Copper plumbing will generally be in good shape. Pipes likely to cause you problems are iron or galvanized pipes. Test all faucets. Poor water flow could indicate a buildup of lime deposits in the pipes. Discoloration of water could indicate some iron pipes.

Many homes built prior to the early 1960s had galvanized plumbing. While ordinarily not a major problem, when buried in a slab or run underground, the pipes tend to deteriorate. Pipes that leak under a slab generally require costly work. Again, you should be aware of this risk and use it in your purchase negotiations to make the risk acceptable.

Property Age

When you check the plumbing in a building, you can also check its age. Until recently, all toilet tanks had the date of manufacture stamped inside the tank. Ordinarily, a tank is installed within six months of manufacture. Unless the fixtures were updated during remodeling, this date gives a fairly accurate age of a property.

Another way to determine age is to check the walls around the water heater and furnace. Building inspectors usually nail their approvals in these areas. Often the approvals say "Do Not Remove." People generally follow instructions, so these original construction approvals are often found on buildings being torn down. A more accurate way to ascertain the age of a building is to check with the tax assessor's office. You can find the first year the improvements were taxed. Don't bother asking real estate agents how old a building is. Unless it is in their listing, they are seldom able to give an accurate estimate on an older structure. Very often the age the agent quotes falls far short of the actual age of the structure.

Basements

In checking a property with a basement, look for water lines on the basement walls. These lines indicate previous flooding or sewer backup problems. Also check the foundation or basement for cracks. They indicate settling but are not usually serious. You can, however, make a fuss over small cracks, which will place an owner on the defensive and help your bargaining position. Check the floor joists in the corners with a penknife. If use of the penknife reveals soft or rotted timbers, then you should immediately bring in a qualified contractor to determine the cost of repairs if you are seriously considering a purchase.

Foundation

You should check the foundation for earthen tunnels running up to the wood. Be particularly alert in areas where the ground level is close to the wood. If the tunnels have been removed, you will see marks that look like a line on a map indicating a road that is not quite straight. If you find indications of these lines, then the structure has or had subterranean termites, and you should insist on or arrange a termite inspection. Again, while the damage may only be slight, the presence of termites places you in an excellent bargaining position. Be sure you know the extent of the damage before you give an offer on a property.

Insulation

If a building has poor insulation, you should consider whether the costs of added insulation would result in savings. Some states offer credits or tax deductions for insulation work. As a rule of thumb, make an improvement if increased revenues or cost reductions will offset the cost of the improvement in six years or less. Of course, improvements can be depreciated for tax purposes.

Other Items to Check

You should also check furnaces and air conditioners. Don't assume that everything is working properly. If a home has pocket doors that glide into the wall, check them out. Frequently they don't work properly and repairs can be costly. In older properties you should check flooring around plumbing fixtures for rot. One sign of a problem is loose tile. If you see neighbors outside, stop and talk with them. You can usually find out if the property or the neighborhood has any problems of which you are not aware.

Bugs are not usually a problem because they can be exterminated, and they can be an ally because their presence is a bargaining point in your favor. A roach running across a floor can knock several thousand dollars off a purchase price.

If repairs are necessary, get estimates. To be realistic, increase the average estimate by 50 percent. That is what you can expect to pay. As repairs progress, it is common to discover additional work that must be done.

Do not be deluded by the furnishings and decorating. A tastefully furnished and decorated property can emotionally trigger your "want" button. Try to visualize renting or selling the property as empty rooms.

HAZARDOUS SUBSTANCES

The presence of asbestos, radon gas, lead, toxic mold, or any other hazardous substance in structures or on land is likely to be perceived by an owner as a significant problem. This perception can provide an owner the self-justification necessary to sell or lease option property at an unusually attractive price and/or terms. While legal liability of an owner to tenants is still a gray area in some states, the presence of hazardous substances has practically panicked many owners in their desire to rid themselves of a potential liability situation.

Asbestos

Asbestos describes a group of fibrous minerals that can cause severe damage and death when inhaled into the lungs. Symptoms of cancer may not occur until many years after exposure.

Asbestos is found in homes and other structures in:

- Vinyl asbestos floor tile
- Duct wrapping for heating and air conditioning
- Insulation on hot water and steam pipes as well as boilers (construction from the 1920s to 1972)
- Insulating sheets near heat sources
- Some roofing shingles and siding
- Ceiling and wall insulation in some homes built or remodeled between 1945 and 1978
- Sheetrock taping compounds
- Some ceiling tile
- Troweled-on walls (it has a textured, firm appearance)
- Ceiling spray applications

Generally, if asbestos is in good condition, it should not be removed because doing so can cause more harm than good. Friable asbestos (easily crushed or pulverized by hand pressure) is very dangerous. Get an engineering study as to the presence of asbestos prior to any purchase of a large structure built before the early 1970s. You should decide if immediate removal is required if asbestos is present. If so, consider an offer that would take its removal into account. There are a growing number of firms that remove and dispose of hazardous materials.

Formaldehyde

Formaldehyde is a colorless gas emitted where formaldehyde was used in the manufacture of various products. These include:

- Pressed wood products
- Urea-formaldehyde foam insulation (used during the 1970s and early 1980s)
- Some textiles

Formaldehyde presence can cause eye and throat irritation. While form-aldehyde use in homes was generally before 1982, some commercial structures built since then utilized formaldehyde products.

Formaldehyde foam was used extensively by remodeling contractors and mobile home manufacturers who filled wall cavities with the foam through small openings. You can usually determine if formaldehyde foam insulation was used by removing a light switch plate. Formaldehyde removal can be costly because of the time-consuming job of ripping out interior wallboard. It is my understanding that because of the relatively short life of formaldehyde emissions, few structures are likely to have dangerous levels of emission today. While removal is likely unnecessary, you can use the presence of urea-formaldehyde foam insulation in a property as a bargaining chip for better price and/or terms negotiations.

Lead

Excessive accumulation of lead in blood and body tissue can cause damage to the brain, kidneys, and central and peripheral nervous systems. At least two-thirds of homes built before 1940 and one-third of homes between 1940 and 1960 used lead-based paint. Since 1978, government requirements have significantly reduced the allowable lead in paint products.

The simplest way to deal with lead paint is to cover it with a durable covering. Removal methods are dangerous as they result in lead-rich dust. Again, the likely presence of lead-based paint, pointed out to an owner, gives the owner additional motivation to be rid of the property.

You must notify buyers or tenants of the presence of known lead-based paint plus provide them with a warning booklet for structures built before 1978.

Many homes built prior to 1988 had plumbing joints that used lead-based solder. Lead levels in water supplies are greatest during the first five years after construction. Mineral deposits generally form a coating over the plumbing and prevent later lead deposits from dissolving.

You can locate certified lead inspectors in your area through the Web site, *www.leadlistings.org*. Home lead test kits are available through *hometest.com*.

Radon

Radon is a radioactive gas that occurs in nature. Odorless, tasteless, and invisible, it originates from the breakdown of radioactive substances. Outdoors, radon dissipates into the air and is harmless. Dangerous levels of radon can be found in many structures. The known health effect of radon is an increased risk of lung cancer. Risk depends upon the level and length of exposure.

Above-average radon ratings can be used as a factor in obtaining seller concessions. However, for high radon readings you should realize corrective action is required, such as vapor barriers over the soil, sealing concrete slabs and wells, repairing cracks, increasing ventilation, and so on. Commercial radon detectors cost from $25 to $50. Also, a number of firms specialize in radon and other hazardous material detection.

Chemical Discharges

Any property that has or had an underground fuel tank likely has a toxic problem. You should have soil samples taken prior to purchase and know the likely cleanup costs. In some instances, leakage over a long period will require the removal of so much soil that the cost of removal and disposal of what is regarded as hazardous waste can exceed the property value. On the positive side, the presence of a fuel tank is likely to be a strong seller-motivating force. By pointing out liability problems, an advantageous purchase is possible, even considering cleanup costs.

Urban property that has been used for many years for a variety of industrial uses could have a number of toxic problems. A major problem in checking for toxic problems is that tests might not reveal the presence of dangerous compounds unless you are specifically testing for the particular compound.

Toxic Mold

The presence of toxic mold or black mold can have serious health effects. It is caused by damp conditions such as a prior flood, water leakage, or extremely high humidity. There may be no visible evidence of toxic mold, as it can be inside walls.

Buildings have been declared unfit for occupancy because of mold problems. In some cases, the correction costs have exceeded the value of the property. Buildings have been torn down because of toxic mold. Home inspectors can test for mold spores. Home Depot sells a do-it-yourself Pro-Lab Mold Test Kit.

Should you consider purchasing any structure where it is likely that any hazardous material or waste is present, you would be wise to use an ownership form, such as a separate corporate entity, that offers personal protection. If any tenant or invitee to the property successfully sues for damages caused by the hazardous material or waste, you want to minimize your risk.

Sick-Building Syndrome

Sick-building syndrome (SBS) refers to buildings where occupants complain about acute health and comfort problems that appear to be linked to time spent in those buildings. Common complaints include, headache, eye, nose or throat irritation, dry cough, dry or itchy skin, dizziness and nausea, difficulty in concentrating, fatigue, and sensitivity to odors. Most sufferers report relief soon after leaving the buildings. A problem is that no specific illness or cause of the illness can be identified.

The problem may exist in just one portion or room in a building or over the entire building.

Since SBS is found in newer buildings with sealed windows, the problem relates to poor ventilation or moisture problems. Ventilation standards are changing to require more fresh air into buildings. Some experts believe that chemical contamination from outside sources drawn into the ventilation systems contribute to the problem. Others believe the problem is primarily biological contamination with molds, bacteria, and insect droppings in ventilation systems and carpeting. Because of construction, newer sealed buildings have a high moisture level that contributes to the problem.

Corrective action has been to clean the ventilation systems and even change the systems to accommodate windows that open. In other words, make the newer buildings as they were years ago. This can be expensive and will result in much higher heating and cooling costs.

As an investor, you should consider possible liability for the discomfort caused by a sick building and problems in renting a building or keeping tenants when the building develops a sick building syndrome reputation.

SBS structures are definitely problems, but they are also opportunities for persons who can solve them.

Professional Inspection

While you should personally inspect any property you purchase because the ultimate responsibility rests on your shoulders, I strongly recommend a professional home inspection for any purchase. The cost for a home inspection is generally between $250 and $300 dollars. Commercial inspections are likely to be at a per-hour rate. While home inspectors are certified in some states, in other states, anyone can call himself or herself a home inspector. It is important, therefore to choose an inspector who is a member of the American Society of Home Inspectors (ASHI). Members must pass two comprehensive written tests plus have performed a minimum of 250 fee inspections. You should ask the inspector, even if a member of ASHI, how many home inspections he or she has performed. If less than 1000, the inspector is considered an apprentice within the industry.

Try to be present when your inspector comes to inspect the property. Be sure to point out any areas you are concerned about.

Don't use an inspector who is affiliated with a contractor that performs corrective work. There is too much likelihood of a conflict of interest. Also, avoid inspectors recommended by sellers' real estate agents. Because they want the sale to be completed, they want an inspector who does not nitpick and seldom makes waves. As a buyer, you want to know about all of the problems concerning the property, even minor ones. While all inspectors have general knowledge, some have specific knowledge. Many inspectors come from the trades, such as plumbing or electrical. If an area is of particular concern to you, ask inspectors what special experience they have had in that field. You might also want to see a sample copy of a property report they prepared.

For a list of inspectors, check the National Association of Home In-spectors at *www.nahi.org*.

For nonresidential properties, you might want an inspector with an engineering background. Many home inspection firms have specialists for commercial property on their staff. You will also find inspectors with spe-cial experience and training by using an Internet search engine to look for "building inspectors, commercial" and indicate your state.

An offer to purchase subject to approval of a professional property inspection provides you with an opportunity to renegotiate the price if any defects are found.

Termite Inspection

Besides the professional inspection, termite inspection requirements are generally written into purchase offers in areas of the country where there are wood-eating insects. The seller generally pays for a termite inspection and any corrective action required.

Evaluating Tenants

Just as we evaluate a building, we can also evaluate tenants. Even though a tenant might be on a long-term lease or on only a month-to-month lease, it is impossible to predict whether or not the tenant will remain. This is of particular importance in special-use structures. The tenant's financial strength is of course important. A Dun and Bradstreet report will show the tenant's financial rating. The location of other businesses of the same type as the tenant's is also an indication. If similar businesses have been mov-ing out of the area, it is a negative indicator as to your present tenant. The nature and extent of tenant improvements and planned improvements can be strong indicators of a tenant's intent. You should consider what you would do if the present tenant left.

APPRAISALS

What a previous owner paid does not determine value. Don't worry that the price you offer is far more than the owner paid. On the other hand, don't feel you must offer at least what the owner paid. Values are based on what willing buyers will pay to willing sellers at the present time, not at any other time. Don't just ask the broker to tell you what the property is worth; if you are unsure about value, get an independent appraisal by an expert. Its cost can save you worry, heartache, and a financial mistake. Look for a professional appraiser who has either the Member Appraisal Institute (MAI) or Senior Residential Appraiser (SRA) designation. But even with a fee appraisal remember, it is your money, not the appraiser's that is at risk. The decisions are yours. Keep in mind that an appraisal is only one person's estimate of market value. It is not cast in stone. Your own analysis may indicate a value greater or lower than indicated by an appraisal.

You can also ask a broker, if one is involved, for a competitive market analysis. These are usually provided at no cost and simply compare similar sales showing location, age, size, special features, and listing and sale prices. By driving by the properties you will get a feel for the value.

Everyone who deals in real estate should have a basic understanding of the following methods of appraisal.

Market Comparison Method

This is the easiest appraisal method to learn and is used by most people when they buy property. They simply compare a property to other properties. When people say a price is too high, what they usually mean is that the price is higher than the price of a substitute property providing similar benefits of ownership. Using this method, we balance out amenities. For example, while one house has a two-car garage, a comparable house might have only a carport but also a fireplace. The homes might balance out, or you might feel that one is worth a particular dollar amount more than the other. We consider tenants, lease terms, and financing in comparing properties. By checking the market, the average investor can get a very good feel for value based on comparables.

Replacement Cost Method

This method of appraisal is generally used on new structures or on service type buildings where there are no comparables. Using the replacement cost approach to value, we determine what it would cost to build a similar structure today that provides similar benefits. We can then deduct the accrued depreciation (reduction in value caused by use and age). To this figure the value of the land is then added. The land value can be estimated by the market comparison method.

cost to build today
- accrued depreciation
+ land value
value of the property

The problem with this method of appraisal is that it is frequently difficult to determine the amount of the accrued depreciation. This is a judgment call based on the condition of the property.

Income Method

This method is for income property. First, the net income is ascertained. In determining net, we deduct all expenses from the gross income. The only expenses not deducted are interest expense and payments on the principal. This net is then divided by a capitalization rate. Various methods are used to arrive at the rate, but it is really just the rate of return that an investor wants on an investment of this particular type. The greater the risk, the greater the rate of return the investor desires.

$$\text{net} \div \text{rate of return} = \text{value}$$

Gross Multiplier

This is not a true appraisal method. It is only a way to get a ballpark figure. Assume that for a particular type of property investors are currently paying prices equal to nine times the annual gross receipts. Multiply the annual gross income times nine, and if the price asked is equal to or less than this amount, then you would want to investigate further.

Since the gross multiplier does not consider unusual expenses, it can be dangerous as an appraisal tool and is of little or no value to a serious investor. In years past, investors talked about cash-on-cash return or the actual cash returned on the cash investment. They also talked about cash throw-off, which is simply disposable cash income or net spendable income.

Things have changed radically in the last few years. Only in a limited number of areas can quality properties be found that produce significant disposable cash returns unless significant down payments are made. While seminar gurus tell you to seek nothing-down properties that have a strong positive cash flow, these situations are few and far between unless purchasers can solve problems or change the use of the property. Some investors now get excited over a good break-even investment. In fact, negative cash flow investments that investors would have laughed at years ago are often snapped up today if the tax depreciation and anticipated appreciation benefits offset the negative cash flow.

The basic economic principles of supply and demand underlie all evaluation. A market in which there are many willing buyers with few sellers means rising prices. The price you will pay today is determined by the marketplace, which reacts to what is anticipated. Current rents will rise in the future. Today's negative cash flows are expected to turn to healthy positive cash flows within a few years. If you believe that inflation is in our future, you can expect a general increase in real estate valuations. What today might seem a horrendous price could very well be tomorrow's bargain. In the same respect, in areas where there are few buyers and many sellers, values have dropped significantly.

WATCH OUT FOR YOUR EMOTIONS

Many investors fall in love with a property. When this happens, the desire to own can result in uneconomic decision making. In addition, if the seller is a skilled negotiator, they will use your emotions to their advantage while you lose all possible bargaining strength.

I like to point out to my students that my finest investment is a huge, ugly warehouse store. The building offers no pride of ownership. What it does offer is a national tenant on a triple-net lease where the annual cash flow has grown to exceed the original total cash investment. This building illustrates that what is important is the bottom line, not pride of ownership. After you have made your millions, you might want to upgrade investments so you can take people around and point out what you own. However, pride of ownership normally costs money. Most buildings you can point at with pride, unless sold under distress conditions, do not make much economic sense.

A danger to be avoided is the "I want to invest now" syndrome. Many people have watched the investment game for years from the sidelines; when they finally decide to be players they want in immediately. Certainly it's a trite expression, but "Act in haste, repent in leisure" does hold true. Take your time. Analyze before you jump at the first opportunity. When you have found a property that meets your needs and you have a feel for its value, you are now ready for the next step—your offer to purchase.

Don't rush to buy the deal that is too good to be true. As I have stated before, normally such a deal isn't true: There is usually something wrong. There are many sharp operators who are willing to lie, cheat, and steal to get your money. A seller may "forget" to tell you that the property is on a floodplain and that a building permit will not be issued or that an addition was built without a permit and must be ripped down because it violates building codes.

10

Your Offer to Purchase

Every man by nature has the right to possess property as his own. This is
one of the chief points of distinction between man and the lower animals.

Pope Leo XIII, 1891

As previously stated, anyone can buy at retail. In fact, some people end up
paying more than a fair price for merchandise. There are, however, people
who seek and find bargain prices, but not for bargain merchandise. They
buy quality at wholesale, close to wholesale, and even at below wholesale
prices. Just as in retail merchandise, bargains await you in real estate, but
you must know where to look and what to look for. Chapters 7 and 8 hopefully will have shown you how to locate wholesale opportunities. Again,
you should realize that a purchase at market value means you have immediately lost at least 10 percent on your purchase.

You would, at the very least, lose 10 percent if you paid retail for an
investment property and turned around and sold it—probably more after
paying real estate fees, loan costs, closing costs, and so forth. If a really
quick sale is required, chances are you would have to discount the price by
at least another 10 percent. You must therefore buy property at a discount
from market value of at least 10 percent to remain even. Any less of a discount means a loss should a resale be necessary.

All right, you have found a property you are interested in and want to
make an offer. First of all you should realize that a "firm" price is seldom
firm. Some bargaining is usually possible. Even when a seller refuses to
reduce a price, he or she will frequently negotiate on what goes with the
property, down payment, or interest rates.

Price is not the same as value. Similar property sells over a range of prices. The range tends to be wider when there are few similar sales (thin market) and narrower in an active market. Sale prices that are significantly above the normal range are usually the result of "must have" or uniformed buyers. Sale prices that are far below the normal range are usually the result of "must sell" highly motivated or uninformed sellers.

Sharing Your Assessment

If you're at all considering making an offer on property you have located and evaluated, keep the information to yourself. Sharing may have been a virtue in kindergarten but it isn't in investing. People telling people who tell other people can create interest and competition for you.

A friend told me of the waterfront property located on a highly desirable lake that he almost purchased. The problem was that he mentioned the great opportunity to a former friend who purchased the property. While there is nothing wrong with telling others after you have made a purchase, don't do it before it is a done deal.

SELLER'S MOTIVATION

If you are dealing directly with the owners or if the owners are present when an agent shows you the property, ask them why they are selling. Owners will normally answer truthfully. The greater the owner's motivation, the greater the likelihood of a purchase significantly below market value.

When a broker advertises a property and uses the word *asking* in the ad, the broker is really saying, "The price is soft." The same inference is given by using the words *submit all offers, motivated seller,* or including a reason for the sale. Unfortunately, some ads don't reflect an owner's views. The broker might hint at a bargain just to bring in traffic. However, such ads are a starting point for your negotiating position. Ask the agent how long the property has been on the market and if the seller is truly motivated. If the property has been on the market for an inordinate period of time, a significant discount on the listed price is almost assured.

While a seller's real estate agent should not disclose the owner's motivation to sell without permission, from my experience at least half of the agents will do so if asked. In fact, many seller agents will volunteer the fact that an owner must sell and provide the reasons. If you are using a buyer agent, the agent is obligated to tell you what he or she has discovered as to seller motivation. Many buyer agents will seek out situations where there is exceptional seller motivation. Knowing why an owner is selling can be worth tens of thousands of dollars to you in negotiation leverage.

With a must-sell owner it is often possible to purchase property far below market value. Property purchased right will have a built-in safety net. Because you paid less than market value, such an investment reduces the possibility of the equity being eliminated by minor market fluctuations. It also allows you to price the property for a quick sale at a profit. The more information you have on the seller, the stronger may be your bargaining position. You should keep in mind that while you don't have to buy a particular property, the seller may have to sell. This can put you in the proverbial catbird seat. You are the one bargaining from a position of strength.

Unmotivated sellers are the reason you should avoid becoming emotionally attached to a property prior to purchase. Unmotivated sellers are will-sell sellers who are willing to part with property at their price. They are under no financial or emotional pressure to sell. Holding the property does not present a hardship, and they have no strong need to use the proceeds of the sale for any other purpose.

Avoid prolonged dealings with unmotivated sellers. This does not mean you should not make offers. Often sellers who claim to be unmotivated are in fact strongly motivated to sell. They have adopted a not-very-interested approach in order to hide the fact that they may indeed be desperate to sell. Therefore, don't be afraid of offering anyone a low offer. I have never been offended by anyone offering me money. The best approach is to give an offer under the assumption the seller is highly motivated to sell.

When buyers believe sellers are not strongly motivated to sell, they generally begin negotiations at a higher figure than if sellers were motivated to sell. They will also set their purchase negotiation goals at a higher price than if sellers were motivated. In this way the unmotivated seller has won before negotiations have begun.

While as a buyer you want to know a seller's motivation, you don't want a seller to know how motivated you are to buy.

If a seller knows you're in love with a property, your bargaining position will be significantly weakened. All your knowledge as to negotiation tactics will become meaningless. When looking for a new home, my wife and I found a property that looked like it could be on the cover of *House and Garden.* After going through the house, my wife said, "I want this house." Within hearing range were the owners as well as the owner's agent. Well, I purchased the property, which turned out to be a great home, as well as an outstanding investment. I paid full price but I managed to get some personal property included in the sale. If at all possible, you don't want the seller to know the extent of your motivation. Don't let your love shine through.

KNOWING WHAT THE SELLER PAID

Before you prepare an offer, it helps if you know what the seller has invested in the property. By knowing when the seller purchased the property, you should be able to get a fairly good idea of what the seller paid. By telling neighbors that you are interested in purchasing in the area, you can lead up to the property and find out when the present owner purchased it. Chances are neighbors who were living there at the time the property was purchased will even know what the present owner paid. You're more likely to get the real reason a seller is selling from a neighbor than from a real estate agent or the owner. In talking with a neighbor, also ask about problems with the particular property and in the neighborhood.

An owner is more likely to accept a price cut when it cuts only profit. If an owner asks $100,000 for a parcel of land and receives an offer of $80,000, he or she might accept it if he or she paid only $40,000. If the owner had recently purchased the property for $100,000, there is much less chance of the offer being accepted. Some years ago, I purchased a condominium for $55,000 when the new units in the development were selling for over $80,000. However, this unit had been purchased in the first phase of a development when the price was $55,000.

The same principle is true for financing. Owners are more willing to finance the buyer from their profit dollars.

HOW THE PRICE WAS SET

When dealing directly with the owners, ask them, "How did you arrive at that price?" This will often reveal very subjective thinking and that the price is by no means firm. A follow-up question to ask them is, "What is the lowest price you will take for the property?" The answer to this question really gives you a new asking price without having made an offer.

Any negotiations would be based on discounts from this price, not the original asking price. This technique is simple, straightforward, and it works. The same technique can be used to receive discounts from contractors whose bids you intend to accept: "What's the best price you can give me for the job if we sign the contract right now?" After you get this price, a further contractor discount is very often possible if you ask "What's the best price you can offer if I pay in *greenbacks*"? While you might pay cash it is still essential that you receive a receipt.

When dealing with a seller's agent, ask the agent how the price was arrived at. Ask for a copy of any competitive market analysis that was prepared. (This is an appraisal prepared for the owner.) Some agents may feel that the analysis is proprietary. If so, ask the agent to prepare a competitive market analysis showing all similar sales in the area in the last six months. In most areas computer printout material is readily available. Having competitive market information that the broker is going to show the seller gives the buyer clout in negotiating at the low end of comparable sales or even lower.

A property is not a bargain just because it is priced significantly below an appraisal. Don't accept appraisals as gospel. They are simply opinions of others and are often too high or too low. While an appraisal can be used to reinforce your evaluation as to value, the basic determination as to what to offer must be yours, since you will be the one paying the price.

TIMING

There are times and situations when bargains are available in both prices and terms. In a buyer's market, where there are few buyers and many sellers, the best bargains are possible. There are always some sellers who for some reason must sell quickly. While a very low offer in a normal market might be rejected immediately, in a buyer's market the below-market offer will usually either be accepted or generate a counteroffer. An outright rejection of offers becomes unlikely when few offers are being made.

In a seller's market, you may have to look hard for sellers who will carry paper (provide seller financing). In a buyer's market this is less likely to be a problem, since sellers realize that they may not get what they want. Owners who want all cash find that they have to carry paper if they want a sale. The better the financial condition of the seller, the greater the possibility that the seller will carry paper.

Besides economic conditions locally or on a national basis, things like weather can affect a local marketplace. One investor purchased two deluxe two-bedroom, two-bath condominiums in a winter recreational area after two years of little snow. He purchased both condos for under $125,000 each, even though similar units had previously sold in the $200,000 range. There were a great many units available, and the investor just kept on throwing out offers until he found owners desperate enough to accept. Incidentally, he resold both units after one year, making a profit of close to $200,000 on a total cash investment of about $40,000. That's a 500 percent cash-on-cash return.

Because there are more buyers than sellers in a seller's market, there are fewer truly desperate sellers. However, they are always out there. You just have to keep testing owners' motivation. You of course test them with purchase offers.

Don't give up when offers are rejected. A baseball player who gets a hit 3 out of 10 times at bat doesn't want to quit because of seven failures. Instead, he rejoices in hitting .300.

HOW LOW TO GO

Your offer must make sense to you. Don't worry that your offer will be rejected. Rejection costs you nothing, but an offer that doesn't make sense to you can cost you a great deal.

Problem properties usually can be purchased at attractive prices and/or terms. When a property has problems such as vacancies or health or building code violations, any offer may look good to an owner. If a property has developed a negative cash flow and the owner must pay a significant sum each month to keep the property, what would otherwise be an unacceptable offer might be accepted. Don't be afraid to make too low an offer.

What you offer is your decision. If you wish to make an offer, don't worry that the real estate agent will say it won't be accepted; it is your offer. Keep in mind that the primary responsibility of a seller agent is to get the best deal possible for the seller, not for you the buyer. Also keep in mind that the real estate agent must present your written offer to the owner.

Again don't ask your friends what you should offer, especially if they aren't in the market. You are the one making the offer and the one who will also have to make the payments. Therefore, while you might want to listen to some others, especially your attorney and accountant, the offer must be yours.

Some buyers set their offers based on the seller's asking price. An asking price should not be the basis of an offer. Because you purchase significantly below an asking price does not mean you are getting a bargain. In fact, you might be overpaying. On the other hand, the offering price might be too low and actually be a better bargain than a discount from a price that is too high. Then it could be wise to offer full price. In fact the following example shows when to offer more than full price:

> I'm Jim S. I formerly worked as a real estate agent, but I found I could make more money flipping (buying and selling) property for myself. Recently, I saw an agent putting up a for-sale sign on a lot. I introduced myself and asked the price of the lot. I was told $5600. I told the agent to please remove the sign, and that I would be at his office within the hour with a cashier's check for a full-price offer.
>
> The price was a bargain. While the price would have been proper a couple years earlier, the area had experienced a spectacular appreciation in value because of local economic conditions, which, by the way, were counter to the national economy. Previously, I had offered full price on another lot soon after it was listed. In doing some checking, the owner felt she had priced the property too low and refused my offer. In another case I offered an owner less-than-asking price for his recently listed lot so as not to alert him that the price was too low. I lost out to another buyer who came up with a full-price offer.
>
> I decided in this case to take an unusual approach. With a cashier's check for $6600 along with my offer for that amount, I told the salesperson at the real estate office I had a full-price offer without conditions along with a cashier's check for the full purchase price. I stated I wanted acceptance by 6:00 p.m. that day or the offer would expire because I was considering other property (which was not untrue). I then handed a sealed envelope to the salesperson and left the office.
>
> It appeared to the agent and the owner that I had misunderstood the price and thought it was $6600, rather than $5600. Less than an hour later I received a call that my offer was accepted. Incidentally, it took me almost three months to get my price for the lot, $30,500.

When making an offer, keep in mind that while psychologically $99,900 will seem to you to be much lower than $100,000, it will appear much lower to the seller as well. It is well worth it to round off the price offered. Don't give offers that barely slice below $5000 or $10,000 increments. The time to come up with the $99,900 prices is when you sell property.

YOUR AGREEMENT

Don't make a verbal agreement or leave any part of an agreement to a verbal understanding. When it comes to a "friendly understanding," you will find that not everyone is "your friend." If it is agreed to, get it in writing and signed.

The word *obfuscate* is interesting in that the definition means to "confuse" or "make obscure." Because the word is not well-known, readers tend to be confused and the meaning to many is obscure. If you use words like obfuscate in your offers to purchase or make it difficult for a seller to understand your offer immediately, it is doomed to failure. They are not going to accept it if they don't understand it. Say it simply and clearly. Obfuscation will mean failure.

The following are elements that you should consider for inclusion in an offer to purchase:

Personal Property Included.   Your offer should specify what personal property is included in the sale. By spelling things out, you can avoid misunderstandings later. For example, if there is a swimming pool, does the pool-cleaning equipment stay? Does a portable metal storage building stay? What about the drapes, slide-in ranges, fireplace screens, and tools? Be specific. You can frequently induce sellers to include personal property such as washers, dryers, and refrigerators, which they did not intend to include, by asking for them in the offer. This really serves as the equivalent of an additional cut in price.

Pricing Personal Property.   Because personal property located in income property can be depreciated in a much shorter period of time than real property, you might want to specify in an offer for furnished units how much of the offer price applies to the real property and how much applies to the personal property. Chances are you will want to allocate the maximum amount possible to the personal property. An accountant can help you in making decisions in this area.

Seller Rent.   If the seller is not giving up possession until after closing, your offer should cover the rent, if any, that the seller is to pay.

Casualty Loss.   The offer should cover who is to be responsible for a casualty loss to the property, such as fire, prior to possession.

Past Due Rents.   For income properties, rent arrearages should be agreed upon. As a buyer you don't want to pay the seller for these arrearages because they may never be collected from the tenants. It can be a bookkeeping headache to try to collect them for the seller and then remit them. As a buyer you should just ask that all claims for past-due rentals be assigned to you as part of the consideration for the purchase price. If they are collectible, it is something extra; if not, you are not penalized.

Estoppel Letters.   If you are buying rental property, you'll want the offer to require the owner to provide you with tenant certificates of no defense. Also, known as an *estoppel letter,* the tenant signs that he or she has no claim against the landlord or offset against rent.

Right to Show.   When buying a property for rental or resale, you will normally want the right to show the property prior to closing. This can save you valuable time later. Consider the following clause for your purchase agreement:

> The purchaser shall have the right to show the property to prospective con-
> tractors, insurance carriers, buyers, and/or renters at reasonable times prior
> to the close of this purchase agreement. For the purpose of this clause, four
> hours' notice shall be deemed a reasonable notification time and reasonable
> hours shall be between 9:00 a.m. and 8:00 p.m.

Such a clause allows you to immediately begin getting bids for renovation work upon closing, if that is desired. It also means you can have the property rented or sold before you take possession.

Release Clause.   If you are purchasing several parcels from one seller or a parcel that can conceivably be broken into several parcels, your offer should contain a release clause from any blanket encumbrance when there is seller financing. A blanket encumbrance is a lien covering more than one property, such as a single mortgage over several properties. The re-lease clause provides for the release of separate parcels from the lien upon payment of stated amounts. Without the release clause, you could not re-sell one parcel without paying off the entire blanket loan.

Liquidated damages.   Unless agreed otherwise, a purchaser who de-faults can be held liable for damages by the seller. If the seller later com-pletes a sale at a lower price, then the difference would be the seller's damages. I believe it is best to include a liquidated damages provision. *Liquidated damages* are damages agreed to in advance of any breach of contract, to be paid should the buyer default. Customarily in real estate transactions, the agreement is that the buyer forfeits the earnest money deposit as the damages. This is then the sole remedy that the seller can have against the buyer. As a buyer you might not want to forfeit the deposit if it were substantial. You can, however, specify a lesser amount as liquidated damages.

Home Warranty.   For a single-family dwelling, consider obtaining home warranty protection. Your purchase offer could require the seller to pay for the policy. The insurance covers appliances and major systems (generally for one year). If there are problems the policy can be very valuable.

Condition at Closing.   To protect against a seller's failing to make repairs if items are broken or become inoperative prior to the closing, you might consider the following:

> Subject to all electrical, plumbing, and mechanical equipment being in good and proper working order as of [date].

Maintenance Until Closing.   As a buyer you will want your offer to include a clause requiring the seller to maintain the garden, pool, buildings, and other improvements until closing. Otherwise neglect could result in substantial damage.

Seller Financing.   When an offer requires seller financing, you want the material terms of the financing spelled out in detail. For example:

> Subject to the seller's taking back as part of the purchase price a second mortgage in the amount of $ ___and payable at $ ___or more per month. Said payment to include interest at ___percent. This mortgage shall be due and payable in full ___ years from date of closing.

You will want the "or more" to be included since it will allow prepayment without any penalty. Most sellers will not accept a long-term second mortgage. Normally, sellers want the buyers to agree to pay them off in five to seven years. Usually, because of appreciation, increased equity will allow refinancing to pay off this second mortgage. However, you should keep in mind the fact that values do not always go up. There is risk.

Warranty as to Financial Statement.   If you have any doubts at all as to the income and expenses quoted, consider the following:

> Subject to the seller warranting that the attached income and expense statement is accurate and complete for the period indicated.

If the statement provided was intentionally prepared falsely, the seller will probably refuse to accept this warranty.

Final Inspection.   Your offer should provide for a final walk through prior to closing to make certain all conditions and seller obligations have been met.

Lease Approval.   Often, what a seller indicates a lease provides is not in fact what the lease states. You might consider:

> Subject to seeing and approving existing leases by [date].

Compliance with Codes.   If you have not checked local codes and have doubts as to a building's compliance with the codes, you certainly would want the following provision in your offer:

> Subject to seller warranting that the building complies with all building, health, and fire codes.

How Title Is Taken.   You should provide in your purchase offer that:

> Title shall be in the name(s) of _____ or nominee.

This allows you to sell prior to closing and for you to direct the seller to convey directly to your buyer. An advantage of this procedure is that you will save on title costs (title insurance or abstract), as well as the other costs associated with two separate closings. This is commonly known as a *double escrow.*

Termite Inspection.   Consider including a termite inspection clause in your purchase contract. The clause generally requires the seller, at his expense, to provide the purchaser a termite inspection. The seller agrees to correct any damage or infestation prior to closing.

Professional Inspection.   Your offer should provide the right of inspection by professional inspectors and provide for an escape from the contract should problems be found and the seller is unwilling to correct them.

Time for Compliance.   If the offer says, "time is of the essence," it means that no delays will be allowed. You might want to remove these words and use, "on or about" for dates to allow some flexibility. Otherwise, you would be in default if a deadline could not be met. Some buyers will state that the closing date may be extended (30) days upon the buyer increasing the earnest money by $____.

CONTINGENCY CLAUSES

You can tailor your contingencies to the special circumstances of a purchase. However, it is wise, to avoid contingencies when they are not really needed. The more contingencies your offer contains, the less chance you have of getting acceptance. Use contingencies only when they are really important.

If you really want a property, get your offer in without delay. If you are worried about something and want to check it out, you can make your offer contingent upon that item.

Approval of Third Party.   You can frequently tie up a property for a few days by placing a contingency on it such as:

Contingent upon the approval of ___ within ___ days of acceptance.

The approval person could be your spouse, a professional real estate counselor, a construction expert, or any other appropriate person.

Loan Assumption.   Don't take it for granted that a loan can be assumed. You should subject your offer to a loan assumption if the assumption is important to you. A clause such as the following is very common:

Subject to the seller's being able to assume an existing mortgage in the amount of $___ at ___ percent interest with payments of $___ per month with _____.

Financing.   If you are unsure of your ability to finance a purchase, the following statement in an offer protects you from being in default should financing not be available:

Contingent upon obtaining a loan in the amount of 80 percent of the purchase price at no more than 8.5 percent interest by [date].

Percolation Test.   If the vacant property does not have sewer, you want to make certain that a septic system is possible. You could state:

> Contingent upon passing a percolation test by [date].

You could require that the seller pay for the test as this is not unreasonable.

Removal of Tenant.   If a property has a problem tenant or if you wish the property for your own use, you can save cost, time, and stress by having the present owner remove the tenant. You might state:

> Contingent upon owner delivering premises in a vacant condition at time of closing.

Prior Sale.   If your old property is highly salable and the property you are purchasing has been on the market for some time, the seller may agree to the following contingency:

> This offer is contingent upon the sale of the property at [address] by [date].

Title Report Approved.   The following contingency is preprinted in many offers. It protects the buyer against easements or other problems that the buyer is unaware of:

> Contingent on buyer's approval of preliminary title report.

Inspection and Approval of All Units.   In an older building where you were only able to see one or two units, what you saw might possibly be the exceptional units, not the typical units. You might therefore wish the following contingency:

> Subject to the inspection and approval of all units in the building by the buyer.

Don't use a zoning change as a contingency. Such a contingency can be dangerous because it may give the seller ideas that could result in a higher price or the property being withdrawn from the market. You are better off getting an option rather than alert the seller to the potential of greater value.

Right to Continue Offering.   An owner who does not want to accept a contingent offer can usually be prevailed upon to do so by the inclusion of the following:

The seller has the right to continue to market the property. Should the seller accept another offer that is contingent upon the rights of _____, then _____ shall have ___ days from receipt of notice to waive his or her condition(s) as set forth in paragraph___. Failure of _____ to waive said conditions in person or by the receipt of a registered letter by___, shall terminate and void this offer and buyer's deposit shall be returned to the buyer.

The seller does not jeopardize the ability to sell the property with such a clause as the property remains on the market.

LEMONADING

Some investors use the term *lemonading*—adding a sweetener to a deal to make it more acceptable. Your lemonading could consist of agreeing to pay an attractive interest rate, agreeing to pay off a loan in a relatively short period, agreeing to step increases in interest rates, or even to simply adding additional cash.

Lemonading can take place in the original offer or in subsequent negotiations. Never give all you can give with your original offer. Leave room so some concessions can be given during any negotiations. You must allow a seller to save face by gaining something in the negotiation process.

The size and form of your earnest money deposit can serve to sweeten what would otherwise appear as a sour offer. Large earnest money deposits in the form of cashier's checks made out either to a broker's trust account or to an escrow agent will make it difficult for an owner to turn down an offer. Don't give large deposits directly to the owner because you might have a situation where an owner can't deliver clear title and has spent your deposit. The offer should provide, where there is no agent, that the buyer shall deposit the earnest money in a neutral escrow account on the next business day. If there is an agent, the money is to be placed in the agent's trust account. Cash can be effectively used by buyers; it seems to mesmerize people. Several thousand dollars in *cash* stapled to an offer to purchase will probably cause a seller's pulse to race. However, make certain the seller does not gain control of the cash.

ASSUMING LOANS

Even if you can pay cash or intend to refinance, if there are advantageous private assumable loans on the property, you should assume them. After the purchase you can then contact the individuals holding the loans and offer to pay off the loans at a discount. You can usually negotiate some sort of discount for early payment. If the individual needs money, then the discount can be substantial. I once obtained a 50 percent discount on a second mortgage, which actually amounted to more than a $5000 price reduction after the purchase.

If the sellers will carry paper, let them, even if you could obtain similar conventional financing. Conventional lenders are not interested in discounting the loan for an early payment, but private individuals frequently are. After about six months, an offer of prepayment at a discount can be made. The seller might not accept at first, but it will be in the back of the seller's mind as a source of cash. There is an excellent chance that eventually the seller will make you a discount offer for prepayment.

AS-IS SALES

If an owner is selling property "as is," be particularly careful. Look for the unexpected. Just because you buy a property as is does not, however, mean that you have given up all your rights. If a seller knows of a hidden defect and fails to inform the buyer or actually conceals the defect, many courts will hold the seller liable despite the fact that the purchase was as is.

USING ATTORNEYS

Use an attorney to help you make your first offers. Legal fees to prepare an offer are very small when compared with the obligations you are accepting with a purchase. You will want to develop a good relationship with an attorney specializing in real estate.

There is a danger in accepting definitions from a real estate agent. The agent is giving you his or her opinion, which may not be the opinion a court would have should a disagreement arise. Also keep in mind that generally the first duty of the agent is to the owner, not you. The agent also wants to make a commission. While most real estate agents are honest, as in any group there are some bad apples.

If you are uncertain as to your rights or need to draft a legal document or even to modify a legal form, you should consider legal advice. The time to avoid legal problems is before they are created. If it is a real estate matter, you want an attorney who specializes in real estate. Don't choose an attorney from your local telephone book. You want an attorney who is a member of the real estate section of your state or local bar association. Bar associations can provide you with names of such attorneys in your area.

ABSTRACTS AND TITLE INSURANCE

In many areas of the country, abstracts are used to verify title. *An abstract* is simply a copy of every recorded document dealing with the property. An attorney will read the abstract and give you an opinion as to the marketability of the title. Even though you use an attorney, there can still be problems with an abstract. An attorney would not know if a prior deed was forged or if a prior grantor had been declared insane or was otherwise incompetent prior to transfer of title. Similarly, a single owner might actually be married and there could be unknown spousal interests. I therefore recommend that your offer specify that title shall be verified by a policy of title insurance paid for by the seller.

You should consider purchasing an extended coverage policy of title insurance. As the buyer, you will be expected to pay this additional cost. An extended coverage policy provides additional protection for items such as incorrect survey or building on the wrong lot. Your title insurance company will explain the availability and advantages of obtaining this additional coverage.

CONSIDER ALL FINANCIAL OBLIGATIONS

Before you complete an offer, carefully consider the financial obligations. Can you make the payments? Don't count on a quick resale for a profit. By using amortization tables, which all real estate agents and investors should have, you can compute your principal and interest payments. To this you should add an estimated amount for taxes, insurance, and maintenance, as applicable.

ACCEPTANCE OF OFFERS

Your offer to purchase should state how long it is good for. Even though you may allow a number of days for acceptance of your offer, you have the right to withdraw your offer any time prior to acceptance.

Acceptance is generally considered to take place upon the mailing of the seller's written acceptance. Once the seller has placed the acceptance in the mail, you can no longer revoke your offer. Revocation, on the other hand, generally takes place upon receipt. Generally, even though you have mailed the revocation of your offer, it can be accepted by the seller up to the time your revocation is actually received.

I do not believe in giving the seller very much time to accept an offer. If the seller is in the community, provide one day for acceptance. This forces a decision and usually avoids a situation where the seller runs around and gets the advice of numerous people. Friends are likely to say what they think the seller wants to hear, "Why, your property is worth lots more than that!" Often inexpert advice causes sellers to lose advantageous sales.

Don't take rejection personally. When the owner rejects your offer, it isn't a rejection of you. Often the owner is just not motivated to sell or the timing isn't right. Many investors let the owner (or agent) know that if the owner has a change of mind, they will consider resubmitting an offer. Often many months later, the owner will contact the investor to see if there is still an interest to purchase.

Few offers are met with outright rejection. What usually happens is that a counteroffer is made. Don't worry if a seller refuses to give in an inch. If the purchase makes sense for you at the seller's price and terms, accept them. Some buyers walk away from advantageous deals just because the seller won't give any concessions.

Buyers feel they are losing face if they give the full asking price. Ask yourself, "If the seller had asked 20 percent more and had come down to the present price, would I want to make the purchase?" If yes, then go ahead with it. However, if the deal doesn't make sense, walk away from it. Don't try to reach an agreement for agreement's sake. You are never going to run out of opportunities.

AUCTION SALES

Auctions are an interesting way to buy property, but don't go to an auction unprepared. Know the property, set your top price, and stick to it. It is easy to get caught up in the emotion of an auction setting. An auctioneer might say, "Are you going to lose this fine home for just $500 more?" A logical reaction would be to go the additional $500, but another bidder will probably top the bid. Your reaction could be to retaliate with an even higher bid. The desire to be a winner pushes many bidders far beyond what they had set as their maximum price. Instead of being a winner, they become losers because they bid away their profit. To help you stick to your predetermined limit, write it down. A written limit is harder to exceed than is a mental limit. While an auction can provide a bargain, there are times when property at an auction will sell for far more than the market would otherwise indicate.

You should prequalify as a bidder before the auction begins. Know the bidding requirements. You may be required to produce a cashier's check or cash for 10 percent of the purchase price. The balance will have to be paid at closing, which will be a specified period from the auction date. Unless the seller has arranged financing, have your financing lined up in advance. An auction setting does not allow you to condition your offer. You as the offeror are usually making an unconditional offer to purchase at a stated price. The offer is not accepted by the auctioneer until the gavel falls.

Auctions may have reserve prices. *A reserve price* is a price below which the owner is not required to sell. In some states the owner can bid against you up to his or her reserve price. The presence of a reserve price does not mean you should start bidding at the reserve price, because the owner is free to accept bids below reserve prices and frequently does. At a recent auction a condominium unit with a reserve price of $150,000 sold at $128,000.

A friend of mine went to an estate auction where real and personal property was being sold by the heirs. My friend wanted the house for his own use. He was high bidder at $111,000, but the heirs turned down the bid as being less than the reserve price (which was not published). The property had a fair market value of about $160,00 to $170,000. My friend walked over to one of the heirs and handed her a folded piece of paper. When the heir opened it and saw written "$125,000" he said, "Do we write up the sale now?" The answer was in the affirmative. The heirs were able to get a quick sale and my friend got a great home for his family at a good price.

When selling a large number of units, owners often set extremely low reserve prices on a few units. This tactic attracts buyers hoping for a terrific bargain. Don't get too excited over low reserve prices; it is what others are bidding that is important. At some auctions reserve prices are not published and the bidders are not informed until bidding ceases.

When an auction is without reserve, it means the property will be sold to the highest bidder no matter what the bid.

A number of years ago a shopping center site was being auctioned in Lancaster, California. Most of the bidders were expected to be from the

Los Angeles area. The morning of the auction there was a storm, and snow chains were required to cross the mountains from Los Angeles to Lancaster. There were only a handful of bidders at the sale, which was without reserve, and the successful bidder resold his bargain for a $200,000 profit later the same day. Poor weather can mean bargains when an auction is without reserve.

Often at estate auctions, the auctioneer will hold the real estate as the last item to be auctioned. The idea is to induce bidders to remain while the personal property is auctioned off. This can backfire in that the weather, like a hot summer afternoon, can mean that most of the bidders will give in to the heat, leaving little competition for the real property.

At an auction, it is not just the thickness of the wallet that determines who gets the property; it can also be a matter of psychology. Bidders may increase the price by $500 or $1000 when there are few bidders. A tactic that often scares off nonprofessionals is to suddenly up the ante and increase the bid by a large amount such as $10,000. When professionals know there will be bidding competition, they will open the bidding at a price significantly above the minimum price. Other bidders realize they can't *steal* the property so they hesitate. Hopefully, their hesitation lasts long enough to allow the auctioneer's hammer to fall.

When you raise the ante, chances are those who are bidding will still top your bid by a low amount hoping you have bid your maximum. If the property value permits, a second major increase will often silence the other bidders. If the bidding had been allowed to increase in small increments, chances are the final price would have risen to the point where a purchase is either economically marginal or uneconomical.

A variation of this heavy-hitter approach is to stay out of the bidding in the early stages, letting others bid by increasingly reduced increments. You can often get the opposition to fold by coming into the game late with a bid that significantly increases the table stakes.

Watch the crowd. Young couples and couples with children are generally bidding on property that will become their home. Single persons, often with notepads, can mean investors buying for rental or resale. When there are a group of properties, the first properties will generally be bid up by buyers who are buying for their own use. The investors will either not bid or will drop out early. (This will give you an idea of their expectations.)

Enter the bidding after about one-third to one-half of the units are sold. Even then, only bid if the sale prices are within an acceptable range to you. Some of the best prices are often when between 60 percent and 80 percent of the units are sold. Bidding for some units will defy any pattern because homebuyer bidders may want particular units. That is, prices will peak up significantly for a property even though similar property has sold previously for less.

Watch the other bidders. If there are a great many bidders remaining who appear to be looking at units for their own use, the final group of homes sold might sell for prices higher than any others. However, if most of these buyers have left, the final units could sell at bargain prices.

If you're not the high bidder at an auction, you should fill out a form for a backup offer. Often high bidders are unable to complete a purchase, in which case your backup offer will be considered.

Not all auctions are for distressed property. Some land companies use them as a marketing tool for raw land having low values, although the promotion of the auction may indicate otherwise. Large developers now use auctions to clear out inventory before starting new projects. In some areas, real estate brokers assemble large groups of property from many owners to attract buyers. Nevertheless, auctions offer exceptional opportunities.

11
CHAPTER

Subdividing—Smaller Can Be Better

No man acquires property without acquiring with it a little arithmetic.

Ralph Waldo Emerson, 1850

Whoever first said that the whole is equal to the sum of its parts didn't have the slightest idea what subdividing is all about. In real estate the value of a large parcel can be considerably less than the value of the same property cut up into smaller, more usable units. For example, a 20-acre parcel might have a market value of $3500 per acre, or $70,000. If that 20-acre parcel were broken into four parcels of 5 acres each, they might sell for $25,000 each, or $100,000 total. If the parcel were broken into 1-acre parcels, they might well sell for $8000 each, or $160,000 total. As parcels are cut into smaller acreage pieces, there is an increased demand, since more buyers can afford to buy and use them. An increase in demand translates into an increase in price. Today we have many different types of subdivisions—recreational, conventional housing, mobile home, and even industrial properties.

THE SUBDIVISION PROCESS

While the subdivision process sounds simple, it can actually be quite involved. There are local, state, and even federal regulations concerning subdivisions. Large subdivisions also require environmental impact reports, which can be costly. The average time for subdivision approval varies by state and community. In some areas it takes only a few months, while in other areas, such as Los Angeles, a three-year period to obtain all approvals is not unusual.

Although the raw land can usually be purchased with little money down, the payments must be made on the land; therefore, a developer must have sufficient cash flow to make the payments during approval and development stages.

Residential subdivisions in some areas must be fully improved. This can mean sewer, water, streets, curb, gutter, and even sidewalks, which can mean expenditures of thousands of dollars for every lot. Because of the development costs, many subdividers develop in phases, such as 50 lots at a time, in a development that contains perhaps 500 lots total.

In some states municipal bonds are issued to pay for the improvements. Buyers of each lot, then, are subject to a bonded indebtedness. This puts the cost of the improvements on the buyer, not the developer.

While large subdivisions can require a great deal of time and effort, a simple split of a parcel into two parcels can usually be accomplished with little difficulty. In many states you can manufacture as many as four parcels from a single parcel with relatively few problems. While you will probably need local approval for a simple lot split, it would not be subject to the entire subdivision process. Your local building department or planning commission can tell you what state and local procedures and regulations govern the subdivision process. There are people who will handle the detail work of a subdivision approval for you at a fee, but if you intend to handle more than one subdivision, you should get involved in the detail work so you fully understand what is required.

Before getting involved in any subdivision project, consider all the costs as well as the time required. As a rule of thumb, carefully estimate the time required from land acquisition to the first sale, and then double this time. After carefully estimating all development costs, add 50 percent to that figure. If the project does not look economically feasible based on these estimations, don't do it. It is seldom that initial time and cost estimates come close to the actual costs. Don't count on being lucky. Because of the many uncertainties involved in subdivision approval and land preparation, you should leave a sufficient profit margin to cover the worst contingencies.

> When I build something for somebody I always add $50 million or $60 million onto the price. My guys come in; they say it's going to cost $75 million. I say it's going to cost $127 million, and I build it for $100 million. Basically, I did a lousy job, but they think I did a great job."
>
> *Donald J. Trump*

The great cost in time and money of getting a subdivision approved opens up an entirely new field for investors with vision—wholesaling parcels with approvals for developers who want to build right now. The investor gets the proper zoning changes, has the engineering work completed, and obtains all approvals. This work can be worth much more than its cost to a developer. Keep in mind that payments must be made on the land while this approval work is taking place. Also, what is finally approved can often turn out to be much less desirable than what was originally contemplated. For instance, the density approved might be much less than what was originally requested. As an added risk, if the approvals are completed in a period of economic contraction, a far longer holding period than originally anticipated might be required. If the developer cannot meet the holding costs, a forced sale might be necessary.

Release Clauses

When you purchase property you are considering splitting, you should provide in your mortgage or trust deed a release clause or a provision for separate liens on the parcels. A release clause allows you to sell one parcel free and clear of the mortgage upon the payment of a specified sum of money. Without a release clause or a provision for separate liens, the only way you could sell one of the parcels would be by land contract. If someone wanted to pay cash, you could not give clear title unless you paid off the blanket lien covering all the parcels.

If you are the person selling you want to make certain that the amount required for release from the lien is as great or greater than the value of the parcel. As an example, four contiguous 10-acre lots were sold to a developer who put down a relatively low down payment. The developer's accepted offer set forth equal payments for the release of parcels from the lien. The developer then paid for the release of two parcels that had commercial zoning and walked away from the deal leaving the seller to foreclose on two parcels that were worth far less than what was owed on them. Because no deficiency judgment was possible in this instance, the seller was legally robbed.

Besides making certain the dollars are sufficient for release from the lien, sellers will often specify the order in which parcels must be released so that the less desirable parcels must be taken before the more desirable parcels.

Making Lots

Most subdivisions are divisions of land for single-family residential use. Location is of primary importance in a residential subdivision because location will be the strongest influence on the sale price of the lots.

> My name is Roger S. I build custom homes. I also subdivide small parcels. As an example, I recently purchased a 10-acre suburban wooded site and subdivided it into 22 large lots. I was required to put in a paved road that I dedicated to the county as well as underground wiring. Since there was no municipal water or sewer, homes would have their own wells and septic systems. When I had final approvals, my costs per lot totaled almost $40,000. I sold two lots to other builders (friends) at $50,000 each providing that they would build a 3000 square foot home with completion within six months. This price was below market value. As an additional inducement, I agreed to carry a second mortgage for the entire purchase price so they could really use my equity in obtaining their construction loans. In other words, I agreed to subordinate my lien to a construction loan. I also started construction of a home. The three large homes under construction created an interest in the area and I was able to sell 12 lots at an average price of $75,000. By selling these lots I was able to recoup more than my land development and finance costs and I had eight lots to build on myself plus the lot I had built a house on at zero cost.
>
> While I took a risk with the subordination loans to the other builders, it was a calculated risk. I knew they were good builders and were relatively stable. I also knew that the construction activity of three builders of fine homes in the subdivision would increase the attractiveness of the property.

Physical features such as trees, rocks, view, and slope will affect value. If land has a creek or spring and proper topography, there is the possibility of developing a lake. Lake developments, whether natural or constructed, offer exceptional investment opportunity for future residential development. Water-related property sells at a great premium. Some developers simply locate property and put in the lakes, after which they wholesale the parcel to another developer for final development.

RECREATIONAL SUBDIVISIONS

Recreational subdivisions are usually located within 100 to 250 miles of a major metropolitan area. Some unusual recreational clubs are "undivided interest subdivisions." Many have a clubhouse and 1000 or more camping or trailer sites. Buyers don't get their own site; they just own an interest in the whole, such as a one ten-thousandth interest, and the right to use an available site. The club sells lifetime memberships. While there are more members than sites, it is unlikely that all of the sites will be occupied at one time. While the profit potential sounds great, the sales costs can eat up even what was originally viewed as an obscene profit.

Own-Your-Own-Lot Mobile Home Parks

Lots are small, usually about 50 by 75 feet. Even with the loss of land for streets and public areas, developers may still obtain from 6 to 10 lots per acre. In many cases these lots sell for upwards of $100,000.

Some park owners have turned existing parks into condominiums. It is a way to sell the park quickly and obtain a premium price. Because of the immobile nature of today's installed mobile homes, the buyers are right there; they are the current renters. Everyone benefits in this type of sale. The park owner gets a premium price and the lot buyers, while possibly paying more each month toward rent, can now deduct the interest from their taxes, and they are protected from future rent gouging. The net effect for many of the buyers will be a lower true monthly cost. A word of caution, in many areas it is difficult if not impossible to get approval for condominium conversions of mobile home parks.

Breaking Up Resorts

Older resorts are generally poor investments for operators, who will often sell far below reproduction costs, with favorable terms. Over the last 30 years, a number of investors have been actively buying lake resorts and breaking them up. While a large resort operating at a loss might not be desirable, individual vacation cabins or condominium units appeal to a large market.

Some investors who break up resorts have had a continuing business for many years.

I'm Anderson. I've been breaking up vacation property in Wisconsin and Michigan for about 20 years. My operation is simple. I give a cash offer for resorts having at least 10 cottages. I look for basically sound structures with indoor plumbing but nothing fancy. My offers are cash offers subject to obtaining approvals for splitting up the property within a set time period. In this way, I am not at risk if there are any problems with a land division. I pay to have the paperwork handled by others. After I get my approvals, I upgrade cosmetically and put the units on the market. After I have my costs out, I will often sell the remaining units to local brokers at a wholesale price. I want to have cleared out on a project before I start another one. In this way my risk is readily manageable. The people who go broke in this business get greedy and let their risk get out of control.

Right now I am doing one resort about every 18 months. My son has come into the business with me and someday I hope my grandson will join us.

FARMS

Large farms can often be broken into several smaller farms or recreational land parcels with the resulting value of the pieces far exceeding the value of the whole. This is especially true for scenic land that really is marginal land for farm use. The increase in value in making small farms out of large farms is unrelated to the economics of farming, where larger is generally better. It is, instead, related to the demand for retirement or hobby farms as well as acreage. The buyers of these 20 acres and independence farms are not interested in productivity figures; they are generally in love with the idea of a rural lifestyle and beauty is of primary importance.

Trees and views are far more important than crop yields. In fact, the least desirable farmland can often be sold for the highest prices when broken up into smaller farm units.

I'm Frank. It's been 20 years since my first farm purchase, and I guess I must have purchased over 60 farms since then.

My formula now is:

1. Find farms of 120 acres or less within 40 miles of my home that have views, wooded land, or other features city people like. Water frontage and orchards are highly desirable features. (I avoid prime farmland.) I like farms where the buildings and 5 to 20 acres can be broken off into minifarms and the rest broken into 3- or 4-acreage parcels offering scenic homesites.

2. Get an option to buy for 30 days. (I don't pay more than $250 for an option.)

3. Check the county as to any problems in splitting the parcel as planned.

4. Have percolation tests made to determine if the homesites will support a septic system. (This is very important if the soil has a lot of clay.)

5. Approach all adjoining farms to see if the owners are interested in buying any of the cropland. I usually offer it at the going price and offer terms. In several cases I have sold the entire farm except for the buildings and from 5 to 20 acres around them to a neighbor. Keep in mind that if the land is good the neighbors will covet it.

6. If I can get an offer on the nonscenic part of the farm or if the purchase still makes sense without selling the cropland, I will exercise the option. I won't buy unless I feel I will make at least a 100 percent net profit on the purchase price.

7. My offers are generally low. I formerly offered 20 to 30 percent down and the balance in six months, but now I make cash offers because I have the money available. The advantage of cash offers is it makes a low offer hard to turn down.

8. After survey decisions, minimum improvements and approvals, I put the property on the market with ads and signs. I will pay a commission to brokers who sell. In fact, I will even pay a commission to a broker who finds me a farm to buy. While others worry about paying fees, my attitude is that I don't care what I pay or what others make as long as the net profit is there for me.

The following investor in farms has taken a different but equally profitable approach:

My name is Gopal R. About 15 years ago, I was selling real estate in a small city. I listed a small orchard with a mobile home on it. My ad brought in dozens of calls and the orchard was sold in three days. My best friend, who also worked at the same office, suggested that we make our own small orchards and that is what our partnership has been doing ever since. We buy orchards, generally orchards that are not economically productive because of overproduction in the particular variety of fruit or nut. We buy orchards rather than other farms because we know orchards have a particular attraction to people. When they see rows and rows of trees, it is different than looking at a plowed field. We make agricultural subdivisions by breaking the orchard into a number of parcels varying from 10 to 40 acres in size. The subdivision process for agricultural subdivisions is much simpler than for other subdivisions in our state. For the parcels that don't have a farmhouse, we put a new double wide, three-bedroom, two-bath mobile home on the site plus a large metal garage/workshop.

Our sales are to people my partner calls "wanna-bes," people who desire to return to a simpler agricultural life. A wanna-be is more interested in joy than in profit. We do, however, provide each of our purchasers with a farm consultant for eight, one-half-day periods to help them get started.

There are a lot of wanna-bes out there—to date we have turned 67 wanna-bes into farmers. Most of our buyers regard us as friends. They are primarily active retirees. Owning an orchard gives purpose to their lives. Wanna-bes have provided my partner and me with a good living. In a few years, I will probably retire. I already own my own orchard. I guess I'm a wanna-be, too.

> Note: Because of their desirability, a number of the mini-orchards Gopal sold have been resold at prices much more than the buyers originally paid.

COMMERCIAL CONDOMINIUMS

In the late 1960s and early 1970s some commercial condominiums had difficulty selling out. They were built at a time when the condominium concept was not widely accepted. In addition, the economy was relatively stable and major rent increases were not a serious threat to business.

Today's businesspeople are sophisticated in tax matters. They realize that ownership offers several tax advantages over renting. Besides interest and tax payments being deductible, ownership also offers the further tax benefit of depreciation. Past increases in commercial space rentals have made many realize the desirability of controlling their outlay for space requirements so as not to be at the mercy of any future inflationary economy. In addition, ownership is an investment that can, over the long run, be expected to increase in value and, as such, is a hedge against inflation.

> My name is Renee L. I inherited a six-store strip shopping center in an older commercial area. I had two vacancies in the building, one for over a year. One of my tenants mentioned that she would be interested in buying her portion of the building. This gave me the idea of turning my building into a condominium. I found that by offering good terms, I could bring in strong tenants who either purchased their unit or leased it with an option to buy. I was able to realize a net sale price 60 percent greater than I had been told my building was worth.
>
> Since this first condominium conversion, I have purchased four similar buildings at distress prices and turned them into commercial condomini-

ums. I have helped the neighborhoods by bringing in good tenants and I have enjoyed a respectable profit.

INDUSTRIAL PARKS

Industrial parks offer exceptional profit potential. Generally, they should be located close to good transportation arteries. A railroad siding is not required for many light-manufacturing plants. However, large water mains and good water pressure are essential for sprinkler systems. Possible heavy electrical demands require the availability of three-phase wiring. Adequate sewage disposal is also required. In some better industrial parks in Orange County, California, lots sold for more than $10 per square foot. This is almost $500,000 per acre. Many industrial park sites are not sold to industrial firms. They are sold to investors. A one-acre industrial site offers intriguing possibilities as a long-term investment.

RESIDENTIAL CONDOMINIUM CONVERSIONS

One of the greatest opportunities for small investors is in the condominium conversion area of subdivisions. In a conversion situation you are usually simply changing from rental units to units owned by the individual occupants.

Condominium conversions become popular in the mid-1970s. Housing could not be purchased in many areas for under $50,000. At the same time, apartment buildings could be purchased at perhaps $25,000 per unit. A person who purchased a 10-unit, two-bedroom building for $250,000 could get the required approvals and convert the existing building into 10 condominium units that could be readily sold for $50,000 each. If the buyer had purchased the building with $50,000 down, then the $250,000 profit would be a profit of 500 percent on the down payment. This may seem like a huge profit, but there have been thousands of condominium conversions with profits of this magnitude and greater. Because of the demand, as more people have realized the potential for conversions, apartment sale prices have soared but so have the prices of condominium units. Substantial profits are still being made.

In areas such as Boulder, Colorado, where there is growth control, conversion can be especially attractive because of strong buyer demand for a very limited number of available units.

In some communities, there are exemptions or short cuts for approval of small condominium conversions. Some developers in such communities target small apartments such as four- or eight-unit buildings for conversion to condominiums.

For a successful condominium conversion, it is necessary to be able to offer the buyer occupancy. In a few areas tenants cannot be evicted simply because the owner wants to sell the unit, more commonly, state law requires a longer notice to tenants to vacate and/or the right of the tenant to buy the unit at the most favorable price and at terms the unit will be offered to the public. The result is that their tenants are a ready pool of buyers for a great many of the units, depending upon the local rental market and financing available. Nationally, around 20 percent of renters become owners of the units when they are offered for sale.

If you are interested in a possible condominium conversion, check with your local planning agency to find out if there are impediments to conversion. Some planning departments wish to maintain their stock of rental units and have restrictions for condominium conversions that make conversions difficult if not economically impossible.

Check all the requirements for condominium conversion. You might want to check owners of other units who have gone through the process as to problems and recommendations for both an attorney familiar with the legal process for condominium conversion and an engineer to prepare plans and descriptions if building plans are not available.

In your analysis, you should be talking with real estate agents as to expected sales prices. You will want to choose a marketing agent who has had experience in marketing condominium conversions.

For a fee, a number of firms handle the paperwork on condo conversions and prepare the package for local and/or state approval. A flexible mind will allow you to see conversion opportunities that others ignore. These opportunities are all around us. There are still opportunities available.

One unusual condominium conversion involved a parking garage near Beacon Hill in Boston. The area's desirability had risen and attracted many younger professionals (gentrification). New purchasers had expensive cars, but many of the older homes did not offer garages or parking space. Developers purchased a commercial garage and turned it into a condominium selling spaces for around $12,000 each. The developers made one error. They did not research the demand. They quickly sold all of their units. While a good profit resulted, they failed to maximize this profit. Reportedly, within a year, units were being resold in the $100,000 range.

Condotels

Some motels and hotels have begun converting to condominiums. They call themselves *condotels*. The management will rent the unit as a regular motel or hotel unit when the owner is not there, and the owner shares the gross receipts with the management. These units have been primarily in resort areas. The success of this concept has been spotty, but some developers have had very successful projects.

CURRENT TRENDS IN CONDOMINIUM CONVERSIONS

Some investors specialize in buying an apartment building, getting the condominium approvals, and selling it. In some cases they can use options and get the approvals during the option period, but this is usually not possible because of time delays in the approval process. The investors can sell the buildings readily with the conversion approvals. In this manner large profits are possible.

If you are interested in any type of condominium conversion, I recommend you contact your state real estate department, which normally handles state approvals. You should also check with the city or county planning departments as to requirements and/or restrictions. You should fully understand the procedures required for conversion. You might find that there are different requirements for cooperatives than condominiums. In some cases additional expenses such as garages may be required, or the local requirements may totally preclude an economical conversion. If you are uncertain as to whether or not approval for conversion will be granted, try to tie the property up with an option while you seek approval.

Fully analyze the market for converted units. Consider whether or not they will be salable to the present tenants and what the individual units will sell for. Then, if the profit potential justifies the risks, go ahead.

For any condominium or condominium conversion consider covenants, conditions, and restrictions (CC&Rs). An attorney specializing in real estate can help you in this area. CC&Rs that meet the needs of other condominium projects might not be applicable to your project. CC&Rs are rules binding on each owner concerning, for example, the use of the premises and the homeowner association organization and operation.

Stock Cooperatives

A *condominium* is an actual subdivision with one property broken up into small units with individual owners. A *stock cooperative* is not truly a subdivision in that the cooperative corporation takes title to the entire building. Each stockholder has rights to occupy a unit but doesn't really own it. There will probably be more buyer resistance to a cooperative than to a condominium. A cooperative has dangers connected with singular ownership. Since there is only one mortgage, if several owners fail to pay their share, the mortgage covering the entire building might be foreclosed.

Cooperative Conversions

Some owners of cooperatives have increased the value of their units by converting the cooperative to condominiums. Because of public perception, cooperative values are likely to be less than for similar condominiums. Resident cooperation is necessary for a cooperative to condominium conversion.

Time-Shares

Time-shares are interval ownership subdivisions. The owners normally buy the use of a resort area condominium unit for one week or more per year. The buyer is thus assured of a place to vacation at a guaranteed cost. While time-share development can be profitable, buying a time-share is a poor investment. Very few have appreciated in value, and resale of time-share units is extremely difficult. Often the time-share management will buy a block of units in a project developed by others. The management sets prices on the units so that the gross profit is at least 300 percent. For example, if a unit is purchased for $100,000, the management might try to sell 50 weeks at prices that average $8100 each. Naturally, some weeks are more desirable and will sell for more than the average, while undesirable periods will sell for far less than the average. Usually the operators leave two weeks free for general refurbishing of the units. The owners of a week can use it, or the management will rent it for them.

Many operators offer programs for vacation trades. In fact, the trade possibilities at exotic places are used as a major sales benefit. Time-shares affiliated with Resort Condominium International (800) 338-7777 or Interval International (305) 668-1867 offer worldwide exchange privileges, but don't think you can exchange an off-season week at Lake Muck for a condominium on the French Riviera during summer season. The properties are graded and exchanged accordingly.

While the markup of the units may sound high, you should consider that time-share developers must make the payments until the units are sold, some weeks are very undesirable and may take a long time to sell, and these sales involve heavy promotional and sales expenses, including 50 sales commissions for each unit. Many time-share promoters have gone bankrupt.

Several developers are offering quarterly time-shares in order to avoid the high sale costs of weekly time-share sales. For example, each purchaser buys a three-month period. The period is one month in the prime season, one month in a less desirable season, and the third month in the least desirable season. A vacation area might offer packages of:

1. January, May, September
2. February, June, October
3. March, July, November
4. April, August, December

In this way, there are only four sales commissions to pay. These longer periods appeal to more affluent buyers who have as much use of their quarter interest as many owners get from their vacation homes.

One group of 36, two-bedroom units with tennis courts and pools sold out in three months at $39,500 per one-quarter share. This translated to $158,000 for units that would have otherwise sold in the $90,000 range. This is a far lower markup than is found for weekly time-shares. This may explain why the one-quarter-share has had good buyer reception.

Because time-shares are difficult to resell, the average resale price is at about a 40 percent discount from original cost. Discounts of 60 percent to 75 percent are not that uncommon. This creates an interesting opportunity for a purchaser buying for his or her own use. A number of brokers handle time-share resales, although you will also see for-sale-by-owner ads.

Assemblage

The opposite of subdividing is assemblage, the process of assembling several small contiguous parcels to make one large parcel. In fully developed areas it is difficult to find any large parcels. While smaller parcels are usually relatively more valuable, large parcels can in some circumstances be worth far more than their separate parts.

12

Trading Up to Wealth

No man but feels more of a man in the world if he has a bit of ground that he can call his own. However small it is on the surface, it is four thousand miles deep and that is a very handsome property.

Charles Dudley Warner, 1871

Exchanging goes back to earliest times. It is the oldest form of commerce. By giving up something desired less, it is possible to acquire something desired more. While some may regard barter as primitive, it has been rediscovered as an exciting real estate technique useful in our society.

TAX ADVANTAGES

One reason for the modern interest in exchanging is the Internal Revenue Code. Exchanging allows an owner to defer paying taxes on a gain. While tax evasion is illegal, tax avoidance is simply good business practice. Exchanging allows a tax-free transaction of getting rid of undesirable property and acquiring desired property.

An outright sale can result in a taxable gain, but Section 1031 of the Internal Revenue Code allows a tax-free exchange between like-for-like properties. What this means is that real property that has been held for investment, trade, or business can be traded for other real property held for investment, trade, or business. Real property must be traded for real property and personal property must be traded for personal property to qualify as a tax-free exchange. A tax-free exchange is possible even though the character of the property exchanged is not similar. For example, vacant land can be traded for an apartment building.

Since a personal residence is not held for investment, trade, or business, it does not qualify for a tax-free exchange. It is possible to change the character of your residence so that it would qualify. If you move out of your residence and rent it, it becomes an investment property. Some exchange experts advise that a residence must be rented a minimum of one year to qualify for a 1031 exchange, but consult with a CPA or tax attorney before you consider such an exchange. There would be very few instances where owners would want to exchange their personal residence because of the generous exemptions from taxation provided when a personal residence is sold (See Chapter 3).

Property of dealers will not qualify for tax-free exchanges if the property has been acquired or developed by the dealers for resale. It may be subject to regular income tax, even though it is traded rather than sold.

If a person would have a significant taxable gain by selling property and would be reinvesting the proceeds in another property, then they would probably want to do so with a tax-free exchange. If they had sold the property, they would have been taxed on their gain, but by using an exchange they have the total sale proceeds to reinvest. Discuss exchanges with a real estate attorney to make certain your exchange is tax-exempt and you understand fully the legal ramifications.

TYPES OF EXCHANGE

Exchanges fall into three basic categories.

Direct Exchange

Two parties agreeing to exchange properties is very rare. It is unlikely that you will find someone with a property you want who will take a property you wish to dispose of in exchange.

Three-Party Exchange

This is the most common exchange. It involves A, an owner who wishes to sell, but also wishes to own another property; B, a buyer who wishes to buy A's property; and C, an owner of property that A desires. B buys C's property to trade for A's property. C gets cash for his or her property. B gets A's property that he desired in exchange for the property purchased from C.

Both of the transactions would be part of the same closing. Everyone gets what he or she wants. For the transaction to be tax-free to an exchanger, the exchanger must never have control of funds involved in that exchange.

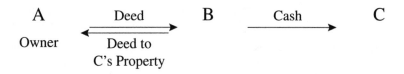

What often happens is that C will not want cash, but will want a tax-free exchange and desires property held by D. In which case, B would buy D's property, trade it to C for C's property, and then trade it to A for A's property. The exchange could become more complicated if D didn't want to sell but wanted property held by E. Instead of three parties, some exchanges expand to complicated transactions involving a great many owners. There are real estate brokers who specialize in complicated exchanges.

Delayed Exchange

A *delayed exchange,* also known as a *Starker Exchange,* allows an owner to sell a property and have the proceeds held in escrow for a property not yet chosen. The seller cannot have control of the funds. The seller must identify the property to be purchased within 45 days of closing and the exchange property must be purchased within 180 days of closing.

By use of a delayed exchange, you can sell your property while you have the ready-and-willing buyer and then locate what you really want.

Boot

Not all exchanges are tax-free. If one person receives "boot," the exchange is fully taxable. Boot is unlike property given to even out a trade. Although *boot* is usually money, it can be personal property such as an automobile or jewels. Assume you were to trade a property that you own free and clear worth $200,000 for a property also held free and clear worth $150,000. If the other party were to give you $50,000 in cash to even up the trade, this boot would be taxable to you. One way to avoid a tax liability would be to have the other party use the $50,000 to buy a second property, and then trade two properties for your one property.

If one party to an exchange gets debt relief because the property traded had a greater indebtedness than the new property acquired, then the amount of debt relief is also considered boot and will be taxable as capital gains. As an example, assume you own a property on which you owe $50,000 and trade it even for a property that is free and clear of debt. The trade has resulted in your being relieved of a $50,000 debt, which is treated as boot and is taxable.

> My name is Steve J. After I got out of service in 1945, I started farming in an arid area of the Antelope Valley in northern Los Angeles County. I accumulated 3000 acres over a period of time. All of it was purchased under $100 per acre and much of it was for $5 to $15 per acre. Even with the amount of acreage I had, farming was still marginal.
>
> Around 1970 I was offered $1000 per acre for my entire farm from a land sales firm. I approached a consultant for advice. He estimated my total tax liability in excess of $1,000,000. He then asked what I would do with the money. I told him I didn't really want to retire and my two sons wanted to be farmers, so I guess I would buy another farm.
>
> He then asked me where I really would want a farm if I could have a farm anywhere I wanted. I told him in Oregon. I would like a large cattle, crop, and apple operation like I've seen in some of the farm magazines. He sent my sons and me to Oregon on a look-and-find expedition. We found a large farm operation that had everything I could wish for. It could be purchased in the $3 million range. We set it up as a trade. The land developer built a new house on the property to my specifications and traded it to me free and clear. I also received $200,000 in cash for operating expenses (this was taxable). My net savings from the advice I received was approximately $1,000,000.

Any property you trade for must make sense. If you would not buy it at the price and terms available, you should think twice about buying it in an exchange. Don't let your desire to defer taxes lead you into a stupid trade.

> My name is Jason C. I parlayed a few thousand dollars into an equity of over one-half million dollars in a series of three land purchases and exchanges.
>
> On my last sale, I had decided to use a delayed exchange. Unfortunately one of the owners of a property I wished to buy refused to sign the sale agreement. Since the period to designate a property was almost up, I made the worst investment decision of my life. I designated a tract of land valued

at $2,000,000. The seller would carry back the difference with no payments for one year. Several "experts" had assured me that the property was a steal and could be split and sold for a significant profit within a matter of months. Well, my experts were wrong. I could not sell the property, I could not make the payments when they became due although I used up my savings in trying to hold on to the property. I had a tiger by the tail and the tiger won. I ended up losing my equity and my savings because I wanted so much to avoid paying Uncle Sam taxes on my gain.

OTHER ADVANTAGES IN EXCHANGING

Taxation isn't the only reason for an exchange. People exchange to solve problems. By exchange they are able to get rid of a set of circumstances they are not happy with for a set of circumstances they desire. Exchange can solve a great number of problems.

Depreciation
Exchanging allows you to change the ratio of land to improvements, which can allow greater depreciation. For example, suppose you own a property worth $100,000 that has a structure on it worth only $20,000. You would be limited to depreciation of the improvements, since the land cannot be depreciated. If you were to trade for a property also worth $100,000 but with improvements worth $90,000, you could depreciate from 90 percent of your original cost basis. Since depreciation is only a paper expense, it could shelter other income from taxation.

Geography
Some people exchange for geographical reasons. Assume a person who owns an apartment building in New York wishes to retire to Florida. Trading for an apartment building in Florida would fulfill the need without the necessity of a taxable sale.

Income Gain
Some people trade to gain income. For instance, raw land, which is a cash drain because it has expenses but no income, can be traded for apartments or commercial property offering a spendable cash flow. On the other hand, some people are willing to trade income property for raw land since they are more interested in long-term appreciation than present income, and raw land tends to have greater long-term appreciation possibilities than income property.

Pyramiding Property

Many other investors use exchange to pyramid their property. "Bullish" investors recommend this method strongly, especially for young investors. Smaller properties, even when purchased with low down payments, can after a few years' appreciation result in a substantial equity. By trading up, you increase the value of the property you own as well as your indebtedness. Assume you traded a property worth $200,000 on which you owe $100,000 for a property worth $700,000 with a $600,000 indebtedness. While your equity in the property is the same, you are in a much better position as to appreciation. An increase in value of 50 percent in seven years with the $200,000 property would have increased your equity from $100,000 to $200,000. For the $700,000 property the same 50 percent increase in value would now give you a $450,000 equity.

Of course, trading up does lower your percentage equity in a property, and there are risks associated with this practice. A high vacancy factor or unexpected expenses could result in a large negative cash flow. A highly leveraged investment is a gamble on the future. If you could not take the loss, don't take the risk.

Consolidation of Property

Exchanging also allows consolidation of property. A number of smaller properties can be exchanged for one large property that is easier to manage. On the other hand, some owners are interested in diversifying. By obtaining several properties, they can reduce their risk, especially in the case of a large property with only one or two tenants.

Fewer Managerial Problems

Some people exchange to divest themselves of management problems. An apartment house with many problems could be exchanged for raw land that requires no real management.

Salability

A property not readily salable might be exchanged for a more salable property. In such a case the exchange is simply an intermediate step toward a desired conclusion.

Avoiding a Realized Loss

There are times when an owner exchanges in order to avoid realizing a loss. Just as there is no realized loss for a stock market investor until the stock is sold, an owner of real property does not suffer a loss until the real property is sold. Some people psychologically do not want to admit the loss. We see this in the stock market when stockowners hold stock that has gone down for many years, hoping it will increase in value enough so they can break even. Even though there are other stocks they would prefer, they still hold on. When the same thing happens in real estate, trading is a solution. A trade allows owners to get into circumstances they prefer without admitting the loss.

> My name is Harold. I wanted to purchase a lot owned by a corporation. The price quoted to me by a corporate officer was far in excess of the current market value. The corporation had purchased the lot several years previously, after it had been announced that a major shopping center was to be built in the area. The shopping center was never built, and land prices, having risen on the speculation of great development, fell.
>
> During a meeting I discovered the corporation did not want to show a significant loss by the sale. It was a fairly small corporation and the loss would upset some of the stockholders. They preferred to hold on to the lot until it was worth what they had paid. I recognized this as an ideal exchange opportunity. I was holding a number of second mortgages on property I had previously sold. These mortgages, if sold, would be worth far less than their face value. My offer was to trade several of these mortgages at face value for the lot. It was accepted. The corporation got its price, although over a period of years, and I got the lot. The trade met the needs of both parties. Since mortgages are regarded as personal property, it wasn't a 1031 tax-free exchange.

More people would be interested in exchanging if they understood it. People usually want cash in order to purchase something else. If they can get that something else directly, then there is really no reason for a sale.

WHAT YOU CAN EXCHANGE

You can trade just about anything—even junk land that has no value or serves no real purpose. You can trade the land and keep the building as a lessee or even trade the building and keep the land as a lessor. In some states mineral rights are considered real property. You can trade all the mineral rights to a property or perhaps half the mineral rights. Whatever has value can be traded.

Personal property can readily be traded, but remember that personal property cannot be traded for real property on a tax-free exchange since the trade is not like-for-like. This problem comes up in trading furnished units. The furniture is considered taxable boot unless the property traded for includes furniture of the same value.

PROBLEMS TO WATCH FOR

Don't take the word of another as to what a property is worth. Even if the other person is an appraiser hired by the owner. It is only good business to personally check out comparable values in the area. If in doubt, you should seek the aid of your own professional appraiser. If taxes are a consideration in a trade, you should seek the advice of an attorney or a CPA who is knowledgeable in exchanges. Because of the specialized nature of exchanging, only a few attorneys and CPAs are really knowledgeable in this area. Most will refer you to a competent specialist.

13
CHAPTER

Optioning Your Way to Success

Endeavor vigorously to increase your property.

Horace

An option gives you the positive right to purchase or lease property at an agreed price and terms for a stated period of time. If you want the property, you can exercise your option and buy or lease it. If you decide you don't wish to buy or lease it, you don't have to. By failing to exercise the option, you only lose the price you paid for the option. An option, by giving you time, allows you to presently take advantage of a favorable situation even though you may lack the capital to purchase or lease the property at the time of the option.

An option provides the optionee (the person getting the option) with fantastic leverage. Just a few dollars can give you rights to very expensive property. As the optionee you should endeavor to obtain an option for the longest term and the lowest consideration possible. Of course, you also want the option to provide as favorable sales or lease terms as possible.

When you consider the bottom line—to make money in real estate—control is what is important. To control property, you need not own it. An option gives you control with the least investment.

CONSIDERATION

To have a valid purchase option, the optionee (potential buyer) must actually give consideration to the optionor (owner). Consideration is anything of value. While usually money, it could be any item or right having value. It is not enough to merely state in the option that it is given for consideration; the consideration must actually change hands. While real estate professionals frequently talk in terms of an option amount related to the purchase price, such as 5 percent of the price for a six-month option, don't worry about formulas. You are dealing with people interested in selling their property. For an option you should pay the minimum amount necessary. The option price is real risk capital because, if the option is not exercised, the price will be lost.

FINDING OPTION OPPORTUNITIES

You can find option opportunities at any time but options are far easier to obtain in a slow sales or rental market than when there is little buyer or tenant demand.

You can use the telephone to locate more option opportunities than you can possibly take advantage of. When looking for option opportunities, begin with the classified ads of owners offering options in their house-for-rent ads. (In some papers "lease options" is a separate category.) Also, look for homes for rent where the owner's telephone number is out of the area. Such an owner is usually highly motivated to sell but is renting because of the need for current income. Call on single-family homes for rent and ask the owner if he or she would consider a lease option. A great many landlords are landlords by necessity, so you will likely get a positive response on 10 to 15 percent of your calls. The slower the resale market, the greater interest you will encounter in your proposals.

For commercial and industrial lease options look for problem properties and those with a high percentage of vacancies and/or long-term vacancies. Properties in need of maintenance and/or repair are also likely candidates for options. Also consider property that has been on the market for an inordinate period of time. Owners of such properties are generally willing to talk to you.

Another source of lease option property is to advertise what you are looking for under a Wanted to Rent category in the classified ads. As an example:

3 BR Needed
Prefer west side with 2 baths, double
garage and basement. Would like an
option to buy. Can pay up to $1400/mo.
Call _____ at _____

Such an ad will bring a response. By advertising, you put the owner in a position of trying to sell you on his or her property. While you should immediately ask about the purchase options, don't go into lease terms on the telephone.

NEGOTIATING THE OPTION

Some unethical dealers will obtain purchase options by use of subterfuge. They will offer to buy property for cash. While their offers will be low, the all-cash nature of the offer will often result in acceptance. They normally ask for a long escrow period, such as six months. The reason given is generally either that an estate has to close or they have property being sold in another state that will not close until that date. The buyer only makes a small deposit, such as $1000, with the explanation he or she won't have more money until the other event takes place. A clause in the purchase agreement provides that the seller's sole remedy in event of default of the buyer is the forfeiture of the buyer's deposit (liquidated damages clause).

What the buyer really has is an option to buy for what would generally be regarded as a low option price. It will be exercised only if the optionee finds a buyer for more money before the option expires.

This technique is pure deceit and cannot be condoned. Besides avoiding such tactics, be on the alert that they could be used on you. Don't tie up your property with a low-earnest-money deposit unless the deposit is to be increased to a stated amount within a reasonable period of time. Be alert for extremely long escrow periods. If the escrow period is longer than normal, the deposit should likewise be larger than normal.

A purchase option or lease option allows you to control property with the lowest possible cash outlay. As the optionee, you want the lowest possible option costs, the longest possible period in which to exercise the option, and, if a lease option, the greatest possible percentage of your lease payments applied to the purchase price. In addition, you will want any option price to apply toward the total price.

You want the right to sublease in your lease option. In this way, you can sublease for a higher rent and give your tenants an option to buy at a higher option price. Check the credit of your tenants so that you know they will be able to buy and structure the option with option price paid in advance that will make the exercise of the option likely.

When you use a lease option as landlord/seller, I suggest that you have an option to purchase separate from the lease. The reason is that a court might determine that your tenant is really a buyer with an equitable interest and not a tenant. This would preclude a quick eviction for nonpayment of rent.

While you may not achieve all your wishes, you must strive for them during negotiation.

In a lease with an option to purchase, of critical importance is how much of the rent shall apply to the purchase price. While an owner may balk at an option price reduction of $1000, the owner might readily accede to a rent application to the purchase price from 30 percent to 50 percent or even 100 percent, which would far exceed the $1000 reduction on purchase price. Keep in mind that you can often give in on a highly visible emotional figure such as sale price and can more than gain it back in the option terms.

If you negotiate an option price above the current fair market value, you will need appreciation in value to make any exercise of the option an advantageous purchase. You would likely be getting a purchase option at no additional cost if you are receiving it as part of a lease that you want. What you are in fact negotiating is the right to profit should the property undergo exceptional appreciation during the option period. However, it would not be wise to pay any significant additional fee for the mere possibility of significant appreciation unless the option period is long enough so the likelihood of such appreciation turns the betting odds in your favor.

> My name is Amat R. I work for a major corporation that tends to transfer employees on a regular basis. I have a simple technique of investing. It is not original, as I learned it from another company employee. I try to lease the best house I can afford in a desirable area. I want a lease for three years with an escape clause that allows me to get out of the lease if I am transferred. I also insist on an option to purchase anytime during the lease. While I try for market value, I will accept up to 10 percent above of what I evaluate market value to be. My results? In the last 15 years, I have had four such options, three of which I have exercised and then resold. My profit to date—$135,000. By a simple option, I obtain the advantage of possible appreciation in value.

You can offer a sweetener, such as rent paid in advance for one year, as an incentive for an owner to give you an option to purchase with a lease. Before you agree to pay out rent for one year, you will want to ascertain the condition of the owner's title by obtaining a property profile. For example, you don't want to be giving an owner going-away money if he is facing imminent foreclosure.

Consider an extension to the option period if you are negotiating for an option to buy or lease. You don't want to be in the position of deciding to buy or lease when you are almost certain you have another buyer or tenant, but it isn't down in writing yet. Consider the inclusion of the following extension agreement.

> This option may be extended for [three months], [up to two periods of six months each] by delivering to [name] the sum of [$], [$ for each extension] anytime prior to the expiration of this option (or extension thereafter). In the event the option is exercised, the consideration for any extension(s) shall apply in full to the purchase price.

In any option or lease option you enter into, consider the inclusion of a mandatory arbitration clause such as:

> Lessor and lessee agree that any disputes arising under this [lease] [lease option] shall be arbitrated in accordance with the applicable laws of the state of [name] as supplemented by the then current rules of the American Arbitration Association. Judgments on the arbitration award rendered may be entered in any court having jurisdiction of the parties.

You will likely also want a clause specifically giving you as lessee the right to record the lease, lease option, or a memorandum of lease or lease option. This will protect you with respect to later buyers, lessees, or lenders.

Don't just go out looking to buy options; procure them selectively. If you feel a property can be turned at a profit, an option is the logical move for an investor with limited capital. The downside risk of buying an option is limited to the price paid for the option. The upside profit potential is limited only by what a buyer will pay.

It is often possible to tie up a number of properties by buying one property, and, as a condition of the offer, obtaining an option to purchase additional properties when an owner has a number of lots (or similar properties of any type). You could buy one lot with an option on 10 more if an owner has many lots for sale. Your options would require you to exercise the options at set time limits and, perhaps, in a set order. Failure to exercise an option would result in termination of the other options. This provision will make sense to an owner and will likely get you the options. For example, the option could require you to exercise the option on the second lot within 90 days of closing of the first lot, the third lot option within another 90 days, and so on.

Why ask for these options if you only need one lot? The answer is control. You now have control on 10 additional lots at no cost. You would exercise the options if you are able to sell additional lots. If not, your cost is only a little effort. You are likely to obtain control of a large group of properties by setting forth a reasonable period for the exercise of each option. Many builders use this procedure to ensure a lot supply at the same price. You can use it to make money on property you don't own. Again, it is control that counts.

Options on Commercial and Industrial Property

Options to buy vacant commercial or industrial property can be extremely valuable. If you can procure good tenants at long-term leases, the property becomes readily salable to investors. Good tenants not only make a property more salable, they can increase the value to the point where you as optionee might be able to buy the property without using any of your own money.

> An optionee found a national tenant who wanted a 20-year lease. Based on the financial strength of the tenant and the agreed rental, the optionee was able to borrow enough on the building not only to cover its full purchase price but also actually to have cash left over. What happened was that the lease so increased the value of the property that a first and second loan totaling 60 percent of the appraised value was actually more than 100 percent of what the optionee was required to pay as the purchase price.

By meeting with national franchisors, you can get to know their requirements. If you can get an option on property that satisfies their needs, a profit is likely. The franchisors normally are happy to work with anyone who can help them obtain desirable locations.

> Some optionees, once they obtain what they consider a good option, will try to put together a group of investors to buy the property as a limited partnership. The optionee will act as the general partner, taking a piece of the investment for his or her efforts.

> With an option it is possible to list the property for sale with a real estate agent. Even after paying a commission, a good profit is possible when the option price is right. You should realize that an option is worthless once it has expired. Once you know you will not be exercising an option, you should be advertising the option or the property for sale. You can do this because you control it with your option.

> My name is Juan J. I am a landscape gardener. Several years ago I leased a house on two acres of commercial land. I needed the commercial zoning to

store my equipment and supplies. The owner agreed to give me a purchase
option for the three-year lease.

Before the lease expired, I asked the owner about a renewal of my lease.
The owner indicated he would not renew because he had other plans. I
then contacted a commercial real estate broker and showed him my lease
option.

The broker listed the property for sale. The owner got very agitated by
the broker's for-sale sign. The owner offered me $5000 for my option.
Based on what the broker had told me, I refused.

The broker sold the property and I ended up with a net of almost
$200,000. The broker had used what he called a double escrow to pass title
from the owner to our buyer.

What had happened was that what had been a fair-priced option became
a bargain price because of changes in the area.

My advices to others, whenever you rent any property, try for a purchase
option. It just might be worth a fortune and you can get it included for free.

Often owners who don't have their property officially for sale will give options at a price they consider desirable. While the price may be high at
present, if the option is for a long enough period of time, such as one year,
inflation as well as specific economic factors of an area could turn it into a
bargain by the time an option is exercised. For instance, raw land options
are usually readily obtainable. Slight changes in the economy can have
great effects on land value.

I know of several investors who buy options in the area of any large
new development as soon as announcements are made, usually at prices
much higher than the property value before the announcement. Their premium prices may become bargains. For example, when Atlantic City made
gambling legal, some investors purchased options for what many considered
ridiculous sale prices. The owners felt that they would be instant millionaires if the options were exercised and were eager to accept the option consideration. While the optionors became millionaires, so did the optionees.
Although we don't often have a situation like Atlantic City, a new college,
hospital, factory, or shopping center all offer potential for option profit.

Zoning Changes Increasing Property Value

Some investors use options to tie up a property rather than buy it. They
then add value by either rezoning or getting approvals for desirable uses.
They then sell the package to a developer.

My name is Al J. I don't buy anything, but I cause a lot to happen. I tie up
property with options, get zoning changes if necessary, arrange for engi-

neering work and get all approvals, and then sell to someone who will develop the property. I present a complete package.

I specialize in residential subdivision property. I have a number of builders I work with, and I usually know the project is going to be sold as soon as approvals are in hand. One risk is a change in the economy where I get stuck with a lot of work for ready-to-build subdivisions that no one wants. I minimize this risk by providing option extensions for a total period of four years.

I also reduce my risk by avoiding communities where I have to fight for approval because of a no-growth attitude. Life is too short to have to fight public opinion. I don't want to try and force anything on anyone.

I occasionally make a mistake, and it can be costly because with engineering, option fees, legal work, etc., my costs for a 100-lot subdivision could be $300,000 or even more, and this is without any work on the land. If it is denied, the $300,000 is gone. Because of the risk, I won't touch a subdivision in which I don't envision at least a $2.50 profit on every dollar I place at risk.

My tactics work for me. I get approval on 80 percent of the projects I start, and I exercise options on over 90 percent of these.

Options for Trading

You can use options you have as trading pieces. For example, if you have some interesting purchase options you are unlikely to exercise due to other demands on your resources, you can use options as part or all of the down payment to buy another property. The options can be particularly attractive to those who have the resources to exercise them and can visualize the benefits to themselves.

Tenant Options

Landlords frequently gave options to purchase to their tenants as part of the lease. The option price is usually set quite high. The landlords never expected values to climb as they have in the past decade. Often these options were for long periods of time such as five years. Tenants with leases such as these were in a position to take advantage of a bargain.

In an appreciating market you should consider subleasing when you have a long-term lease/purchase option, such as three years. In this way you can put the property on the market in, say, two years and your sale price would reflect this two-year appreciation. In such a situation, a lease option would be interesting even if you couldn't get enough rent to cover your lease payments. For example, assume your lease payments on a three-year lease with option to buy were $1200 per month. If you could only sublease for $1000 per month, you would have a negative cash flow of $200 each month. Over three years, your rental loss would be $7200. If your purchase option was at market price, and the price was $250,000, a 10 percent annual appreciation would offer you $75,000 appreciation (without compounding the appreciation). While you normally should avoid negative cash flows, in a rapidly appreciating marketplace, you might want to consider such a situation. While we don't know what future appreciation will be, if history is any indicator, values will rise.

OPTIONS TO RENT

Options to rent open up an entirely different area of profit potential. For these options you should look for rentals that have been vacant for some time. Usually these will be stores, offices, or industrial properties. While sale options are frequently difficult to obtain, options to rent are easy to obtain for periods of from 30 to 60 days. Owners often desperately want a tenant and are willing to tie up the property for one or two months at a very low option fee.

I recommend you try for an option to rent for a one-year period at as low a price as you can negotiate, plus options to renew for at least two five-year periods at stated rentals. The option should also allow you the right to sublet or assign the lease. After the owner has agreed to the option, ask that an option to purchase be included. In this way a purchase option can often be obtained without additional consideration.

Once you have the option to lease, get to work looking for a tenant at a higher rental than you have agreed to pay. In some cases this profit can be substantial. It can increase each year if you are paying a flat rental figure and your tenant's rental increases with the Consumer Price Index.

As previously mentioned, one very effective way to find tenants is to go through the Yellow Pages and look for categories of tenants who could use your space. Simply call each listing in each applicable category and ask if the business can use the location at a desirable rent. Although this method is time-consuming, you will not only rent property, you will also get many leads for people looking for other properties as well. While calling on the phone eight hours a day, day after day, is tedious work, it can pay off.

There are people who look for shopping centers and office buildings in trouble. They will offer to lease all the vacant space on a long-term lease at an extremely low rental, usually just enough to allow the owner to make the payments on the mortgage. If an owner is desperate, he or she will accept this type of arrangement. The lessee is not a thief, since he or she is taking a high-risk gamble. While the owner could not lease this space or keep it leased, the lessee is betting that he or she will be successful in subleasing it. This type of arrangement requires a strong financial position as well as a great deal of courage and ability.

Not Exercising the Option

If you decide not to exercise an option but would exercise it if the price or terms were different, you should keep in mind that while an option price gives you the right to buy or lease at that price, you are not precluded from attempting to renegotiate the price or terms. Your chances of renegotiating would be affected by the owner's motivation to sell or lease.

Granting Options

While as a buyer you may want to buy options because of the huge profit potential they offer, you should be hesitant about giving options as an owner. Just as when buying an option you considered possible changes that would increase the value, consider the possibility of something happening of which you are not aware. You should check to see if other owners in the immediate neighborhood have been offered money for options. If they have, then the optionee knows of or hopes for something of which you are not aware.

If you as an owner are going to give an option for a long period of time such as several years, I suggest that the option be tied to the Consumer Price Index so that inflation does not lower your real price. If you have a purchase agreement to buy a property that you intend to lease, you can recoup part or all of your down payment by looking for a lease-option tenant before you have closed your purchase. The option money you receive can significantly reduce the cash needed for your purchase.

Many prospective buyers have good incomes and significant down payments but have problems such as credit that precludes them from becoming homeowners. If you advertise a home under lease-option you will get far more responses than if you offered it for sale.

An advantage of lease options, besides ease in selling is that tenants are not as concerned on price as they are payments. A premium price can usually be obtained with a lease option.

You want a lease option that will be exercised. You can increase this likelihood by requiring that a significant option fee be applied to purchase as well as having a percentage of rent apply toward purchase. The greater the option fee, the greater the likelihood of the option being exercised.

While selling using lease options can be profitable and relatively easy, there is a problem of capital. If your down payment is more than the option price received, you will have reduced your ready capital for future investments. Of course, your rent payments must equal your loan payments plus taxes and insurance or you will have a monthly negative cash flow.

While you want a separate fee when you give an option in a lease you don't want to pay an option fee when you are the one leasing the property. The rent is considered legal consideration for the option to purchase.

Right of First Refusal

If you lease, you should of course try for a purchase option, which can be frosting on the cake in the form of another profit potential. However, if you are the landlord, resist giving a tenant a purchase option as you could be giving away appreciation. You can, however, safely give a right of first refusal.

Under a right of first refusal, the tenant does not have the right to buy if you don't want to sell. However, if you want to sell to a buyer, before you can complete the sale, you must go to the tenant and offer the property to the tenant at the same price and terms you are willing to accept from the other buyer. You are not giving up anything when you give a right of first refusal.

Options, if used properly, can result in great profit. They avoid the down payment and risk of a purchase while offering profit potential by leasing or sale. Again ownership isn't necessary to reap the profit; only control is. Additional uses of options are included in Chapter 14.

14

CHAPTER

Special Situations

You make money in real estate doing what other people say can't be done.

Frank Curry, 1980

IMAGINATION AND DETERMINATION PAY OFF

William Zeckendorf, a legendary New York investor and developer, made millions of dollars because he was able to see opportunities where others only saw problems. A national periodical headed an article about Bill Zeckendorf with "He Turns Lemons into Lemonade." By looking for opportunities in problems you can also find ways to sweeten the lemon.

In 1948 a very successful attorney accompanied a friend to a boat show and fell in love with one of the larger yachts on display. It has been said that the difference between a man and a boy is only in the price of his toys. Well, the attorney purchased his toy that day. The next day was not as pleasant when he discovered that all the public moorings in the area had long waiting lists. About the only way to get a public mooring was to buy a boat already tied up at a mooring, which wouldn't help him as he had just purchased a boat. A number of the private yacht clubs had moorings available but required club membership. In those days, memberships were 100 percent Gentile; a Jewish attorney could forget about even applying. One of his friends in the real estate business told him that he could help temporarily. The friend had listed for sale a coal yard on the river not too far from the ocean. The yard had a dock and since it was closed, the real estate agent thought he could arrange with the owners for temporary docking privileges.

The attorney went to look at the dock. Although located in a run-down commercial and industrial area, the yard had five acres and over 600 feet on the river. The existing dock was for large ships, so it was more than ample for his yacht. The attorney knew that this was only temporary; he wanted a place to keep his boat permanently. After checking with the city planning department, he offered $50,000 cash for the old coal yard. The offer, while low, was accepted. This acceptance set in motion an amazing series of negotiations.

The attorney thought that if he had so much trouble getting a place to keep a boat, other people also would need mooring space. Before the sale of the coal yard was completed, he had an architect draw up preliminary plans for a private marina.

With the preliminary sketches he contacted the major oil companies to see if they would be interested in handling the fuel sales at his marina. This was at a time when oil companies were producing more than they could sell. There was fierce competition for retail sales. Oil companies built new service stations not so much for profit as for distribution. As could be expected, a number of companies were very interested, since large boats use tremendous quantities of fuel. The attorney not only wanted the oil companies to build their own facilities, he also wanted a percentage of the gross as rent, coupled with a minimum rent. In addition, he insisted on $50,000 being paid in advance rent when the facility opened. Several of the oil companies backed off at this demand, but one agreed to it and was given the oil and gas franchises.

Next, the attorney approached a firm that ran other mooring facilities. This firm agreed to construct the yacht slips and a boat ramp and to split all mooring fees 50–50 with the attorney. The company also would set up boat hoists to handle winter storage. The attorney was also to receive a percentage of this business as well as a percentage of any repair business. This agreement was for 20 years, after which all improvements became the property of the attorney.

Then the attorney looked into finding an excellent club manager. He hired away the manager of one of the exclusive clubs with a generous contract. The manager was given the job of selling 300 full memberships for $1500 each, which included the right to rent a boat slip. These memberships were all sold within three months (all memberships without racial or religious restrictions). Social memberships were sold for $500 each. These memberships allowed the members to use launching facilities as well as to rent temporary dock space on a daily basis. After the memberships were sold, the manager's job was to handle special social functions and to oversee the entire operation.

A magnificent clubhouse was constructed, using the membership money collected. A restaurant operator put in the restaurant and bar equipment and agreed to pay a minimum rental plus a percentage of the gross (members were required to spend a minimum amount each month at the restaurant and/or bar).

In less than one year from the date he had first seen this rundown coal yard, the attorney had transformed it into a quality yacht club. What is amazing is that not only did he build it without leaving any of his own money in it, but also the attorney now owned the entire property free and clear of all liens.

PROBLEM PROPERTIES HAVE POTENTIAL

One of the most interesting problem properties I know of was a house of ill re-
pute built in the late 1930s. The building, of log construction, was in a northern
resort area set far back from the highway on a large parcel of land, making it
quite isolated. Downstairs was a large room that originally served as a bar and
dance area. It also had kitchen and bathroom facilities. Upstairs were 12 extremely tiny rooms off a central hall. Each room had a sink and a window.
There were also bathroom facilities on the floor. The building had a succession
of owners. Several restaurants had gone broke on the premises, and the building had been vacant for several years. The house was finally listed with an
imaginative broker. She wrote several hundred letters to psychologists in
nearby cities and also advertised in a psychology magazine. She sold the building to a psychologist who was engaged in various types of encounter groups.
The property was ideally suited for groups such as this or for training purposes.

Many small communities have serious unemployment problems. Some of
these communities have set up industrial development corporations that
have sold low-interest bonds to raise funds to attract industry. Many communities will build buildings for employers and rent them at very low
rentals. Others even make loans to firms that will come into the community. Unfortunately, in the desire for employers, many communities have
built structures for firms with financial problems with the result that many
of these development groups have vacant buildings. These situations offer
great potential for problem solvers. Options can often be obtained on these
completed structures at extremely low rentals if the use will provide an
agreed number of jobs. If you can find firms that would benefit by moving
to the area, you can make a profit by the rental differential and solve a
community need.

If you own a lot suitable for low-income housing or can tie up such
property, contact your local Department of Housing and Urban Development (HUD) office about low-income housing programs. HUD has a number of programs where you can obtain below-market financing for
low-income housing. Generally, allowable rents will provide a positive
cash flow. Depending on the program, you may be free to raise rents when
the loan is refinanced. Your HUD office can also give you information on
urban renewal programs.

Your local redevelopment agency might have redevelopment money
in the form of both grants and loans for developments in designated areas.
While these areas generally are not likely to experience great value appreciation, they can offer money that could mean an immediate positive cash
flow. When real estate has a problem, problem solving can offer financial

rewards. See Chapter 3 for additional information about enterprise and empowerment zones.

MOBILE HOME UNITS

A couple in California lived in a 10- by 50-foot mobile home. They decided they wanted a double-wide unit but discovered that they could only get about $1500 by selling their unit and, although they could get several thousand dollars on a trade-in, they could actually buy the double-wide they wanted for almost the same amount if they had no trade-in. This couple purchased their double-wide unit but kept their old mobile home, moving it to a fairly rough family park where space rentals at the time were only $40 a month. They rented their old coach for $130 a month furnished. In fact, they had a great many calls on the rental ad. The couple did some figuring and realized that they were clearing $90 a month on their old coach, or $1080 each year. In a year and a half this would give them as much as they would have received by selling the unit. They visited several mobile home dealers and said they were interested in buying, for up to $2000, 10-foot- and 12-foot-wide units that had been taken in on trade. The couple wanted the dealers to finance the units at 10 percent down on four-year loans. Several of the dealers were interested, since very few buyers wanted old single-wide units.

The couple then made deals with several older mobile home parks having vacancies. While better parks wouldn't take in an old singlewide, many of the smaller parks with vacancies would do so. In one park they rented 10 spaces for $25 each per month and were able to get a five-year lease at that rent. In a little over one year both were able to quit their jobs to handle their mobile home rentals full-time.

This couple saw a need and a means to fulfill it. Unlike many people who just talk, they acted. Now they own well over 100 rental units and, while not prestige property, it is highly profitable.

Note: A recent conversation with the couple revealed that they have sold most of their units to their tenants in order to have more time to enjoy their wealth. They had, at one time, over 200 units rented. They now own three mobile home parks.

There are a number of own-your-own-lot mobile home parks. Some investors have purchased lots for rental units or have worked with mobile home dealers to offer a packaged deal, home and lot.

You can become a landlord by looking for mobile homes for sale that include the lot. By buying the mobile home and reselling it without the lot, you will have your own one-space mobile home park. Be sure to check the restrictive covenants of the park to make certain such action is permissible.

Because mobile homes that are not on permanent foundations are regarded as personal property, if you sell units and finance the buyer, you don't have to foreclose should the buyer default. Repossession of personal property is, in most states, relatively quick and easy.

FACTORIES

Because of manufacturing inefficiencies, many multistory factories have become obsolete. They have often been sold at very low prices and excellent terms because their use has been limited. Some people with imagination have turned these structures into productive buildings. Some have been leased to crafts people who each rent space. This draws many tourists as well as local shoppers to the buildings. An example is Giardelli Square in San Francisco, a former chocolate factory. Others have been converted to large nightclubs, restaurants, skating rinks, and even legitimate theaters. Others have been converted to apartments. Conversion costs are high, but may still be far below the cost of building new units.

> My name is Seymour T. I was a cap maker until lower-priced caps by foreign manufacturers came on the market and made it impossible for me to operate my business at a profit. I gave my employees severance pay and sold the equipment, supplies, and remaining inventory of my business at an auction.
>
> Going out of business left me with an old seven-story, brick, steel, and concrete building 80 feet wide and 120 feet deep, with truck doors on both streets, which gave ample access for delivery shipments to the inside of the building. The building, which extended between two streets, was located about six blocks from the city's mercantile center. The area itself needed rejuvenation. I didn't have any takers when I tried leasing the building at bargain rent. One big problem was that there was absolutely no parking area. My employees had mostly used public transportation, although there were commercial garages in the immediate vicinity.
>
> I listed the building for sale without success. It sat vacant for two years. My son came up with a one-word idea: lofts. He suggested we turn the building into loft apartments. Based on the pillars we could have eight apartments to the floor. Each loft could be approximately 20 feet wide with about 1000 square feet of floor space, face a street, and utilize the almost floor-to-ceiling factory windows. The building was also equipped with a centrally located automatic freight elevator (about 10 years old), stairways,

and front and rear steel fire escapes and a balcony that ran the width of the building of each floor on both streets for fire escape access. There was a full, dry basement and 16-foot-high ceilings. The building had an excellent fire suppression (sprinkler) system.

My first thought was that the loft idea was crazy. Some research by my son and visits to a former hosiery factory that was converted to lofts in Milwaukee, and a two-square block "Cobbler Square" complex in Chicago (the former home of Dr. Scholl's foot products) convinced me that my son's idea was not so crazy after all.

An architect agreed to do some preliminary work. He had an engineer check out the building, and I received some rough estimates of costs (actual costs turned out to be about 50 percent higher than those initial estimates).

My son prepared a feasibility study based on various costs to convert the structure to lofts and estimates of selling prices based on the information of several knowledgeable brokers. (Incidentally, from these conversations, we chose a broker to work with the architect to make certain we would have a really salable product.) Even if our costs doubled and the sale price estimates were 20 percent too high, the feasibility study indicated the loft conversion would still make sense.

The architect recommended a real estate attorney who had extensive experience in subdivision approvals and local zoning changes. Approvals took over one year. A big problem was that there wasn't enough room on the first floor for parking space for each unit. We considered ramping into the basement, but the engineer ruled out this idea. Our solution was to have local parking garages agree to lease space on a long-term basis to our tenants. We also obtained statements from the city traffic engineer and parking structure operators that street parking was not a problem in our area on weekends or between 4:00 p.m. and 8:00 a.m. on weekdays, which was when most residents would require parking.

I was ready to give up on the project several times, but what kept me going was that I had so much time and money invested in a building that would otherwise be practically worthless.

After approvals, we sandblasted the building, partitioned the units, and put in zone-controlled heating to each of them. We roughed in kitchen plumbing, but except for a model unit, we didn't put in any cabinetry or appliances. However, we did complete a bath for each unit. We built a 500-square-foot open second level in our model unit.

We refurbished the elevator, installed keyed electronic door controls, built storage rooms and a laundry room in the basement, and turned the first floor into a parking area. The units were priced bare (walls painted white), with additional prices provided for finishing the kitchen and building a full or half second level, etc.

All units were sold out within five months. I estimated my investment in each unit at about $40,000, which we sold for base prices at $69,500 and going up to $84,500, depending upon floor, view, and inclusion of parking. My net cash was $1.5 million for a building I couldn't sell at any price.

> Note: While costs have escalated since Seymour converted his factory to lofts, so have sale prices. The units Seymour sold are now selling for about 300 percent more than Seymour sold them for. Loft conversions are still viable investments.

LAND

When an owner is holding land for appreciation, an attractive lease is possible where the owner gets little more than his taxes.

> My name is Chris B. I own a swap meet. I have 400 seller spaces that rent for $25 each per day. (I have a waiting list for spaces.) This gives me $20,000 in rental receipts every weekend. I charge visitors a 50-cent fee to enter. This fee more than pays my lease, as well as operational and promotional expenses. I also lease the concession stands on a percentage basis. While I currently give free parking, I am considering a charge for this. Parking takes up the greater part of my 40-acre site.
>
> I am considering going public and opening up swap meets across the country. My wife asked, "Why? Our net is well over $1 million per year!"

It is possible to make money from land while it is being held for appreciation. Some states pay small amounts per acre if the land is declared a game preserve. Many states also give a property tax break if land is turned into forest. Some owners have planted fir trees, getting the trees at nominal costs from state reforestation programs. These owners also take whatever tax benefits are available. Before developing their land, they harvest their crop of Christmas trees.

Ask yourself, "What use could be made of my land for 1 year, 5 years, or 10 years?" It could be temporary storage or parking. It might even be for raising nursery stock. Use your imagination and you could reduce holding costs or even make a profit.

BILLBOARDS

While there are many restrictions on billboards, where allowed, they can contribute significantly to a property's income and value.

> My name is Yvonne L. I obtained an option to buy an old garage building on a site that backed up against a major highway. There were two large bill-

boards on the property that had been erected by a prior occupant of the property advertising his business. My option was for $100,000 with 10 percent down and the owner to carry the balance at 6 percent interest. After determining that the billboards could remain, I signed a lease with a sign company and exercised my purchase option. The rent from the building plus my billboard income gives me over $5000 per year spendable cash on an investment of $10,000.

BUSINESSES

Many businesses are sold with real estate. Often the value of the real estate is the major value of the business. Don't buy a business for the real estate unless you can cash out of the business quickly. Don't try to run it. Running someone else's business is an invitation to disaster.

SINGLE ROOM OCCUPANCY (SRO)

Single room occupancy (SRO) describes one-room permanent living units. They are often converted hotels and motels.

Small motels and cabins located on good highway frontage can be operated as low-cost SRO units. They could be stopgap operations until the property can be developed for a better use.

The Windsor Hotel in downtown San Diego was renovated to include 32 SROs. While they have communal bathrooms, they still rent for $250 per month to low-income downtown workers.

In Las Vegas, a 320-unit development is in construction. It is intended for casino workers, and planned rentals will start at $475 per month.

SROs have generally high occupancy rates and the average stay is quite long. In Atlanta, an SRO has an average resident stay of 218 days. Some SROs are used by individuals on probation but most units house workers, single retirees, or individuals receiving public assistance.

HUD funds are available for SROs. There is a Section 8 housing provision for SROs.

The following is an example of turning a lemon into lemonade that William Zeckendorf would have been proud of.

> My name is Ira R. and I formerly owned a small shoe store in a city of approximately 50,000 people. My lease was not going to be renewed, and I was desperately searching for a new location. A small hotel nearby had a large corner restaurant that would be an ideal location for a shoe store. I checked with the owner of the hotel, who told me that while he was not interested in renting the restaurant space to me, he would sell me the whole

hotel for $100,000 without any down payment. The owner operated a small bar in the hotel (like the restaurant it also had outside exits) and this would be included.

I had a builder friend check over the hotel. The roof was in good shape and the heating plant was adequate, but the 24 rooms in the three-story hotel were in miserable condition. The hotel portion of the building wasn't even paying the utility bills and the clerk's salary. The restaurant was losing $400 to $500 a month. The only positive income came from the bar. I readily saw why the owner was offering me this opportunity to purchase the hotel. After checking with the city building and planning departments to make certain the hotel was up to code and I could make some desired changes, I took the owner up on the purchase offer. I held an auction of the restaurant equipment and supplies, which netted $6300. I closed the restaurant off from the hotel, converted the kitchen to a storeroom and office, and made minor changes for my shoe store.

I offered to sell the bar (license) and fixtures to a bartender who worked for the former owner. We agreed on a price of $20,000 cash, which he obtained by refinancing his home. He agreed to a long-term lease beginning at $450 a month. We closed the bar off from the hotel.

One of the hotel's permanent residents was a rather energetic woman in her mid-60s who was on Social Security. I asked her to be my manager. The hotel was to be for permanent guests only. We visited several hotels in a nearby city that catered to permanent guests to find out about hotel operations and house rules.

Hiring a painter and handyman with the money from the sale of the bar, we began refurbishing the 24 rooms. We installed coin-operated washer/dryer units on the first floor in what had been the hotel clerk's office. We also put in a cold drink machine.

We offered the refurbished rooms at $85 per month for a single without bath to $150 for a double occupancy with bath. Cooking was not allowed, but we did install a small refrigerator in each room. My manager took to her job with great zeal (she received her room rent free plus $150 per month). In a matter of weeks, we had a room rental waiting list. I had not realized the demand for single-room occupancy was so great. Not only did I now have a shoe store where I paid no rent, I had disposable income as well.

About a year after my successful hotel purchase, I learned about a 44-room motel that had just come on the market. It had been a chain motel with a large restaurant and large two-bedroom manager's suite. The motel was no longer on a major traffic artery because of a new freeway and was in a rather run-down condition. The motel was listed for sale at $750,000, which appeared to be a bargain price. There was a $360,000 mortgage against the motel that could not be assumed. I decided against the purchase when I realized how difficult new financing would be.

About a month after I looked at the motel, I learned from a talkative real estate agent at a Rotary meeting that the motel was in foreclosure.

I contacted the county to ascertain if I would be allowed to change from a motel operation to a permanent residency operation. I then contacted the lender and indicated that if they would allow a loan assumption, I would give the owner an offer; otherwise, they might find themselves managing a motel that was losing money.

After several days I was informed they would agree to the loan assumption providing the 8.5 percent interest rate was raised to 9 percent and I made the loan current. (The owner was about $20,000 in arrears.)

I offered the owner $430,000 for the property. I was to assume the first mortgage and give a second mortgage at 9 percent interest to the owner for the balance of the purchase price. The broker agreed to share in this second mortgage for her commission. My offer was accepted. I now took over the motel with the only cash being that for the loan arrearage. I had a second mortgage of approximately $50,000 (based on credits for paying the loan arrearage).

I hired a retired army sergeant and his wife as managers, giving them the large two-bedroom apartment plus $400 a month as salary. We immediately began refurbishing units, painting the exterior and planting flowers. My manager supervised all the work. Some permanent residents were obtained from the hotel waiting list, and we began advertising.

The restaurant was advertised for lease. I found a good operator and leased it at $500 per month, which was an extremely low rent; I wanted to ensure the operator's success. (The restaurant had been a big money loser for the prior owner who hired a manager to run it.)

Within four months of purchase, we reached 100 percent occupancy on a monthly basis.

I have long since sold my shoe store and my first hotel. I now own seven former motels over a two-state area consisting of over 300 units, all of which are rented on a monthly basis. I purchased every one of them without a cash down payment using the same purchase techniques. I found very few instances where lenders failed to realize that it was to their advantage to let me assume the loan. Most of the purchases were made through a motel broker who knows what I am looking for and keeps his eyes and ears open. Even then I turn down most deals either because there is too much debt or the area will not support my SRO conversions. (In several cases, I could not get approval to change the operation to permanent residency because of zoning restrictions.)

Right now, we are operating at over a 90 percent occupancy with significant positive cash property.

My secret—I offer clean, nicely furnished rooms with private baths in well-maintained buildings at a reasonable monthly rate. I include no housekeeping services, other than common areas. My tenants are mostly either single working people or pensioners. All tenants understand our reasonable rules, which we strictly enforce. One key element I feel is my managers. I take care in hiring good people and I expect a lot from them, but I treat them with respect.

We have a computerized property management program and computer terminals and modems at each unit. At a glance, I can discover problem areas and make plans for corrections. I visit each of my properties every month and usually spend a full day with each manager.

Note: While sale prices, rents, and salaries have increased since Ira started his SRO conversions, the basic concept is still economically viable and Ira is looking to increase his holdings.

Many local residents will oppose single room occupancy developments and property conversions because they fear this will be the home of prostitutes, drug addicts, and alcoholics. If zoning changes or permits are required for an SRO, there is a possibility of rejection. If the SRO will be "over-55 housing," then there will be much less opposition and in some cases communities will welcome the SROs as they meet a need.

STUDENT HOUSING

If you live in a college or university area, you might check the college housing office to get a feel for this special housing need, as well as current rents being paid. If you are interested, you should follow up by viewing available student housing, relating quality and amenities to the rents being paid. You can then determine if conversion of property to student housing or new student housing construction will make economic sense. Your analysis must consider possible reduced rents and occupancy rates during summer periods although year-round demand is strong in some areas.

Several major investors own large student housing projects. Sterling University, a Houston-based company owns 15 student housing projects across the nation. Intergroup owns six large student apartment communities. Other large developers are discovering the profit potential in this niche market.

When apartments are rented to students, rents tend to be 15 to 25 percent higher than for similar apartment space. Some Texas investors show even greater returns as they separately lease bedroom and bath suites in apartments with rights and obligations as to common areas.

Private dormitories can be economically viable although they are more management intensive. Some offer amenities such as shuttle service to campus and high speed Internet access.

Many parents have found that buying a condominium unit for their child at college can cut college costs and in some cases result in recouping all college expenses. Because of this interest in investing by parents, there is a large riverfront luxury apartment complex in Brisbane, Australia, that is being marketed as student housing and the units are being sold to parents and investors.

> I know a very young investor who, while a freshman at college, found that the rooming house he lived in was for sale. The owner, a businessman, had purchased it a year earlier. What looked good on paper had turned out to be a nightmare for him. Besides rent collection problems he had constant maintenance and health orders from the city and generally a lot of grief. This student offered the owner $2000 for his equity, which was accepted. He obtained the $2000 from his parents by telling them the rooming house would pay for the rest of his education.
>
> The young student evicted several troublemakers and commenced to clean up the place. He now owns 18 rooming houses in a university city. They are rented to students only. He has a full-time maintenance man and a student manager at each house. His full-time job is watching over his investments. This is not bad for starting with a borrowed $2000.

HOUSING FOR THE ELDERLY

While our fair housing laws prohibit age discrimination, an exception is housing where 80 percent of the units are occupied by at least one person aged 55 or older. Advantages to owners of such property are:

- **Easier Rent Collection.** Elderly people tend to pay rent on time. Fewer tenants need to be evicted for nonpayment of rent or other problems.
- **Lower Renting Costs.** In many areas of the country, there are long waiting lists for apartments. Some apartments have three- to four-year (estimated) waiting lists. Some new units are filled before they are completed. It is common to rent units to friends of occupants.
- **Longer Occupancy Period.** The average tenant in elderly housing stays longer than the average tenants in nonrestricted apartments. Residents who are not out in the job market tend to develop friendships with other renters and are reluctant to relocate.
- **Less Maintenance Expense.** Because units are rented for longer periods of time and tenants do no have small children, units

rented to elderly people show less wear and tear and the longer occupancy period reduces renovation between tenants.

The baby boomers of the late 1940s and 1950s will be fueling the demand for this type of housing. To determine the feasibility of converting a building to over-55 housing or building a new facility, check the available over-55 units in your area for vacancies and rent schedules. While some units offer special amenities for seniors, many do not. Special amenities might include shuttle service for shopping and a recreation area. Units with special amenities for seniors generally have higher rents. For older less desirable units, you could consider Section 8 housing for seniors. Section 8 is discussed in Chapter 15.

I do not recommend investors get involved in assisted living housing unless they have a medical administration background. Assisted living housing generally requires a 24-hour staff, some meals, and a great many personal services.

If you want more information about elderly housing, contact the U.S. Department of Housing and Urban Development.

GROUP HOMES

Many investors have turned larger residences into group homes for developmentally disabled adults. Normally, the residents work at a sheltered workshop during the week.

You can find out about the need for a group home in your area by checking your local Association for Retarded Citizens (ARC). They can also give you information about payments available per resident.

Many people have found that by simply taking in one or two of these individuals, they can become homeowners, when they otherwise could not afford to be owners. Before any decision is made to own a group home or take developmentally disabled persons into homes, you must realize that it is a commitment in both effort and emotions.

RENT-CONTROLLED COOPERATIVES

There is interesting speculation in rent-controlled cooperative apartments. While you can buy the units (converted from rental apartments to cooperatives or condominiums), in many communities you cannot always get the tenants out. Under some rent control ordinances, they can remain in the units until they voluntarily move out or die. Because the rents bear little relationship to the sale value if occupancy were available, the tenant's age and health affect the price. While a little on the ghoulish side, some investors buy these units betting on the early demise of owners.

A preferable approach used by at least one investor is to offer the tenant a large share in the sale profit to vacate. While many elderly owners don't like the idea of moving, if the investor is able to contact any of their children and tell them of the offer, the children will often be allies in persuading a tenant to vacate so the unit can be sold.

Some syndicators have discovered these rent-controlled units and have set up limited partnerships for investment. The fact that such units can be purchased for 40 percent to 60 percent of market value, intrigues many investors.

MEETING SPECIAL GROUP NEEDS

Several apartment buildings in the Sunbelt have in recent years gone "clothing optional." These are apartment units with private interior courts, usually with a pool. Dedicated nudists have filled up the units at premium rents. In the Los Angeles area these units command rents from 25 percent to 50 percent higher than otherwise comparable units.

CREATIVE CONVERSION OF OLDER PROPERTIES

For many years consumers have had the idea that new means better. While *new* may be good, for many people *old* is better. Old office buildings with iron railings and open iron elevator cages were torn down in the 1950s and 1960s to make room for new glass towers. Today many old buildings have regained their former luster and command premium rentals. Attorneys, accountants, and other professionals like the solid image these structures provide. A building should have a basically sound structure and classic lines if you are considering restoration. Old schoolhouses and train depots can at times be purchased at very low prices. They offer exceptional possibilities for shops, restaurants, and even apartments.

THE VALUE OF OLD FURNITURE

In cleaning out the basement and attic of a huge old home I purchased, I received an indoctrination into the world of antiques. I mentioned to a friend that the place was loaded with old junk. My friend was an antiques buff and drove up to look at the property with me. My friend agreed to clean out the attic and basement, throwing out the real junk and selling what was salable. In exchange I agreed to let her have several old bureaus. Over the next few months she gave me a number of checks totaling over $1000. After this experience, I started looking differently at the "junk" left in old buildings.

I have purchased a number of older furnished homes and apartments over the years. In several cases the resale of the furniture has gone a long way toward returning the down payment. Those old 1912 Sears oak chests are now regarded as valuable antiques. In the basement of one apartment building I found six old oak iceboxes, which I sold for $200 each.

A close friend purchased a lake cottage that had been part of a resort. On the same lot as his cottage was an old four-car garage full of old wicker porch furniture. The sale of these pieces gave him back more than double his down payment.

TREE AND TIMBER VALUE

If you should find a property with a fine old black walnut tree on it, this would be like finding gold. One tree, depending on size and configuration, could be worth over $10,000. I heard of one country home that was sold with nine such trees on the front lawn. The purchaser harvested his lawn and received more than the price of the entire property from the sale of the trees.

One of my fishing companions purchased a heavily wooded lot of several acres for $5000. In building his home and driveway he had to clear away a number of trees well over 100 years old. Rather than pay for their removal, he called in a logger who not only cleared the site but also paid him almost $3000.

Not all timber is valuable, but much of it is. People with smaller parcels of land often fail to consider the fact that there may be value in the timber.

MINERAL, OIL, AND GAS

An acreage parcel may have potential value for mineral, oil, and gas. Rights can be sold and separated from the land, in which case the landowner would get a flat sum. Some sellers will retain all or part of the mineral, oil, and gas rights when they sell the land. They are hoping that what they retained might someday have great value. By giving a mineral, oil, and gas lease, the owner gives a person the right to take minerals, oil, and gas from the property subject to a royalty agreement. Lessees or buyers of mineral, oil, and gas interests are probably either small oil or mining companies or brokers who intend to resell the interests. To explore sale or lease feasibilities, check with local real estate brokers. They most likely would know if any MOG (mineral, oil, and gas) brokers are active in your area.

Keep in mind that if you sell or lease mineral, oil, and gas rights then other parties will have the right to enter your property to extract minerals, fluids, or gas. In some areas of the country, ranchers sold their rights, and strip-mining for coal has left their homes and barns sitting on small plateaus surrounded by deep depressions of land where the coal has been extracted.

In the early 1970s I was offered 200 acres near Cabazon, California, for $20,000. The property had road frontage but was in a desolate and very windy area. Nevertheless, I was tempted because I thought expansion in the Coachella Valley might make the site valuable for warehouse or storage purposes. Well, the opportunity I turned down is now leased as a windmill farm generating electrical power and cash to the lucky owner. I say "lucky" because luck played a big role since no one at the time could have predicted those giant turbines giving value to a desolate stretch among the desert mountains.

In a few areas of the country where there are underground thermal conditions, hot water and steam rights can be sold to power generating plants.

RECYCLING BUILDINGS

Redevelopment and highway construction often create situations in which good structures are available at very low prices. However, they must be moved. In planning to buy such a building, you must first consider local regulations. Can the structure be put on a lot in the area? Besides the zoning, the covenants, conditions, and restrictions could prohibit it. In addition to the initial cost of the building, you should consider moving costs, cost of a lot, foundation expense, water and sewage costs, electrical hookups, driveways and walks, and even insurance for the move. There will be additional electrical expenses for a basement, and some new ductwork could be required. Building codes could require a new hot water heater or a new furnace. Apparently, despite all these costs, moving a structure can be a valuable investment. A few investors specialize in buying buildings that must be moved, so it must offer a profit potential. Some larger buildings are actually cut into pieces to be moved.

Home movers also have buildings for sale. They will price the building moved to your site and set on your foundation. Many home movers have online sites where you can view their offerings.

HISTORICAL DESIGNATIONS

The National Park Service Administers the National Register of Historic Places. The purpose is to protect property of historical and cultural significance. Each state has an office to administer the program.

Owners can benefit from a historical designation in several ways. The historical designation on a home validates its significance and can materially increase its value. Therefore, many owners work to have their homes registered.

An owner of an income-producing property with a federal designation can receive a major benefit, a 20 percent federal investment tax credit for certified rehabilitation. Many states also provide state tax credits for rehabilitation for income- as well as nonincome-producing property.

Your state government probably has a historical preservation commission that designates historical properties as well as historical districts. These properties need not be listed on the federal register. There are also state architectural designations. Proving the architect could mean additional value. Some states also offer tax deferrals and tax reductions for designated properties.

On the negative side, a historical designation could impede demolition and make it costly to remodel, as changes in the exterior would be limited. A property might be kept in a use less than one that would maximize income.

> My name is Allan D. I own three large Victorian- and Colonial-style homes that I have converted into offices. I began investing by buying a home on a commercial street for my own office and found that I was able to rent out the additional space at attractive rents.
>
> I recently looked at an older home that would need extensive repair and remodeling to use for offices. I had pretty well decided to pass on the property when the owner mentioned that the home, which was built in 1790, had

been built by one of the signers of the Declaration of Independence. I verified this fact with the local historical society. I managed to quickly obtain a state historical designation. I was also assured that a federal designation would be forthcoming.

While I never turned the home into offices, I did advertise it in the *New York Times* based on the historical significance of the property. I sold the home for almost 60 percent more than I had paid with no changes to it.

GIFTS CAN BE PROFITABLE

The Betty Ford Center is part of the Eisenhower Medical Center, a world-class facility, in the heart of Rancho Mirage, California. This hospital was made possible by a gift of land from Bob and Dolores Hope. In addition, the annual Bob Hope Celebrity Golf Tournament benefits this hospital.

At the time of the gift of land, the area was undeveloped and land value in the vicinity was relatively low. Before the center was completed, adjoining land values rose and have continued to rise. While substantial acreage was given, the Hope family owned a great deal of adjacent property. While the intention of the gift may have been purely altruistic, the result for the giver was a charitable tax deduction as well as a significant financial gain due to the increase in value of the Hope's remaining property.

Being in close proximity to a major hospital, college, or similar institution will of course help property values. You can see that it might pay to give away some land for a particular purpose if that purpose will aid the area and if you retain the surrounding land. In addition, a charitable gift, of course, means a tax deduction.

IT'S UP TO YOU

The uses and development of real estate are limited only by your imagination. These examples are not given to show you what to do so much as to show you that you should be flexible in understanding and solving real estate problems. And remember that finding solutions to problems is meaningless unless you act upon them.

15
CHAPTER

Managing Your Property

The instinct of ownership is fundamental in man's nature.

William James

UNDERSTANDING PROPERTY MANAGEMENT

Bernard Baruch gave a four-word plan for riches: "Buy low, sell high." It sounds simple, but what do you do with the property between the time you acquire it and the time you dispose of it? What you do will be an important factor in what the property will bring at a sale, as well as the operational results of ownership.

Property management includes a very broad area of planning and decision making. It involves goal setting, improvements, changes in use, tenant selection, rent collections, policies and procedures, and a great deal more. Property management requires skills in management, bookkeeping, and interpersonal relationships.

Good real estate management will maximize the net return. A higher net means a greater value. An income property should be analyzed in terms of what use and type of tenant will provide the greatest return, and a plan should be devised to achieve that goal. Costs reported by the former owner should be analyzed for need and accuracy. Realistic operational and improvement costs should be estimated.

While there are some excellent management firms, professional management will not provide you with an education in property management. There is no substitute for personal involvement. The management experience you gain will be invaluable in making future investment decisions.

BEFORE YOU BUY

Before you purchase, you will want to see all current leases, as well as service contracts. At the time of closing you will want to make sure all lease deposits are turned over to you.

Before the sale is completed, you should have considered your insurance needs. While existing policies might be assumed with the approval of the insurer, they may not be adequate for your needs. You will probably desire coverage that provides replacement of real and personal property without deductions for depreciation. Boiler insurance protects owners of large buildings for casualty losses; another benefit is the fact that insurers inspect the boiler and make certain it is maintained properly. You will want a high liability coverage, as well as coverage for vandalism, accidents, and so forth. You may also want plateglass coverage. Rental interruption coverage will reimburse you for lost rents because of a casualty loss. If you are taking over maintenance employees with the property, you should consider the necessity of workers' compensation coverage as well as unemployment compensation. I suggest you review the property fully with your insurance broker prior to closing the transaction.

At closing, the former owner should turn over a complete set of keys to you. You can require this to be done in your purchase offer. Nothing is more annoying than having tenants move out and take the only keys with them. Keep a key file with a complete duplicate set of keys for all of your properties.

SETTING RENTS

As soon as the property is yours, you should immediately notify all tenants that you are the new owner and that all future rents are to be paid to you. Often units have below-market rentals. Tenants usually know when they have been getting a good deal. In such cases, they will be expecting a rent increase.

Before you raise rents, try to make some sort of repair or improvement in order to show the tenants that you care about the property and will keep it up. It improves the landlord–tenant relationship if the tenants feel they are getting something for their increased rent.

You should not be influenced by what similar property is renting for in evaluating rental rates. Similar rented property does not compete with vacant property. The only competition will be similar vacant property. When there is a high vacancy factor, your units must be competitive to other similar properties in condition, amenities, and price. However, when there is a low vacancy factor, you don't have to be competitive. An above-market rental might be in your best interest considering the overall effect on the net income.

A vacant unit will give you an opportunity to reassess your rents. You should consider the law of supply and demand. You should also analyze the rental market. In analyzing competing units, you should consider the following:

- Size of unit
- Condition of unit
- Appearance of building
- Security of building
- Parking or garage
- Utilities furnished
- Neighborhood
- Transportation
- Elevator or walkup
- Pets allowed

The higher you raise the rent, the greater will be your vacancy factor. Some tenants will move simply because they cannot afford to remain, while others will bear the cost of moving if they feel they can find similarly desirable property at a lower cost. If other tenants are available, don't worry that a particular tenant will move.

In your evaluation of rentals, ask yourself what effect a 5, 10, 15, or even 20 percent increase in rents will have on the long-term vacancy factor. Your goal as an owner will be to achieve the highest rent and lowest vacancy factor combination to maximize your net. This is really no different than price setting for any other goods or services.

A higher-vacancy factor not only means rental loss; it also means increased maintenance costs because it is seldom that a vacated unit can be rerented without additional work. An increase in vacancies can more than offset a rent increase and result in a net loss. For example, suppose you had 10 units, each renting for $800 per month, or a total monthly rental income of $8000. If you raised the rents 10 percent, you would now have an

$8800 per month gross. Assume this increase resulted in a 10 percent vacancy factor. You would now have only a $7920 gross, or a decline in total gross of 1 percent without even considering increased maintenance costs. Therefore, you must carefully evaluate the effect of a rent increase on your vacancy factor.

Rents should be consistent. If you rent one unit at a higher rate, you must raise the other units also, although you may have to wait until leases expire to do so. People don't mind paying a fair rental unless they find your other tenants are paying less than they are for similar units. An alternative to a rent increase is a charge for services previously provided. For example, charges for cable TV, high-speed Internet access, water, trash removal, or even parking spaces are equivalent to a rent increase but are regarded slightly more favorably.

In periods of high vacancies, commercial tenants have negotiated long-term, fixed-rate rentals with motivated owners. At times such a rental can be significantly increased prior to the expiration of the lease. To do so you must have a competitor for the premises when the lease expires, and the current tenant must want to remain on the premises.

My name is Jeffrey S. I am an attorney. About 10 years ago, I purchased a large commercial building that had a long-term net lease with a national industrial tenant. The only problem was the terms of the net lease were so favorable to the tenant that I was looking forward to years of a break-even cash flow. The unattractive lease was the reason I was able to buy the building at an attractive price with only a $25,000 down payment.

After several years of exchanging checks each month, I decided to seek a rent increase. I discovered, from checking rents in the area, that I should be charging close to $5000 a month on a net lease (with a net lease, the tenant pays taxes, insurance, and all maintenance). This was about four times what I was now receiving.

I knew someone in the same business as my tenant and asked if they would be interested in renting my property when the lease expired. They were very interested because they regarded the building ideally suited for their use, which included light manufacturing, storage of highly flammable material, and a showroom for wholesale sales. My friend was willing to sign a lease right then even though occupancy couldn't be given for more than five years. Not only did my friend agree to a rental, he agreed to the inclusion of the CPI, so when the lease started it would be at a significantly higher price. It turned out that my property had a number of important factors going for it. The building had a very heavy-duty sprinkler system and met fire codes. It had loading docks and some of the only zoning for miles around that met the needs of the tenant. The 30-foot ceiling allowed for forklift storage. In addition, large commercial users of the product were located close by. A discussion with my tenant's local manager revealed that this was the highest grossing regional operation that my tenant had.

I told my friend at the beginning of discussions that if we reached an agreement, I would give my tenant 30 days to agree to the same terms, although they would have to agree to pay the new rent within 60 days. If my tenant agreed in writing to the lease terms, the lease agreement with my friend would be automatically terminated. My friend realized he would get the premises only if the current tenant failed to agree to pay a market rent for the five years plus left on the original lease. My friend and I signed an 18-year lease starting with the date the current lease expired. We included a paragraph that allowed for the lease to be nullified by the current tenant agreeing to the new lease. I contacted the main office of my tenant and talked to a vice president in charge of real estate. I basically explained to him what he had to decide and indicated I would forward the terms in writing.

The vice president called back about two hours later and stated he would fly right out to meet with me. After a three-hour meeting, we had a new lease memorandum giving me market rent. The net effect was that I had a significant positive cash flow and the value of my building greatly increased in just 24 hours.

Giving away rent is giving away profit. Even though I generally don't believe in giving free rent to fill vacancies, giving free rent at times has advantages. It can be used to induce tenants to sign leases at above-market rent. Since appraisers use rental income to evaluate property for loan purposes, you want the scheduled rents to be as high as possible if a sale or new loan is likely. In addition, in the event of the enactment of rent control, your rentals will be on a higher base than owners of similar properties who reduced rents to fill vacancies.

Another advantage of free rent is that once a tenant is in on a higher rent, they will be more likely to remain when the lease expires. On the other hand, starting tenants with a low rent and later raising the rent when leases expire will result in a greater number of tenants deciding to vacate the premises.

FILLING VACANCIES

Over half of apartment rentals come from the cheapest method possible: a sign. Indicate on the for-rent sign if the unit is furnished or unfurnished. You should also consider newspaper classified ads to fill vacancies. If an ad doesn't bring much response, change it. Advertise the high points. Negative points such as no pets can be explained later. An ad is merely a teaser to excite interest and result in an inquiry. It is not a rental agreement.

If you do not reside in your units, you will want to designate one tenant to show the units and ask for deposits. You don't want someone actually renting; all you want is a deposit that gives you the right to accept or reject. I have learned from past mistakes that a prospective tenant may not be what he or she appears to be. Have the applicant for a rental fill out a questionnaire. Also make a copy of the applicant's driver's license to make certain he or she is who they claim to be. This also gives you a former address. Then you will want to verify the applicant's employment and rental history.

One rule you should have about tenant selection is that you should avoid renting to a friend or relative. If you have a close friend or relative as a tenant, there is a great danger that your personal relationship will suffer. How, for example, would you go about evicting a close friend or relative?

Generally, units that rent for lower amounts require more management effort than more expensive units. Units with lower rentals tend to be older and more crowded. They require more maintenance and greater renovation between tenants. Rent collection problems seem to increase inversely to the amount of rent charged.

Allowing pets will reduce your vacancy factor and mean longer-term tenancies, which also reduce refurbishing costs. However, you do need rules for pets as well as a higher security deposit because of possible damage to the premises. Keep in mind that you cannot charge a greater security deposit because a tenant has a guide dog or some other support animal. You should also realize that maximum security deposits are set by state law, usually at no more than one months' rent.

If you have a commercial or industrial vacancy that you have been unable to fill, offer leasing agents full commission for a tenant. In fact, you would be smart to offer the agent an additional incentive. One owner offered a Rolex watch to find a tenant for a large space when there was a high vacancy factor. Vacant space means lost rent that can never be recovered. Six months of additional vacancy at $3000 per month means $18,000 that is gone forever.

When you have a number of rentals to fill, you cannot take a lot of time for people to make up their minds. I recommend what many would consider a hard sell. When you get a call on a rental, give only bare information such as, "Yes, that is a lovely three-bedroom, first-floor unit in a newer building. The rent is $800 per month and an $800 property damage bond is required. It is available on a one-year lease. I can arrange to show it to you this afternoon at 2:00 p.m. Is that time convenient?" If there are any restrictions such as pets, mention them at this time. The caller's response will either be that 2:00 p.m. is fine or that he or she can't make it, in which case ask when he or she will be available. The caller thus sets the time to see the unit and you have an appointment. You should average close to 50 percent showings from ad inquiries using this approach.

When showing the unit, point out any features that are not obvious. It isn't necessary to tell someone, "This is the kitchen." You should repeat the rental terms and state, "If you would like to apply for this rental, I will be happy to take your deposit. The customary deposit is [$50]. Is that all right with you?" This straightforward approach works well. At the same time, have the prospective tenant fill out a credit information card. Indicate that you will contact the prospective tenant within 48 hours. Usually you should be able to complete employment, rental history, and credit checks in a few hours. Then contact the prospective tenant and ask that he or she bring in the balance of the first month's rent and the property damage bond, usually at least a week before occupancy. (Some owners charge a nonrefundable fee for checking credit and references. This is possible when it is a landlord's market with more prospective tenants than units available.)

MAINTAINING THE RENTAL UNIT

In periods when demand for housing exceeds the available supply, it is possible to rent a vacated unit without doing any work. Nevertheless, at the very least you should see that a unit is properly cleaned before it is rented. Tile floors should be stripped and waxed and rugs steam-cleaned. Although all tenants are not neat and clean, they deserve to start out with a spotless unit. When a unit is vacant, it is a good time for minor upgrading such as new light fixtures or carpets. If the walls need it, they can be painted or wallpapered. Use wallpaper only in baths and in dining areas— and then a vinyl-type paper that can be wiped clean. Use only a few standard colors for paint, so you can touch up walls rather than repainting between tenants. Use light colors (off-white) that make a unit appear both cleaner and larger. Some owners will provide the tenant with the paint, but I have found from sad experience that many people are completely inept. Therefore, it is generally best not to allow tenants to paint their own units.

Instead of cleaning or replacing drapes, consider new vinyl vertical blinds. The cost is relatively inexpensive even for made-to-measure blinds, and there is almost no maintenance cost.

When you upgrade a vacant unit consider the following where needed:

1. New light fixtures in kitchen and bath.
2. A large mirrored medicine chest with a built-in light fixture.
3. A quality vinyl wallpaper on at least one wall in the bath.
4. A 40-inch wainscoting of a washable wallpaper topped with a molding strip in the dining area.

    5. Several rows of ceramic tile behind the stove, applied with a special mastic.

The unit should be clean and free of vermin, and all appliances and utilities should sparkle and work properly. While the unit must meet the minimum standards of providing protection from the elements, it does not need to be of a quality you would like for yourself. Remember that to many people your unit will be offering an improvement in their quality of life.

    In planning, economics must be considered. I know of owners who have spent more money on improvements than could possibly be recouped in increased revenues. When considering improvements, consider the principle of contribution. Ask yourself how much the improvements will contribute to the net income. If you do not believe the improvement costs will be paid for within four or five years by an increased net income, don't make them. I feel you can use your money better for other purposes.

    A normally shrewd investor purchased a small office building. All the tenants had several years left on their leases. After purchasing the building, the investor did extensive landscaping of an interior court. He also repaved the walks with red brick and installed a very large fountain as well as several benches and tables. His costs for this work amounted to more than $20,000. At first glance these improvements appeared unnecessary, but these were his reasons for the improvements:

    1. *Tenant satisfaction.* A happy tenant is likely to remain, thus reducing the vacancy factor. When leases expire, the owner will be competing with many newer buildings. He does not want to lose his tenants. Increased net can be in the form of a reduced vacancy factor as well as higher rents.

    2. *Property appreciation.* When the property is eventually sold, the improvements will help sell the building and should increase the sale price.

    3. *Tax benefits.* Part of the work was repair, which can be written off completely as an expense in the year of the repair. The work that was an improvement can be depreciated over the life of the improvement. The federal and the state governments, therefore, will pick up the tab for a significant part of the expenses.

In deciding if a unit should be furnished, analyze the market for furnished units. Furnished units generally rent at a premium. However, tenancy for furnished units is usually shorter. Unless there is very strong demand, furnished units will have a much higher vacancy factor than unfurnished units.

Some owners of larger apartment complexes make arrangements for a furniture package with a furniture store. They then tell prospective tenants that for a stated amount (rent plus furniture payment) they will have a furnished unit and own the furniture after three years. What they actually do is to arrange 100 percent financing of the furniture package. The tenant makes two payments, one for rent and one for furniture. This allows the owner to state on his sign "furnished and unfurnished."

Security

Never advertise that a building is secure or otherwise indicate that your tenants will be safe, as some courts have held this to be an owner's warranty of safety. However, you can advertise security features such as "lighted parking areas."

There are a number of ways you can help make your buildings more secure. You should let your tenants know what security precautions you have taken and why. They might include:

- Trimming shrubs and trees around entryways and walkways or removal of shrubs in favor of low plantings
- Lighted parking areas (You might want motion detector activated floodlights.)
- Well-lighted hallways and entries
- Locking circuit breaker box (key with manager)
- Battery operated emergency lighting in hallways and lobbies
- Replacement of hollow core apartment doors with solid core doors
- Installing peepholes in doors
- Security chains anchored by at least one-inch screws
- Installation of quality deadbolts
- Quality window locks

Keep in mind that no property will ever be fully secure against a professional burglar, but your security can act as a deterrent. Tenants will appreciate your security efforts and will be less likely to leave for another unit offering poorer security measures.

HANDLING TENANT PROBLEMS

Often property is sold at an advantageous price and terms because an owner has had problems with tenants. Visit such tenants personally and listen to their problems. I believe in complete honesty; tell the tenant either that corrections will be made and when, or if not, why not. Procrastination only causes further problems. If the tenants say they will move, write out a statement as to when they will move and ask them to sign it. If you feel a residential tenant will be a problem, you will usually prefer that he or she leave. It is normally best to allow a problem tenant to break a lease without any penalty.

While most people are really great, unlike Will Rogers, I have met people I didn't like. Some people are just unreasonable. They expect more than is reasonable of a landlord and complain about everything imaginable. You must explain to people that in apartment living they must expect to give up some of the quiet and privacy of a single-family dwelling. Nevertheless, you should usually do all you reasonably can to satisfy tenant problems. Occasionally a tenant will go on a rent strike, saying that he or she will not pay the rent until something is done. Counter by immediately starting eviction proceedings. Do not submit to extortion of this type. From experience I have found that in most cases this tenant action is simply a means to avoid paying the rent. The tenant really hopes that you will take several months to make the demanded repairs, thus giving the tenant several months' free rent. Keep in mind that a tenant defense to an eviction action would be an owner's failure to maintain the premises in a habitable manner.

If a court determines that the premises are not habitable because of a breach of duty of yours (the landlord), you could find yourself with a non-paying tenant as well as damages to pay. Don't evict for nonpayment of rent if you have failed to keep the premises habitable. The premises must be in habitable condition at the time of the rental, and you as lessor have duties to maintain the premises.

For residential property you cannot generally evict a tenant for complaining of unhealthy or uninhabitable conditions. Nor can you evict a tenant for forming a tenant organization. Such evictions are considered retaliatory and can expose you to damages and civil penalties.

In managing property you will come across people who will try to take advantage of you. When a tenant cannot pay rent on time or the rent check bounces, you want to know why and when you can expect a check. You have the tenant agree on a date of payment and then send the tenant a letter showing this agreement. If the tenant does not pay as agreed, you then start eviction proceedings. I don't believe in giving a third chance.

Tenants will frequently try several ploys to gain time in paying their rent. The two most common are the wrong checks with the letter (you receive a check for a charge card while the credit company receives your check) and unsigned checks. You must also be alert for the tenant who wants to go on a 40-day month. The tenant will be 10 days late with the first check and then send a check every 40 days, thus falling farther and farther behind in his or her rent. In three years the tenant will be one year behind. Some owners won't evict since they continue to get checks on a regular basis, and the tenant will promise to make it up. The owner hopes this is true and is afraid that the tenant, if evicted, will never pay.

Most tenant problems can be solved before you rent by checking up on the tenant. As previously stated, don't make a rental agreement. Use a rental application that authorizes you to obtain:

1. *Employment verification.* Verify with the employer the length of time a tenant has been employed and earnings. (Some landlords ask to see a pay stub, but this only shows gross and deductions for one particular pay period.) If the prospective tenant is newly employed, find out where he or she worked before and check the previous employer for length of employment and earnings.

2. *Credit check.* If you do not have access to a credit bureau, ask the prospective tenant to obtain a copy of his or her credit report.

3. *Check prior landlords.* Check with the current and a prior landlord as to any problems with the tenant such as rent payments, treatment of the premises, violations of rules, and the like. (A prior landlord is better than a current landlord because the current landlord could be so eager to be rid of the tenant that they will lie, making the tenant sound perfect for you.)

You should be leery when a credit report shows that a person has had very short or sporadic work history or where you are unable to verify prior rent history.

As a rule of thumb, if you are unsure of a tenant's reliability, don't accept them as a tenant. You must keep in mind that under our Civil Rights acts, you can never turn down a prospective tenant because of race, religion, sex, marital status, sexual preferences, Seeing Eye dogs or assistance animals, mental or physical handicaps, or even having AIDS, but you can turn down an applicant for poor credit, for lying on the application, for a poor rent payment history, violation of rules at other rentals, damaging other property, and/or failing to keep their rental in a sanitary condition. Your rental rules must be applied to all rental applicants in the same manner, and you cannot discriminate in your tenant qualification or rental process.

Uniform Residential Landlord and Tenants Act

The Uniform Residential Landlord and Tenants Act has been adopted by all the states, although many states have modified provisions of the act. The act sets forth obligations of the landlord and the tenant, some of which are set forth below:

Landlord Obligations:

- Keep common areas clean and in safe repair.
- Provide garbage receptacles and arrange for garbage pickups.
- Make repairs necessary to keep structure in a habitable condition.
- Comply with health and safety codes.
- Supply reasonable hot water and heat (unless facilities are under tenant control).
- Provide working plumbing.
- Provide smoke detectors in common areas.

Tenant Obligations

- Keep premises clean.
- Place garbage in receptacles provided.
- Use appliances and fixtures properly.
- Abide by reasonable rules and regulations.
- Do not by negligence, or intention, damage the premises.
- Conduct themselves so as not to disturb the enjoyment of other tenants.
- Surrender premises at end of tenancy in a clean and proper manner.

EVICTIONS

At one time I owned and managed a great number of low-rent units. Tenant problems were quite common. I often found it was cheaper to pay a tenant to move than to evict. For instance, if a tenant had problems and it appeared that rent collections would be difficult or impossible, I would agree to give the tenant $100 or more when he or she turned over the key to me. If I had evicted, I would be faced with the legal expense, a rental loss during the eviction, and possible property damage. Vindictive tenants can leave a property in shambles. However, when they know you are going to inspect the property before paying them, the property is usually clean with the exception of normal wear and tear.

In most states you can handle evictions without an attorney. The clerk of your local county court should be able to show you what papers to use and how to fill them out. Normally, the first step is a notice to quit or pay rent (usually a three-day notice). If the tenant doesn't leave after this notice, and he or she seldom does, it is followed by an unlawful detainer action, which is the court eviction proceedings. The court usually gives the tenant from a few days to several weeks to leave. If the tenant does not leave, you can get the sheriff to move the tenant, although you will probably pay the moving expense.

Never evict a tenant in late December. Courts and the community will regard you as a Scrooge for pre-Christmas evictions. If a property owner evicts residential tenants for a condominium conversion or a change in use, I feel that the owner has a moral obligation to his or her tenants beyond the bare legal notices to vacate that are required by law. Whenever I have evicted tenants because of a change in property use, I have actively sought other units that would meet their needs as well as helped in relocation costs. Moral values are not incompatible with profit.

ON-SITE APARTMENT MANAGEMENT

An owner can delegate many of the management tasks to a tenant. Reimbursement may be in the form of reduced rent, free rent, or even free rent and a salary, depending on the duties required and the number of units involved. Consider retired couples for this job, since they have the time to devote to problems. An on-site manager also gets a psychic income in that he or she gets recognition from other tenants as a person in authority. Give your on-site manager calling cards with his or her name and a title such as "Property Management Officer."

You should carefully spell out the duties of your apartment manager. If your manager is to collect rents, you should consider a fidelity bond. (It is generally preferable to have tenants mailing the rents directly to you.) Notify the on-site manager if there is any problem with rent collection. The on-site manager's job, besides taking rental deposits and handling minor maintenance, is to solve tenant problems. Tenants sometimes expect the management to solve every personality conflict that comes up. Recommend to your managers that they try to have the parties work out their differences before becoming involved. Each year you should set a realistic budget for maintenance supplies and outside services. The manager knows the budget. If your manager cannot make a repair, then you should call a particular plumber, electrician, or other tradesperson with whom you do business. By asking for recommendations at your local hardware store or lumberyard, you will be able to locate persons who do small repair jobs. Generally, independent handymen will perform work at significant savings over large contracting firms, and they are usually competent in a number of trade skills. I suggest that work always be done by an independent contractor rather than by an employee. If the worker is your employee, you will have Social Security, income tax, unemployment compensation, and workers' compensation costs or responsibilities. If the annual operation costs are below budget and the manager has not deferred maintenance to achieve this, consider giving him or her a cash bonus. What will happen is that managers are suddenly able to make repairs they would have otherwise called in a tradesperson for. A little bonus system can save money for you and help keep your managers happy.

MANAGING TO MAKE AND SAVE MONEY

Coin-operated washers, dryers, and vending machines actually provide a profit in many units, especially in smaller units for singles. Some owners allow the managers to take this money for a petty cash fund. This isn't sound procedure because the money will likely end up becoming part of the manager's compensation rather than cash to be used for materials.

Any petty cash fund should be unrelated to machine receipts and all funds should be accounted for. In a lower-income housing I formerly managed, the coin boxes for the washers and dryers were constantly being broken open. I found that for this building it was cheaper to remove the coin boxes and provide the washers and dryers free of charge.

In larger units it is best to use a vending company rather than own your own machines because of the constant repair problems caused by the heavy use and abuse the machines suffer.

In these times of high utility cost you must consider ways to save. Outside lights should be on timers. Instead of 150-watt spotlights for outside lighting, consider going to 12-volt, low-wattage systems or exterior fluorescent lighting. Keep in mind that outside lighting must be adequate for security purposes. One apartment complex I visited has put in a meter for the tennis court lights. Fifty cents allows 20 minutes of lighting.

One way to cut lighting costs is to use fluorescent hall fixtures. Besides operating on lower wattage, they actually give more light. While ordinary light bulbs tend to disappear in halls, the fluorescent tubes stay because your renters don't have any use for the long tubes.

Cutting heating and cooling costs can mean the difference between a profit and a loss. I presently don't own any units where I must supply heating and cooling, but there are many buildings with central systems. When utilities were cheap, it was an economical way to build. Many such buildings have now replaced central heating and cooling units with separate units so each tenant can pay his or her own bills. If this is not feasible, an owner of such a building should avoid long-term leases without a provision for increased rents based on utility costs.

With central heating and cooling, costs can be reduced in a number of ways. Locked thermostats and thermostats that change by a clock can mean significant savings. The days when landlords provided 80-degree heat and 70-degree cooling are part of the past.

Double insulation in crawl spaces or attics, weather stripping, and storm windows and doors all help. Planting a windbreak close to the building will also significantly reduce heat loss. Simple furnace modifications such as automatic flue controls will reduce the amount of heat going up the chimney. Consider having a heating and cooling consultant evaluate your system.

In managing property, a dollar's savings in management costs is equivalent to another dollar in income, and every dollar in income means about $10 to $15 in additional property value upon sale. Therefore, while you will want to maintain a property well in order to protect your investment, you don't want any unnecessary or wasted expenditure.

You should insist that every tenant sign a lease. Even a tenant on a month-to-month tenancy should sign a lease, as the lease will clearly set forth the duties and obligations of the owner and the tenant. Leases can reduce vacancies. The best rental periods are different in various areas of the country, but suppose in your area the best rental period is from May to September. By having all one-year leases expire on either May 1, June 1, July 1, August 1, and September 1, you will have fewer problems renting units if a tenant fails to renew the lease. You don't want leases to expire at periods when few people are moving. As an example, vacancies occurring on December 1 in many northern cities might be hard to fill unless there was a great shortage of housing.

A property damage bond is better for an owner than collecting the last month's rent in advance. Rent collected in advance is considered accrued income and must be reported by the owner in the year it is collected for income tax purposes. However, a property damage bond is not taxable as income until it is forfeited, which may never happen. You should also require at least a $20 key deposit. With a deposit this large, you will seldom fail to get keys returned. (For garage door openers, a $50 deposit should be considered.)

RECORD KEEPING

You must keep accurate records of your income and expenses for tax purposes as well as to aid you in decision making. While I prefer to put records on a computer, a simple yet effective method for record keeping for a single property is to set up a separate checking account for the property. Use the large checks that provide adequate room for the purpose of each check rather than the much smaller personal-type checks.

Deposit all of your income from the property into the account. For each tenant use a large tenant card that shows payment period, when payment was received, and check number. Keep a large 9 × 12 envelope for each property for expenses paid. On every check you write, reference a billing or clearly show the purpose of the check. When a bill is paid, indicate on the bill the check number and when it was paid. Put it in the 9 × 12 envelope.

If your checking account gets too large, transfer some money out to a savings account. If you need more money, transfer more into the account. By using a separate account for the property, you will readily realize the operational status of the property. Of course, as the number of your properties increases, a simple system such as this will no longer be adequate. There are a great many computer programs available for property management. Choose a program based on your particular needs.

Many of the available programs are relatively low in cost as well as easy to use. Features available include lease files, lease expiration date, security deposit balances, work orders, maintenance-cost history, vendor files, tickler files for payments, insurance registry, tenant rent payment history, late charges, appliance inventory, repetitive correspondence, and much more. Two of the many computer companies offering property management software are: Yardi Systems at *www.yardi.com* and Realty Automation at *www.fullhousesoftware.com*.

Programs available differ as to capability and price. Some are available for Macintosh as well as DOS users. By checking on the Internet, you can obtain information so that you can make a software decision based on your specific needs.

ACQUIRING MANAGEMENT SKILLS

If you obtain professional management, your costs will probably range between 4 and 10 percent of the gross. One problem with professional managers is that they have numerous properties to consider and many problems. You are only concerned with your own property. If you can acquire the management skills needed, you can do a far better management job on your own property than a management firm can possibly do. You can obtain these skills not only from experience but also from courses in property management given by a number of professional organizations.

The Institute of Real Estate Management (IREM) of the National Association of Realtors is a large national organization of professional property managers. They provide courses of training leading to the professional designations of Certified Property Manager (CPM) and Accredited Resident Manager (ARM).

An applicant for these designations must be a real estate licensee. For information on their programs, contact the Institute of Real Estate Management of the National Association of Realtors at *www.irem.org/*. The Real Estate Management Brokers Institute (REMBI) is an affiliate of the National Association of Real Estate Brokers, which is primarily an organization of minority brokers. They offer the professional designations Certified Resident Manager (CRM) and Certified Real Estate Manager (CREM). They also offer courses of study particularly relevant to urban property. For information, contact them at *http://rembi.org/ join.htm*.

The National Apartment Association represents owners of apartment and multiple-family units. As an owner, you can benefit from the courses they offer. They offer the professional designations Certified Apartment Manager (CAM) and Certified Apartment Maintenance Technician (CAMT). For information about their educational programs, go to *www.naa.learnsomething.com/*.

The Building Owners and Managers Institute International (BOMI) offers a number of excellent courses for investors and managers. They also offer the professional designation Real Property Administrator (RPA). For information, *go to www.boma.org/*.

The National Association of Residential Property Managers (NARPM) offers an effective professional learning environment for owners of single-family and small residential rental properties. For information, go to *www.narpm.org*.

In addition to the these associations, many community colleges offer courses on real property management, and many books are available on property management in general as well as for managing specific types of investment property.

After you understand the day-to-day management problems, as well as management planning, you may want to give your property to a professional management firm in order to free your time for what, to you, could be more profitable use. In choosing a management firm, talk to owners of similar property who are using professional management. This choice can be very important. I do not recommend signing a management contract unless you feel the management firm fully understands your goals and you have a feeling of trust in turning over your property to the firm.

16

CHAPTER

Tenant Selection and Leases

Men honor property above all else; it has the greatest power in human life.

Euripides

Your tenant and the lease terms will materially affect the value of your property. Whether it is a rooming house or a shopping center, you want to obtain the best tenant possible. Quality tenants mean fewer management problems, a lower collection loss, a lower vacancy factor as well as lower expenses, which make the property more desirable to purchasers and less stressful to own. Credit reports, as discussed in Chapter 15, can eliminate many marginal or problem tenants before the property is rented. Generally, a poor credit report and disregard for maintenance of your property go hand in hand.

SECTION 8 HOUSING

Section 8 housing is a Department of Housing and Urban Development program of rental assistance for low-income families.

Under the Housing Choice Voucher (HCV) program, tenants are given housing vouchers and they seek housing in the private market. The local housing authority must approve the unit. The tenant generally pays 30 percent of income as rent with the balance paid to the owner through the voucher program. The payments continue to the landlord as long as the tenant remains eligible for assistance.

Landlords can still screen tenants although the local public housing authority does some screening. The government is not responsible for damages to the property or for the tenant's portion of the rent.

The advantage to landlords include a guarantee of partial rent (portion paid by the government), ease in finding tenants (some local public housing authorities will help you find tenants), and the fact that generally the tenants will remain as long as they are eligible.

Landlords' negative experience with Section 8 housing has been primarily related to the local housing authority operation.

Delays, hassles, unrealistic requirements, and ridiculously low rents set by some housing authorities have resulted in many landlords refusing Section 8 applicants. However, some local public housing authorities are extremely helpful to landlords and realistic in their dealings. You should be able to make a determination if Section 8 housing makes sense for you by checking local property owners associations as well as your local public housing authority.

PROBLEMS WITH COMMERCIAL TENANTS

A commercial tenant going through bankruptcy or corporate reorganization can mean uncollected and even uncollectible rent. If financial problems have arisen prior to the rental, then a credit report will indicate that the tenant is unable or unwilling to pay obligations on time. While others may disagree, I feel that a vacant store is generally preferable to a tenant with serious problems. Besides the financial loss from a problem tenant, you can expect an emotional loss in the form of stress. More important, having a problem tenant occupying premises under a lease will preclude you from making the premises available to a quality tenant. Any tenant is not preferable to *no* tenant at all. When you consider the fact that it is estimated that over 50 percent of new businesses fail within the first year and fewer than 25 percent are still in existence after three years, you can understand the problems relating to renting to new businesses.

Failing businesses can hurt your ability to rent to qualified tenants. Several business failures in succession at one location can give a location a bad reputation, discouraging other firms from moving in.

GETTING SUCCESSFUL BUSINESSES

Successful leasing agents actively seek out tenants. They look for successful businesses within the area and analyze what advantages the property has over their present locations. They then contact the businesses. While these businesses are often on leases, they may open up second locations.

Some of the important points that will allow you to get successful businesses and professional people to move include:

1. More space
2. Better parking
3. Better location for the type of business
4. Lower rent, when a business did not require the quality location it had

For example, a plumbing wholesaler might be induced into moving from a main street to a side street that offered better parking and about half the rent.

In a tenant search, particularly look for businesses of the same general type as are already located close to your vacancy. Businesses like to be in an area where others in the same business are located. Several firms of the same type together generally attract more customers than if they were separate. Also, many businesses generate business for allied firms.

You should consider businesses such as franchises that are expanding geographically. If you feel a location is suitable for a franchise, call the executive offices and talk to someone in their real estate department. Follow up the call with a letter. Often franchises want desperately to expand. One limiting factor is the ability to obtain new sites. I have usually received a very positive reaction when I have contacted franchises.

ASSUMING LEASES

Tenants can be induced to relocate if you will assume their present leases.

My name is Gary A. I had 40,000 square feet of vacant space in my office building. The office vacancy factor in our area was about 27 percent. My vacancies were killing me. Because of my reduced revenue, I was having a hard time making my mortgage payments. I came up with a plan to obtain new tenants.

I contacted all of my present tenants and asked for names of firms they did a great deal of business with who might want to be located closer to them. I followed up on the leads and was able to lease about 3000 square feet of space. One lead was interesting. The tenant needed about 8000 square feet, but was on a lease with four years to go for their present 5000-square-foot location.

After some thought I negotiated a lease where I agreed to assume the tenant's current assumable lease with four years remaining. In return, they leased my space on an eight-year lease with increases based on the CPI. I then advertised the space obtained for auction. Well, the high bid was about 55 percent of what I was obligated for, but the net result of my lease loss and renting the additional space was very positive. I then advertised stating that I would assume tenants' current leases. I was able to rent all my space, auction the leases I assumed, and end up with a positive cash flow. In addition, my new tenants are all on leases at least twice the life of their old leases, so I will begin to obtain a significant return in a few years.

NAME THAT BUILDING

To obtain a major tenant for a commercial building, consider offering the tenant the building name. During rent negotiations, present the prospective tenant with a color rendering or a pen-and-ink drawing of the building with the name of the tenant on it, such as *The Preston Center, The Preston Building,* or *Preston.* Having the name on the building or center will give the tenant prestige in the community and will give its employees a sense of pride. One developer who gave a prospective tenant a pen-and-ink drawing of the building with the tenant's name displayed on the structure and gateposts later saw the drawing used by the tenant on the company stationery.

TENANT EQUITY

If you are a major tenant or prospective tenant in a building, ask yourself how badly the owner needs you. IBM has done this and has negotiated leases where the building owners have given them an equity position in property in order to sign their leases. They thus became limited partners in the buildings and shared in the profits. The owners of the building obtained a prime tenant on a long-term lease that enhanced the rentability of the rest of the building and thus increased the value of the building. A tenant can have a great deal of economic clout, especially in an overbuilt market. However, most tenants don't realize the power they may possess.

Owners as well as tenants can use the idea of tenant equity as an effective tool.

My name is Clarence R. I make money giving buildings away. Well, at least one-half of buildings. What I do is look for troubled single-tenant commercial properties, and in my area I have no trouble finding them. I then try to tie them up with a purchase option. I try to negotiate purchase terms where little or no cash will be required. I want the owners to carry a large part of their equity with a second mortgage.

Next I look for possible tenants. When I find a strong local tenant who needs space and can use what I have, I give them an offer they can't refuse. I offer a long-term net lease at a fair rent that will pay any debt service. The lease must be tied to the CPI. As part of the lease agreement, I give the owner of the company a one-half interest in the building as a limited partner. The firm pays for the building with the lease payments, the owner gets equity buildup, and has half the landlord's interest. It is an offer that is difficult to say no to and when explained is often accepted. Based on the lease, I can usually arrange new financing if required. The balance of the seller's equity is paid off by the second mortgage that the seller carries. In other words, I strive for 100 percent financing.

NEGOTIATING ACCEPTABLE LEASES

After you have located a tenant, you must negotiate a lease acceptable to the tenant that also serves your best interests. Month-to-month rentals should be avoided for commercial rentals unless you want to keep the property available for some reason. Either the tenant or the owner can generally terminate this type of rental agreement by giving one month's notice. In all fairness, I would not enter into such a rental without full disclosure to the tenant. Keep in mind that a tenant willing to take a short-term rental will generally be fairly shaky. Even for residential property, a month-to-month tenancy is not desirable. Tenants who want such a rental usually do not expect to remain long. When tenants have short stays, it means greater expenses to the owner for advertising and related rental expenses, much greater maintenance, and a higher vacancy factor.

Rental agreements should generally be for at least one year. As the desirability of a location increases, the length required for the lease can be increased. In inflationary periods we experience a change in attitudes of landlords toward leases. Landlords are unwilling to sign multiyear leases at fixed rents or even leases with fixed-step increases. They want either short leases, such as one year, or multiyear leases tied in with an inflationary index such as the CPI. During our present period of low inflation, landlords again want long-term leases.

Net Leases

A triple net lease, which is normally just called a net lease, is a lease in which the tenant pays for all maintenance and repair expenses as well as taxes and insurance. The owner is guaranteed a net amount each month.

Net leases are usually long-term and provide the owner with a fixed income from the property. However, during periods of inflation the real value of the net rental decreases every year. The solution is, of course, to tie the net rental into either the CPI or one of the wholesale indexes, which allows the lessor to retain the same relative purchasing power originally bargained for no matter what happens to the economy.

Percentage Leasing

If you have an exceptionally good retail location, you don't have to be satisfied with a set rent. It is possible to share in a tenant's success through a percentage lease. Under a percentage lease the lessee pays the lessor an agreed percentage of his or her gross income. Generally, businesses having higher markups pay higher percentages of the gross. A percentage lease should also require a minimum rent, with inflation increases, as well as a covenant to remain in business. This protects the landlord against a tenant closing down and paying only the minimum rent. Because each business in a shopping center brings customers for other businesses, if one business closes down it will hurt the gross of other nearby businesses as well. The percentage lease should also set forth the period of time the lessee has to begin operation. Otherwise the lessor could receive only the minimum rent for a protracted period of time.

In a shopping center, an *anchor tenant* is the *prime tenant.* In a new regional shopping center, a number of anchor tenants would be department stores. The center would seek out the most desirable anchor tenant and offer that tenant attractive lease terms in order to attract other anchor tenants who would not receive as attractive rental terms. The shops between anchor tenants benefit by the presence of anchor tenants, which bring in the traffic. They would pay higher percentages for their leases than the anchor tenants.

Some percentage leases have graduated percentages. As the gross increases beyond a particular amount, the percentage decreases. This encourages a firm to advertise and have sales. The net effect of graduated percentages can be greater net income for the lessor.

Many percentage leases contain recapture clauses. If a tenant fails to attain a particular gross, the lessor has the right to end the lease, thus protecting him or her against a poor operator. With percentage leases, you want your tenants to advertise. Leases in shopping centers frequently require the tenants to pay an additional percentage of their gross for cooperative advertising such as shopping-center-wide sales. Remember, you as the lessor want an increased gross, as this means higher rents. Percentage leases in shopping centers usually set forth the hours that stores must be open. If some stores would stay closed on a Sunday afternoon, for example, it would reduce the gross of the stores that are open because every store helps to attract customers to the center. Percentage leases normally also prohibit the tenant from having a warehouse sale or other off-premise sale where the gross would not be subject to the rent percentage.

Lessors usually require tenants under percentage leases to use a specified type of cash register that keeps a running total and cannot be set back. Honesty in reporting is not usually a problem with larger tenants. There can be problems with some smaller stores. There are protection services that will check to see that all sales are properly run up on the registers. Besides the minimum, percentage leases have built-in protection against inflation. As the costs of the goods increase, the gross increases without any real increase in the number of sales.

OTHER LEASING PROVISIONS

Design Approval

In some malls the leases require design approval, allowing for desired uniformity.

Assignment or Subletting

Unless a lease prohibits assignment or subletting, it can be assigned or sublet. In a lease assignment, the new tenant assumes the lease and pays rent directly to the owner. In a sublease the new tenant is the tenant of the old tenant, not of the owner.

If you are leasing commercial property for a long period, the lessee (your tenant) will most likely want the right to sublease the property. If the lessee subleases for more than the master lease payments, the sublessee makes a profit. While this is fine if you are the lessee, it is not so fine if you are the original lessor.

As lessor, you should consider a profit-sharing agreement such as:

Assignment and subleasing of the premises will be made only with the approval of the lessor. However, approval will not be unreasonably withheld. Should any sublease be at a rent greater than the rent under this lease, then the lessor and lessee shall share equally in this additional rental amount.

By sharing, the clause encourages the lessee to sublease at the greatest possible rent. If you wanted it all, the lessee would simply sublease at the same rent or assign the entire lease giving you just the same old rent.

Use of Premises

Commercial leases normally specify the use that must be made of the premises. You may want a restaurant in a location to help other rentals you have. You might not want the lessee to open a pornographic bookstore. Some uses can also increase your insurance costs. Therefore, your lease should include a provision that if the tenant's use of the premises increases insurance costs to the lessor, then the lessee shall be obligated to pay the increased costs. For example, use or sale of highly flammable material could increase an owner's fire as well as liability insurance costs.

You should also require a tenant to carry stated high-limit liability insurance coverage naming the lessor as an insured party.

Leasing Raw Land for Storage

You should be wary of leasing raw land for storage or disposal of chemicals. A few months' rent has left some owners with worthless property. There have been several cases in which tenants have been in the business of disposing of toxic waste. The tenants have stored tens of thousands of barrels of waste on a property, ostensibly temporarily, but have then walked away, leaving owners with a horrendous problem. Besides specifying use, you can protect yourself by a lease clause prohibiting the storage of toxic, explosive, or otherwise hazardous materials.

If you are leasing raw land to a corporation, consider having your attorney draft a clause similar to the following:

The undersigned agree to be personally liable for any and all damages to the leased property and/or necessary corrective action resulting from the storage, accidental discharge, or disposal of hazardous and/or toxic materials on the premises.

Without the personal liability of the corporate officers, the corporation could declare bankruptcy, leaving you without any recourse.

Television

Today, television interference can be an important problem. Some leases prohibit use of powerful radio equipment. The installation and removal of antennas for communication can damage the roof. Many leases prohibit them. Some commercial and residential buildings have a master antenna for the tenants.

Noise

Leases frequently have clauses about noise to protect against residential tenants playing loud music or commercial tenants using disturbing loudspeakers. Some leases actually specify decibel levels. Residential leases frequently have clauses as to loud music and making other noise after a particular hour.

Weight Restrictions

Second-floor commercial and residential leases often have weight restrictions. Overloading a building can damage the structure. Some older apartment buildings ban waterbeds both because of the weight and because of the damage that can result from rupture. If waterbeds are allowed, waterbed insurance should be required of tenants who have waterbeds. It indemnifies the landlord for damage caused by leakage.

Injuries on Premises

Liability for injuries resulting from the condition of the premises is normally covered in commercial and residential leases. Many leases require the tenant to indemnify the landlord for any losses suffered because a third party is injured on the premises. Often commercial leases require tenants to carry high-limit liability insurance.

Number of Occupants

Residential leases customarily specify the number of occupants allowed. Lessors have an interest in this because a higher occupancy means higher utility costs and greater wear and tear on the premises. Occupancy limits must be reasonable as to the size of the unit or they could be considered discriminatory and subject the owner to significant damages.

Other Restrictions

Leases can also specify whether pets are allowed and, if allowed, set forth the restrictions. You cannot prohibit children unless the property is exempt from the 1988 Amendment to the Civil Rights Act of 1968. Exemptions can be obtained for property where 80 percent of the occupants are over the age of 55.

You cannot discriminate based on sex, marital status, or AIDS. You cannot discriminate against the mentally or physically handicapped. You must allow Seeing Eye dogs and support animals.

Anticompetition Clauses

Shopping centers often prohibit tenants from opening another location within a defined radius of the center because it reduces their gross sales.

Often strong tenants will negotiate leases prohibiting other stores from selling particular items. The lessor then places the prohibition in subsequent leases.

Attorney's Fees

Leases often provide that in any lease dispute the prevailing party shall be entitled to attorney's fees. Such a clause reduces the likelihood of frivolous suits by tenants who wish to either reduce rent liability or escape lease provisions.

Guaranty of Lease

For a new business or a business with a history of financial problems, you should consider a guaranty of lease by individuals or firms who have good credit.

Security Deposit

Most states limit security deposits for residential leases. A number of states also prohibit nonrefundable security or cleaning deposits.

For commercial leases, however, there are generally no such limitations. As lessor you should try to negotiate the largest security deposit possible. Generally, security deposits don't earn interest for the tenant unless provided by the lease.

Holdover Clauses

At times a tenant will stay after the end of a lease or after notice to vacate has been given. This can create a serious problem, especially if you have rented the premises to a new tenant. The problem can be solved with a holdover clause. What this clause does is to set a higher rental for a holdover. It forces a tenant to either renegotiate a lease prior to its expiration or to vacate as agreed. An example of a holdover clause would be a month-to-month rental at $1200 per month if the tenant remains in possession after the $600-per-month lease expires. With an increase like this, you know the tenant will not hold over.

Fire

Leases customarily cover the rights and duties of the parties if the premises are totally or partially destroyed by fire, storm, or flood. The lease may merely be suspended until the premises are rebuilt, or the landlord may have the option of notifying the tenant that the premises will or will not be rebuilt. If the tenant's use caused the fire, the lease could provide that the rent continue.

Electrical Service

Some tenants require greater electrical service than a building can provide. A commercial lease normally requires the tenant to pay for any additional electrical installation service required.

Right of Inspection

Leases should allow the lessor the right to enter the premises for inspection purposes, to make repairs, and to show the premises to prospective buyers, lenders, contractors, and so forth.

Options

If an option to purchase is given, it should be for a very short period of time or tied to the CPI so that you are not giving away the benefit of inflation. Often leases provide options to renew for set periods. You should be certain they reflect economic changes. At a particular time $2000 per month might sound great, but you don't know what this amount will be worth in 10 years. Options to purchase are covered in Chapter 13.

Form

Even though a tenant is on a month-to-month rental, a lease is neverthe-less important. A lease sets forth the rights and duties of the parties and will serve to prevent problems or disagreements. You can purchase many types of lease forms from stationery stores. While they will save you money in attorney's fees, it might very well be the kind of savings you cannot afford. Except for simple fixed-rent residential and commercial leases, I recommend that you have a knowledgeable real estate attorney draft your leases. Unless a standard form includes everything you wish to cover when preparing a commercial lease, see an attorney. Avoid trying to draft your own with a cut-and-paste process where clauses from a number of other leases are used. The dangers involved in drafting a lease are not worth the few hundred dollars it will cost to do it right.

Lease Insurance

If you have a property that has a long-term lease with a major tenant, you might consider checking on the cost and availability of a lease insurance policy. This policy insures that your tenant will pay the rent for the term of the lease. There are two advantages of obtaining lease insurance besides your own protection as landlord. They are:

1. A lease insurance policy will make it easier to borrow on the property, and the lender will probably make a larger loan than if the lease was not insured. (The loan agreement would likely provide for an assignment of rents in the event of default of the borrower.)

2. The presence of lease insurance makes the property more attrac-tive to conservative investors. It might result in a higher sale price.

17

Selling Your Property

Give a man the secure possession of a bleak rock, and he will turn it into a garden, give him a nine-year lease of a garden, and he will convert it into a desert. The magic of property turns sand into gold.

Arthur Young, 1787

When should you sell real property? There are really only two primary reasons to sell. One is when you need money for other use and cannot obtain it without a sale. The second is when you believe another investment will better meet your needs.

REASONS FOR SELLING

Some of the reasons for changing property include:

1. The belief that another property offers greater appreciation potential.
2. The desire for a greater spendable income.
3. The desire for greater depreciation.
4. The desire to reduce management problems.
5. A desire to exchange a more speculative investment for a more secure one.
6. A belief that anticipated changes will lessen the desirability of the property.
7. The belief that a property can be sold at a price greater than the purchase price of similar property.

If you didn't have the property that you now own but had the equity you now have in that property, would you invest that equity in the property in question? If you would not buy your own property for your equity, you should consider selling it to get an investment that you would prefer to own. When you don't sell property, you are really saying, "It is worth at least as much to me as I could realize from a sale." If this is the case, hold on to it.

Don't hold on to property because "It isn't costing me anything." A break-even investment is still costing you money. To hold such an investment you are losing the opportunity value of your equity. For example, if you have $200,000 equity in a property that breaks even after tax considerations, the property is still costing you money. If you could invest the $200,000 in an investment with similar safety that would yield a 7 percent return, then by keeping the investment you are losing $14,000 in potential earnings. Unless other benefits will offset this $14,000 in lost income, you should consider selling.

Most real estate investors are slow to sell. While this buy-and-hold policy may be successful over a long term, it fails to maximize income. A prudent investor should cull out properties that are underperforming the market and where significant improvement cannot be reasonably anticipated for the future.

If you want to sell to reinvest in another property, the market conditions are not really very important. In a buyer's market with many sellers and few buyers, you will probably have to accept less than you would like to receive in order to effectuate a sale. In the same vein, you will likely be able to purchase replacement property in such a market for a lower cost than you had anticipated spending. In a rising market you might receive top dollar for a property, and if you have to pay more for the replacement property, your net situation could be similar to having sold in a buyers' market. What you should be concerned with in upgrading properties is exchange value. What can I buy for what I can realize from a sale?

Don't sell just because a purchase offer means a profit. Unless you can place the proceeds in a more desirable investment, don't sell. Prior to accepting a purchase offer or placing your property on the market, you should fully understand the tax consequences of a sale. If you will have a large gain and expect to be investing the sale proceeds in another property, you don't really want a sale; you should be considering an exchange. Exchange techniques and advantages are covered in Chapter 12 and taxes are covered in Chapter 3.

You don't want to be in a position where you have to sell quickly. Real estate is a relatively illiquid investment, and when an owner needs a quick sale, the way to avoid a lengthy sale period is to cut the price. As a purchaser it means a below-market purchase. As a seller you are the one giving away the bargain. While cash traps should be avoided, consider financing alternatives before you become the highly motivated seller sought by other investors.

THE BUYER MAY BE OBVIOUS

The easiest sale I ever made was a residential lot I received in trade. All I did was ask the next-door neighbor if he would be interested in doubling the size of his lot.

For investment property, the logical purchasers are owners of adjacent property or owners of similar property in the area.

For raw land or agricultural properties, contact adjacent owners as well as persons who have recently purchased similar property in the area.

If a property is rented, check with the tenants. Nothing is more aggravating than paying a commission to an agent who sells to your tenants.

While I generally use real estate agents to sell my property, I do so after I have checked out the obvious.

USING AGENTS

Many people avoid real estate brokers simply to avoid paying commissions. This avoidance is a classic example of cutting off one's nose to spite one's face. Don't worry about what others are making. What is important is that you make an acceptable profit. Brokers know the market, have buyer and seller contacts, and can help you sell.

There are some good reasons for paying a commission to a broker rather than trying to sell your property on your own. To start with, when you advertise your own property, you will be spending a good deal of time talking to brokers who will be trying for the listing. Besides brokers, owner ads attract the jackals that are out to steal your property rather than pay a fair price. They will often try to trade near-worthless property for yours. The most important reason for selling through an agent is qualified buyers. Consider how you purchased your present home. Chances are you went to brokers because you realized that they would know what was available and could show you a number of properties.

Other qualified buyers are no different from you. They seek the help of experts and don't want to waste their time running down individual owner ads.

Another important reason for selling through a broker is that it is often very difficult to handle negotiations with a buyer. Direct negotiations often become emotional. Many deals are lost because of the natural emotional reactions of the parties involved. I have purchased and sold property directly as well as through agents. In most cases I don't feel that selling directly actually saved money.

Chances are, you will find an agent you can really relate to, an agent who fully understands your needs and will make every effort to meet them. When you find such an agent, show your loyalty to that agent with your listings and trust.

HELP IN CHOOSING AN AGENT

Real estate agents will usually try for as long a listing as possible. In most areas, exclusive listings for homes are generally for a three- to six-month period. In resort areas they could be for longer periods. Vacant industrial or commercial property could be listed for one year or even longer. Generally, the more salable a property is, the shorter the listing. Since a listing ties you to a broker for a set period of time, you should only sign with a broker you have confidence in.

With the number of real estate licensees around, everyone seems to know people in the business. Many owners give listings out because of friendship rather than expertise. Don't mix business with friendship. It is bad business to give a listing to an office that is not active in the particular geographical area of your listing or in the particular type of property that you have for sale. In addition, real estate has attracted many retirees and part-time people. Because these people do not have to be successful in real estate, they usually are not. You want your listing handled by an office staffed with successful people who really want your property to sell and are willing to work to accomplish that sale.

You might want your prospective agent to prepare a marketing plan for you as to how they intend to market your property. You might also consider asking to see the ads the office has run on a similar property that they currently have for sale. Some real estate offices will not advertise a property adequately.

For residential property you are usually better off giving a listing to a larger office. The large firms with many salespeople and offices, as well as franchise brokers, usually specialize in residential property. However, many small offices specialize in particular geographical areas where they may actually dominate the market. In such cases they might be preferable.

Smaller offices often specialize in nonresidential property. For example, I know of a number of smaller brokers who sell only industrial property and a few who sell only mobile home parks. These specialists can usually do a far better job for nonresidential property sales than large general brokerage offices.

Some brokers just want to get listings, which they give to their multiple listing service (MLS) in the hope that someone else can sell them. This type of broker won't do enough for you; you want a broker who will use his or her best efforts to obtain a buyer. Nevertheless, you would generally want to list with a broker who belongs to a major MLS so that the property will get maximum coverage. However, MLSs are generally dominated by residential listings and don't do much for specialty property such as farms, motels, or industrial buildings. Giving these listings to large groups of salespeople who primarily sell residential property isn't really going to help you in finding a buyer.

EXCLUSIVE RIGHT-TO-SELL LISTINGS

Consider giving an exclusive right-to-sell listing to a broker whom you trust. Under an exclusive right-to-sell listing, the broker earns a commission if the property is sold during the listing by anyone, including you the owner. If you don't want to give an exclusive right-to-sell listing because you have already talked to several possible buyers, I still recommend the exclusive right-to-sell listing with exclusion. Most brokers will agree to exclude several named buyers for a short period of time such as 10 days. Now you will have a real club for the buyers. If they are at all serious, they have 10 days to buy without obligating you to a commission. They will realize that they can make a more advantageous deal right away than they can expect to make after the 10-day period. The exclusion will often result in a quick sale. If the named individuals don't buy, chances are they were lookers only and not serious buyers. People such as this could have wasted a great deal of your time.

OPEN LISTINGS

Some real estate agents agree to work with an open listing. Under this type of listing the licensee earns a commission only if he or she actually sells the property. If the owner sells it or any other agent sells the property, then the agent with the open listing has not earned a commission. While an open listing might sound like a good deal to you since you can sell the property yourself without paying a commission, it is actually a very bad deal for the owner. Very few brokers will advertise an open listing, since it means he or she really doesn't control the product advertised. If a salesperson has the choice of trying to sell a property on an exclusive listing, where a commission is assured, or an open listing, where the owner is trying to sell the property without paying a commission, you can guess which property will get the greatest sales effort.

What is everyone's responsibility will turn out in practice to be no one's responsibility. The Chinese have a saying that expresses this thought: "A pig that has two masters shall surely starve."

DETERMINING VALUE

Before putting your property on the market, consider what it is worth. What you may have paid for it does not determine its value and may bear little relation to what it will sell for. Value is of course influenced by supply and demand. Demand is meaningless unless the demand is coupled with purchasing power. If there are more buyers than sellers, prices tend to rise; while, conversely, a market with more sellers than buyers tends to reduce prices.

When a supply becomes limited, property may sell for far more than similar property in the past. For example, the last available lot in a desirable subdivision could conceivably sell for far more than the price received at the last comparable sale. By checking similar property available on the market, you can find asking prices. Property is usually listed for sale at the high end of the sales range or above it. The fact that property similar to yours is listed at $100,000 does not mean that either that property or yours will sell for $100,000. What are important are actual sale prices and terms for recent sales of similar property. Terms given are important because they can affect the price paid. When your checking has given you some general ideas of value, contact one or more competent real estate brokers who are active in your area. A professional real estate agent will usually have accurate sales figures of comparable property.

If the real estate agent asks what you want for the property, do not give a figure. This can be very dangerous. If you quote a low price, some unethical agents will tell you that you really know the market and that is exactly what they think it is worth. Some listing agents forget that their first responsibility is to the owner and not to earning a commission. By taking a listing at a below-market price, such agents seek to enhance the likelihood of selling the property and earning a commission. Often owners sell at huge profits only to later learn that they actually sold their property at a bargain price. Other agents will try to buy the listing by quoting an unrealistically high value. They are offering more than the other agents in order to appeal to your greed. After the agent gets the listing, he or she will then start coming up with good comparables and try to prepare the owner for a much lower price.

When an agent suggests a listing price, ask why. You want the agent to defend the price suggested. If an agent cannot adequately support his or her recommendations, you should not be interested in working with him or her any further. You want to work with a professional, not an amateur.

I have mentioned the extremes for your protection. Most real estate licensees are honest and knowledgeable. As I have previously stated, you will probably develop a relationship of trust and respect with one or two agents. When such relationships develop, try to deal exclusively with those individuals.

If, after your own investigation and checking with agents, you have still not decided what price to ask, hire an independent fee appraiser. The dollars you spend will be well worth it. Besides peace of mind, a professional appraisal can save you the time wasted in trying to sell a property at an inflated price or the dollars lost if you sold the property at too low a price. (See Appraisals in Chapter 9 for recommendations about finding a professional appraiser.)

No appraiser can tell you exactly what a property will sell for, but a professional appraiser can usually predict the price range into which a sale will fall. For example, a lot may be worth between $45,000 and $55,000. An appraiser could determine this range by various means, most commonly by analyzing actual sale prices of similar property.

When you want to sell in a market where prices are declining, don't chase the market down. An example of an owner who chased the market is a case where an owner listed a property for sale at $795,000. A $650,000 price would have been a fair price based on an appraisal. The owner took the position that he could always lower his price if he got an offer. Well, the market declined and the owner lowered the price to $695,000. Since the value at the time was closer to $575,000, he failed to find a buyer.

The owner again lowered the price to $550,000, which is $75,000 more than the market would indicate was a fair price. You can see that this owner chased the falling market. While pricing above market makes sense in a rising market, it almost ensures that the property will not sell in a falling market. The owner, however, did not understand this. He only saw that he had cut his price $245,000 and had not found a buyer. In a falling market, the price should have been set to appear as a bargain compared to similar properties in order to increase the likelihood of a sale.

There are times when you should price property above what appears to be market value. In many areas of the country, prime residential property is selling within hours of being listed. Owners are receiving multiple offers and they may be above the list price. If this is the case when you wish to sell, I suggest pushing the envelope a little further. Add another 10 percent to the price that you feel is indicated by market sales.

HOW YOU WISH TO SELL A PROPERTY

You should have fully considered how you wish to sell a property before it is placed on the market. If you want cash, you should ask yourself why. Many people ask for cash but really don't need it. If you intend to invest the cash in a safe, interest-bearing account, you are probably better off leaving some of the purchase price in the real estate. You will probably get a higher rate of return, and you will have the security of the property.

Down Payment

The likelihood of default bears an inverse relationship to the amount of the down payment. This means the larger the down payment, the less likely the purchaser is to default. You can reduce the danger of a buyer default by getting as much of a down payment as possible. If the buyer does not have cash, accept personal property such as a snowmobile, or even jewelry. I once took a boat as a down payment. You want the buyers to feel they have an equity that needs to be protected.

Further protection is possible by having the buyer supply you with a computer printout of their credit information. The printout can be obtained from one of the credit reporting agencies.

Wraparound Loans

If there is an assumable loan on your property at a favorable rate of interest, you might want to consider carrying part of the purchase price using a wraparound loan. In this way you will obtain the benefits of the loan, not the purchaser (see Chapter 4).

Balloon Payments

Chances are you don't want to leave your money in property for 20 years after you have sold it. If this is the case, consider a balloon payment, which requires the buyer to pay you off in full at a particular time. For second mortgages five to seven years is about average. Normally the buyer will have sufficient equity in the property, because of appreciation, to refinance it. If the buyer cannot refinance the property when the balloon payment is due, you can either foreclose or rewrite the loan with an increase in the interest rate. The latter is the course many people take in these cases. There is a lot of money to be made in real estate, and it isn't necessary to prosper by forcing foreclosure on a buyer who is making payments on time.

Graduated Interest Rates and Payments

You can structure mortgages to encourage buyers to pay off early with a graduated interest rate and graduated payment mortgages. For the first one to two years I may agree to accept a below-market interest rate. For the third year the rate will rise to the market rate (at time of the sale). Each year thereafter the interest rate rises 1 percent. The buyer has a strong incentive to refinance and pay off as soon as possible. In most states when the seller carries back the loan, the state usury limits don't apply. You should, however, check with a real estate attorney in your area prior to using this method.

Lease Options

Many people who have good incomes and can make significant monthly payments nevertheless don't have a sufficient down payment or credit qualifications to buy a home. Real estate agents who lack knowledge and experience to tailor a purchase to their needs have rebuffed many of these people. These people will often be very responsive to a lease option.

The advantage of selling with a lease option is that a lease option is a relatively easy way to get a premium sales price. If structured properly, there is a high probability the tenant will buy plus take good care of the property and possibly even make improvements. A tenant with a lease option will normally pay a higher-than-normal rent if he or she really hopes to buy. A significant portion of the payments applied to the purchase price means the tenant will build up an equity that is lost if the option is not exercised. If you want to get several thousand dollars at the time of the lease option (as the option price), it practically guarantees that the tenants will do their best to exercise the option. The option price can also apply to the purchase price.

Lease options are a quick and relatively management-free way to flip (turnover) property purchased with a very low or no down payment. Other advantages of selling by using a lease option are that you retain the income tax advantages of ownership, there is less haggling over the purchase price, and in a slow market it is easier to find a tenant on a lease option than it is to find a buyer. I like the lease option forms from Professional Publishing at *www.profpub.com*.

PREPARING PROPERTY FOR SALE

Before you place your property on the market, make sure it is ready to be shown. You want your property to present as favorable an image to a prospective buyer as possible. Owners who don't prepare their properties for sale lose many potential buyers.

While every improvement will not improve the sale price, many will. Consider possible improvements and how they will affect the value. If an improvement cannot be expected to return at least 200 percent of the cost in added value, then don't undertake it. I also know from experience that actual costs generally exceed initial estimates.

Besides increasing profit, improvements also increase salability. A dirty property is difficult to sell; cleaning it up will increase its salability. Paint and landscaping expenses usually improve salability as well as increase value.

Repainting

When you repaint, colors are important. Don't try to copy the decorators with currently fashionable colors. Although people like to visit far-out models, they are usually more traditional in their own homes. You seldom go wrong with light interior colors such as white or cream. They tend to make rooms appear larger and convey the impression of freshness. For exteriors, light colors accented with slightly darker complementary colors usually work very well.

Wallpapering, Paneling, and Carpeting

A little textured wallpaper, perhaps on one wall in a living room or as wainscoting in a dining area, can help a sale. If a wall needs plastering, it will usually be less expensive to put up prefinished paneling than to re-plaster. Carpets should be in medium to light colors such as beige.

Flowers, Plants, and Trees

Seeding and seasonal flowers can help a building. Blooming petunias or other flowers outside an apartment building, home, or even a commercial building, can do a great deal to attract a potential buyer. You can buy many plants and even young trees at stores like Home Depot at very reasonable prices. If you need help in planning your plantings, consult a nursery. Many have reasonable planning services.

Lighting Fixtures

For older residential units I have found that new lighting fixtures in the kitchen, dining area, and bath are well worth the investment. For the bath I usually combine the lighting fixture with a large, modern, mirrored medicine cabinet. Remember that as a seller you are competing with other sellers. You want your property to be more desirable than competing properties.

Furniture

If a property is being sold furnished, you must avoid overfurnishing it. Too much furniture or furniture that is too large makes rooms look crowded and small. Upgrading the furniture will improve salability. It is difficult to sell a unit furnished in "Salvation Army modern" and get the maximum market price.

When I formerly owned a number of furnished units, I would watch the for-sale ads. Frequently, because of divorce, death, or the high costs of moving, an entire household of quality furniture could be purchased very reasonably.

Other Features

Cleanliness is of course important. The kitchen appliances and bath fixtures must shine. I actually use a wax for this purpose. A roach or a rodent will usually ruin an otherwise favorable impression. A pest control company can quickly solve this problem. The property should be well lighted when you show it and as airy as possible. Drapes should be open and lights on. If a building has air-conditioning, in summer you should turn it on at least an hour before showing the building.

The Offer

Should you receive a verbal offer to purchase property, ask that the offer be put in writing even though it may be unsatisfactory. Once a person actually gives a written offer, he usually starts to think in terms of actually owning the property. While he might have thought, up until the time of the written offer, that he would not exceed a certain price, a written offer often makes a potential buyer ripe for a counteroffer. I know that I have reevaluated my position and have accepted counteroffers at prices I originally would not have considered for an initial offer.

Counteroffers

When you receive an offer, realize that your acceptance will form a binding contract. If you give a counteroffer, you are rejecting the buyer's offer and are saying that you won't accept the offer as made but that you will agree to sell at the price and terms stated in your counteroffer. You are giving a nervous buyer an opportunity to back out of the purchase. Many buyers get "buyer's remorse" and look for opportunities and reasons not to buy. Therefore, don't counteroffer if the basic offer is acceptable. If you try to wring the last penny from a property, you could lose the entire deal.

When you refuse an offer or give a counteroffer, you are competing with the buyer. You are really saying, "No! I will pay more for the property!" Not accepting an offer indicates you feel the property is worth more to you than the offer provided. If, on the other hand, you wouldn't consider buying a similar property at the price and terms offered, then you should seriously consider accepting the offer.

You should generally give a counteroffer rather than an outright rejection. Try to make the counteroffer appealing by giving in on one or more of the following areas:

1. Price
2. Personal property inclusion
3. Time of possession
4. Other loan terms

People want to think they have driven a hard bargain. They want to obtain some advantage from the bargaining. It really helps a buyer's pride to have purchased property at better terms than were originally offered. I have seen excellent deals fail because an owner wouldn't allow a buyer to save face by giving even a token concession from what the listing was asking for.

When to Seek Legal Help

If you receive an offer that you don't fully understand, see an attorney. Don't accept the buyer's or broker's explanation as to what the written offer means. While most people are straightforward, there are some who will try for an advantage any way they can get it.

18
CHAPTER

What's for Me?

Mine is better than ours.
Benjamin Franklin
Poor Richard's Almanac, 1756

What others are investing in may not be the right property for you. Real estate investments should be tailored to each person's needs and abilities.

UNDERSTANDING YOURSELF

In determining what areas of real estate you wish to invest in, you must ask yourself: "What are my goals?" "How much money do I want to make?" and "Am I willing to endure the risks and devote the effort required to reach that goal?" Risk is of course related to return. Low-risk investments generally offer the likelihood of more modest returns than high-risk investments. If you are willing to endure the risks and devote the effort necessary to reach your goals, you are ready to become a real estate investor. If you are not, you must either modify your goals or hope that you can live comfortably in your retirement years off your pension.

I rate the order of risk in real estate investments from least to greatest as:

1. Your home
2. Duplex in which you live
3. Apartment unit in which you live
4. Single-family homes purchased for rental or resale
5. Multiunits purchased for rental and/or resale
6. Smaller commuter-type farms

7. Single-family lots
8. Commercial property
9. Larger farms requiring management
10. Industrial property
11. Raw land and lots (other than single-family residential)

Your investment plan must be based on the risk you are willing to endure as well as the negative cash flow you can live with. While buying right, careful analysis of a property, the area, and the marketplace can reduce risks, they are still present. You can also minimize risk by buying without personal liability and with a low cash investment. Risk doesn't mean you should invest as you would approach a crap table and leave success or failure to the game of chance. Risk can be managed. You can also increase or reduce risk by tenant selection, the loan terms you negotiate, the price you pay, and so forth.

To help you in understanding yourself I recommend a self-analysis. Start by asking yourself the following questions:

1. Why am I interested in a real estate investment?
2. How much time am I willing to devote to seeking out and managing real estate investments?
3. Am I willing to devote time at inconvenient hours to property or tenant requirements?
4. What types of maintenance and repair work am I capable of handling myself?
5. Am I willing to get my hands dirty in maintenance and repair work?
6. Can I visualize the effect of paint, landscaping, remodeling, etc., on a property?
7. How do I react to pressure situations and personal complaints?
8. How much do I have in savings?
9. Do I have an insurance policy with loan value? If yes, how much can be borrowed on it?
10. What other property do I have that can be mortgaged or used for trade purposes?
11. How much capital am I willing to invest?
12. Do I require a positive cash flow from my investment?
13. What would happen if I lost my entire investment?

14. How much actual negative cash flow am I able or willing to pay out each month?

15. What, if any, change in income do I expect over the next five years?

16. How will this affect my ability to make payments?

17. Am I willing to decrease my present standard of living for future benefits?

18. Do I like the excitement of a gamble or do I prefer greater safety?

19. Do I like the challenge of games like chess, which require organized plans, as well as changes in tactics to meet changed conditions?

20. Am I willing to make decisions that might adversely affect the lives of others?

21. Do I like working with people?

22. Is the nature of my investments, such as prestige, important to me?

23. My last year's federal tax return shows that my highest dollars of income were taxed at what percentage?

24. My last year's state tax return shows that my highest dollars of income were taxed at what percentage?

25. Within five years I expect my regular income to put me in what percentage bracket (state and federal)?

26. What type of property I am most interested in for my investment and why?

YOUR GOALS

Your goals must be compatible with the effort you are willing to put out and the risks you are willing to endure. If not, your goals will only be wishes that are unlikely to be fulfilled unless it's by chance.

With realistic goals based on your willingness to succeed and willingness to take risks, what would otherwise be merely a daydream can be yours by design. In setting goals you should really be setting a plan. You must have a plan to reach a goal.

Keep in mind that goals are not cast in stone. Changes in your needs, your experiences, and even opportunities can change your goals. When this happens, commit your new goals to writing. A written goal is much better than a mental one.

Show your goals to your spouse or a close friend. Discuss the goals. When you have revealed your goals to another, it acts as an incentive for you to make them happen.

Your goals must flow naturally from your plan. If your plan is to buy one house every five years, your plan to reach a monetary goal of $5 million in 10 years is not likely to be fulfilled.

While goals are not always fulfilled, wishes are seldom fulfilled. Again, goals must be integrated into working plans. Without them you are likely to sit on the sidelines of life watching the investors play. With goals and a plan to implement them, you can be a player.

E P I L O G U E

OK! I have told you what took me years to learn. It will be meaningless if you don't put it to work.

Based on your analysis of the market and your resources and goals, after completion of the questionnaire in Chapter 18, decide on the type of investment that is right for you. This decision must be yours. Your next step is to look for your first investment.

I suggest an investment plan where you devote a particular period each week to checking out properties, learning values, and analyzing your local marketplace. You should plan on at least eight hours per week dedicated to these tasks. I would suggest that you look and learn for at least two months before you even consider making a purchase.

Don't rush, but when you find an investment that meets your requirements and you have fully analyzed it, act by making an offer. If negotiations fail, keep on looking.

I never said getting rich was easy, but if that is your goal you can get there, as many thousands of us have, in both good markets and bad markets. In a poor market, it may be harder to do, but it can be done.

I hope that you will become excited as well as feel comfortable with at least some ideas expressed in this book, but some of you won't overcome inertia. It takes time and effort to break free, but it can be done. Don't become one of those people who after 40 years of earning wages is sent off with a gold watch and a modest pension to live a frugal coupon-clipping retirement. Don't be one of those who sits all day at the seniors' center and tells cronies of all the great opportunities you let pass by. "I could have . . ." are the saddest words of the almost investor.

INDEX

ABOUT THE AUTHOR

William H. Pivar, J.D., besides being a successful real estate investor, has taught thousands of students in his classes and seminars. He is a professor emeritus of the College of the Desert in Palm Desert, California, where he coordinated the real estate program. He has practiced law as a private, corporate, and government attorney and has served as an arbitrator with the Federal Mediation and Conciliation Service.

Dr. Pivar is the author of over 30 real estate books as well as numerous articles.

If you have an investment story that you feel would be of interest to readers of future editions, I would like to hear from you. Please contact me at *pivarfish@webtv.net.*